Beyond the Bear

How I Learned to Live and Love Again
after Being Blinded by a Bear

Dan Bigley and Debra McKinney

LYONS PRESS
Guilford, Connecticut
An imprint of Globe Pequot Press

Lyons Press is an imprint of Globe Pequot Press.

Project Editor: David Legere
Text Design: Sheryl P. Kober
Layout Artist: Justin Marciano

Library of Congress Cataloging-in-Publication Data is available on file.

ISBN 978-0-7627-8455-4

Printed in the United States of America

10 9 8 7 6 5 4 3

CONTENTS

Prologue: "It's Terrible, Just Horrible"

The beeper on Dr. James Kallman's bedside table went off brutally early that midsummer morning in 2003, jolting him from sleep like an elbow to the skull. His head sprang off his pillow. His eyes shot open, then narrowed.

The dark-haired, dark-eyed, thirty-nine-year-old surgeon with a J.Crew look about him was a gifted sleeper, and not easily distracted from it. When his first daughter was born while he was still in residency, he slept right through a raucous bout of colic even after his wife placed their wailing newborn upon his chest. But his pager was fail proof. He propped himself up on an elbow and fumbled for it. Recognizing the number illuminated on screen, he swung his legs out from under the covers, sat up, and, hunched over the edge of his bed, called the emergency room at Providence Alaska Medical Center.

Normally, he'd shuffle off to the bathroom to make the call so he wouldn't disturb his wife. But Sara and the girls were away, gone to Philadelphia to visit her folks. She'd been through enough of these on-call weeks to know how disruptive they could be. So her trip and his rotation were well timed. For Dr. Kallman, being on call often meant running ragged, bad food on the fly, and way too much coffee in Styrofoam cups. Toss in whitener and a packet of sugar and call it lunch. It could be that bad. And so he braced himself.

It was 4:30 a.m., and Kallman, a plastic surgeon and ear, nose, and throat specialist, had a day packed with patients ahead of him. Although frivolous wake-up calls made him crazy, he hoped this was one of them, a problem quickly resolved over the phone so he could go back to sleep. Like the classic: "The patient's IV fell out. Should I put it back in?"

This was not one of those. Dr. Kathleen McCue was on the line. He'd never heard an ER doctor sound so rattled. Something about a fisherman being attacked by a grizzly on the Russian River. Multiple claw and bite wounds. And the guy's face . . .

"Massive facial trauma," Kallman remembers her saying. "It's terrible, just horrible."

He waited for her to describe the injuries, and when she didn't, he pressed for details. Was the brain involved? If so, a neurosurgeon would need to be called in, too. The young man's face was so mangled she couldn't tell what was what. McCue was rarely at loss for words, but what she was seeing made no sense; it was "not compatible with life."

"We can't see anything," she told him. "Please, we just need you to come."

Specialists tend to get snappy with ER docs who roust them from bed. Kallman knew that and didn't want to be one of them but couldn't help thinking, *Get your wits about you.* They went around a couple more times, and then he gave up. Annoyed, he hung up the phone and sighed.

On autopilot, still too groggy to think much, he plodded over to his closet, threw on a sweatshirt and a pair of blue jeans, grabbed his shoulder bag and a banana from the kitchen counter, and went out the door. He backed his Toyota Highlander out of the garage and headed out of his hillside neighborhood, an enclave of stately houses, matching mailboxes, and perfectly manicured yards. Given the time of day, he had the road practically to himself as he drove down the Chugach Mountain foothills toward Providence hospital in midtown Anchorage, a gritty city of 296,000, sprawled between a blockade of skyscraper mountains and the tide-sculpted mudflats of Cook Inlet. Normally he'd use his drive time to get a game plan going in his head. But he had no idea what he'd be dealing with, other than it was going to be bad, bad enough to unravel an experienced trauma doctor. So he allowed his mind to wander.

Because Alaska is both beautiful and mean, doctors dread being on call on sunny summer days like the one July 14, 2003, turned out to be. Not only do planes crash, boats sink, and mountaineers vanish, but after a long, oppressive winter, the reprieve from light deprivation has an amphetamine effect. In their manic states of mind, people blast off for the great outdoors without seatbelts or helmets or common sense, bringing surgeons like Kallman some of their grimmest business. But being mauled by a bear, with the exception of the occasional bonehead who practically asks for it, that's just plain bad luck.

Although this would be his first bear-attack patient, Kallman had dealt with massive trauma, the kind so complicated it takes a team of specialists to sort out. His most recent case came after a semi-trailer truck crossed the centerline of a slushy highway and slammed into a prison van, killing four inmates and a corrections officer. Handcuffed and not wearing a seatbelt, the injured prisoner Kallman worked on looked like he'd slammed headfirst into a machete.

A Dartmouth grad and Fulbright Scholar, Kallman had become a surgeon relatively late in life, after becoming disillusioned with his first career. Although his degree was in chemistry, he'd been hired straight out of college by Bain & Company, a leading global business and strategy consulting firm, a major score for a twenty-one-year-old. Bain even held the job for him for a year while he completed his Fulbright program in Freiburg, Germany. He soon realized that working with data more than people left him feeling flat. So he got his midlife crisis out of the way early, at twenty-five, when it became obvious that financial management, though lucrative, was not fulfilling. Living in San Francisco at the time, he did a lot of soul searching before his epiphany moment. He remembers the exact corner, the exact spot, halfway through a run in the Marina District: *BING. You could be a doctor.* That option had been off the table since a field trip to Stanford University School of Medicine as a teenager when the sight of a refrigerator full of blood bags almost made him lose his lunch. So beginning at twenty-eight, an age most medical students are about to head out into the world, he was just getting started.

He spent eleven grueling years on that treadmill—five at the University of Pennsylvania School of Medicine, followed by a five-year residency, followed by a yearlong fellowship in facial reconstruction. Since he'd been practicing in what he considered "the real world" for only a year, he still felt pretty green. He felt even greener when it came to fixing the kinds of trouble Alaskans get themselves into. Like flying off four-wheelers and into trees. Like hitting moose at highway speed, sending a thousand pounds of muscle and bone crashing through windshields and into drivers' laps. Like crossing paths with rogue bears. He wasn't even supposed to be on call that night. It was his well-seasoned colleague Dr. Dwight Ellerbe's turn and they'd switched.

By the time he pulled into physicians' parking at Providence, adrenaline had kicked in. He walked up to the side entrance, dug his security badge out of his bag, got through one set of double doors and then another, and walked at a steady clip down a long, windowless corridor bathed in beige light.

A detour to the radiology reading room gave him a look at what lay beneath his patient's skin. In the room alone, he called up the CT scan. A three-dimensional skull glowed green on a computer screen, teeth bared, mouth open in a silent scream. The anterior skull base was shattered, and the entire midsection of the face, from the bottom of the nose to the middle of the forehead, was confetti.

Ho-ly shit, Kallman thought as he slumped back in his chair. *How the hell am I supposed to fix that?*

Heart thumping, he stood, then steeled himself and walked out, closing the door behind him. He backtracked to the hallway leading to the emergency department, stopped at the security doors, and swiped his badge. The double doors swung open. He walked through, took a turn at the nurses' station, then another into the biggest and best-equipped trauma bay at Providence, a room of harsh light and gleaming stainless steel. With the patient stabilized, the ER team was going over him head to toe to make sure nothing had been missed—an easy mistake when the main injury is a catastrophic. Everyone looked up as Kallman entered the room.

Before handing the patient over to the critical care team aboard a LifeGuard helicopter, the emergency medical technicians who'd hauled the young man out of the woods had stopped the worst of the bleeding, put in two IVs, and fixed a cervical collar around his neck. He'd been coherent enough to tell them his name was Dan Bigley, that he was twenty-five, and that he was allergic to penicillin. He'd started vomiting in the ambulance, and continued after the medevac crew took over and got him into the air. By the time he got to the emergency room, he was gagging on blood. His skin was cold to the touch. His speech was clear one moment, unintelligible the next, and he was fading in and out. When cognizant, he appeared to be in severe pain, and kept trying to touch his face. Yet unlike many trauma patients, who scream, cuss, and thrash about, he had remained calm and thanked Dr. McCue for helping him. She then sedated him and worked a breathing tube down his throat so he wouldn't drown.

Other than that, he looked just as the bear had left him, stashed in tall grass below the Kenai Peninsula's Russian River Campground just off a trail traveled day and night by thousands of anglers each summer. One look and Kallman got it, why McCue had sounded so unnerved. In addition to deep, dirty puncture wounds on his extremities, as if he'd been hit by shrapnel, he seemed to be missing the upper half of his face. The closest Kallman had seen to anything like it was the botched suicide attempt of a man who'd tipped his head back, put a shotgun in his mouth, and pulled the trigger.

"Upper nose, eyes, forehead anatomy unrecognizable," is how the medevac report had put it.

Covered in dried blood, with shreds of skin and forest debris all mashed together, the top half of Bigley's head was skewed to the left. His scalp was split open at the forehead, and on the left side a flap of skin was peeled back, exposing a jumble of tissue, shards, and bone. Kallman knew from the CT scan that the dura mater—a membrane protecting the brain—was probably torn. He could see exposed brain tissue behind the ruins of the nose.

Then there were the eyes. At first, Dr. McCue had been unable to find them amid the blood and grime. The force of the bear's jaws had popped them from their sockets, snapping the optic nerves, leaving one hanging by a thread of conjunctiva, and the other by just a few threads more. Both were intact but were on the same side of Bigley's shattered nose. It was obvious one was hopeless. The other had just enough connective tissue to possibly survive, although with the optic nerve severed it would never see. If Bigley lived, there was no doubt at all that he would be blind.

Of all his injuries, his shattered anterior skull base was the one most likely to kill him. With nothing to hold it up, the bottom of his brain had herniated down into his nose, exposing it to the world.

Bigley was conscious, but with a tube down his throat, he was unable to speak. Kallman leaned in close: "Can you hear me?"

Bigley gave a slight nod. Dr. Kallman introduced himself.

"Listen, you've got some pretty bad injuries to your face. Do you understand?"

He nodded.

"I'll be taking you into the operating room to take care of you."

Bigley squeezed his hand to show he understood.

Sometime around 6:30 a.m., Kallman woke up Sandy Glaspell, office manager of the private practice where he worked, calling her at home to give her a heads up.

"I'm going to need you to reschedule my patients," he told her. "I won't be making it into the office today. I got called in on a bear mauling. The guy's whole face is chewed up."

Later that morning, with an operating room team mobilized and an anesthesiologist in place, everything was ready to go. Dressed in blue scrubs, hands scoured and snapped into Latex gloves, Kallman walked into the operating room and up to the stainless steel table where Bigley lay on his back, prepped and draped, his ravaged body covered by a warming blanket. He stared down at the chaos before him and froze.

There was no manual for this one. Bear maulings were hardly on any East Coast medical school's checklist of commonly encountered traumas for residents to master. Where to begin? Kallman figured he must have looked pretty lost, because one of the senior operating room nurses walked up, put a hand on his shoulder, and asked, "Doctor, would you like to shave the hair?"

Kallman turned to her. "Right. That's where we'll start; we'll start with shaving the hair."

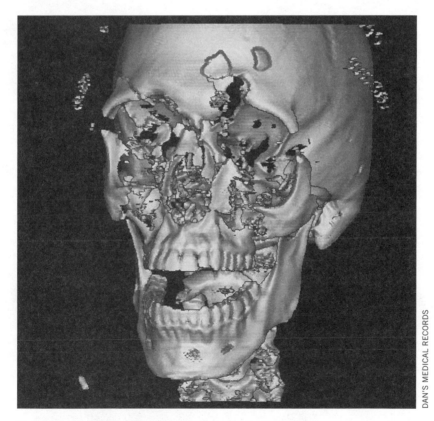

DAN'S MEDICAL RECORDS

Dan Bigley's CT scan after his medevac to Anchorage.

CHAPTER 1

Until That Day

THAT HALF-DEAD MAN ON THE OPERATING TABLE WAS ME, DAN BIGLEY. For a day that started with such promise to end this way was beyond comprehension.

The person I had been for the first twenty-five years of my life had died close to midnight. Slammed to the ground, clawed and chewed, I'd tried to play dead, fingers clamped around the back of my neck, elbows tucked in tight, shrieking through gritted teeth. The mauling had come in wave after wave. Between explosions of pain, the bear had stood over me panting. I could feel the power of its breath on the back of my neck. Just when I thought the bear was done, it started dragging me like a rag doll, facedown over ground as jagged as broken glass. It then flipped me over, cocked its head sideways, and bit me across the face.

A loud, hideous pop. Then quiet. Suspended in luminescent blue. No up, no down, my long-dead grandfather nodding at me in the distance.

One of the first rescuers to get to me that night was a former US Army Ranger, a combat veteran who'd served three tours in Vietnam. What he saw lying in the grass took him straight back to the jungle. It looked as if a grenade had gone off in my face. Colonel Frank Valentine knew a dead man when he saw one. *This kid doesn't have a chance,* he remembers thinking. A chance was all I did have, and I fought for it with every ounce of strength that hadn't yet drained out of my body.

That morning, before heading out for a day of fishing, I'd said goodbye to my new girlfriend, holding both of her hands in mine, interlacing our fingers.

"I'll give you a call when I get back from fishing to see what you're up to," I'd told her.

The way Amber looked at me with that sleepy smile of hers made me wonder what the hell was I thinking. Just this once I should pass on fishing and haul this woman back to bed. But for me, fishing was just shy of an obsession. I'd go fishing in cat-and-dog weather. I'd go fishing when the mosquitoes and no-see-ums were thick as smoke. That day it was pouring neither rain nor bugs, but was shaping up to be one of the bluest days of the summer, one for the tourist brochures. Plus my buddy, John, was waiting—waders, pole, and cooler already loaded into the back of his Subaru. So I hugged her, fingertips brushing the back of her neck. Then a quick kiss goodbye before I could change my mind.

I walked her to the door and watched from the deck as she ambled down the steps and over the footbridge that crossed the creek separating my place from the gravel road out front. She rounded up her dog, Hobbit, an imposing brute resembling a cross between a husky and a riding mower. The door of her old truck groaned as she swung it open. Hobbit hopped in, and she climbed in after him. She started the engine, glanced up, gave a quick wave, and drove off.

It would be the last time I'd see her face.

The morning after, as I lay within a huddle of blue scrubs, stainless steel instruments, and probing Latex fingers, she lay sleeping beneath a patchwork quilt. She'd later rise to public radio and shuffle into the kitchen. She'd pour water into her coffeemaker, add freshly ground French roast to the filter, and push the "brew now" button. She'd make herself Cream of Wheat. She'd go about the rest of her day afloat in thoughts of our night together, but wondering, too, why I never called after fishing like I said I would.

The timing was exceptionally cruel. Over the previous six months, one thing after another had fallen into place in my life, beginning when I landed the most challenging and rewarding job I'd ever had—working with severely emotionally disturbed kids. Then just the week before, I'd become the new owner of a cabin in Bear Valley, high above Anchorage in the Chugach Mountains with a view that went on forever. After signing closing papers and shaking hands with the seller, I'd celebrated back at my rental place by pouring a Crown Royal on the rocks, sitting alone on my deck in the evening light, feet propped up on the railing, thinking about how phenomenal it was going to be living up there. The universe, it seemed, was looking after me.

Just when I thought it couldn't get any better, after a year of being attracted to one Amber Takavitz, the planets had finally aligned, and we woke up that morning tangled in each other's arms. Had that bear not come barreling down the trail, its eyes locked on mine, July 14, 2003, would have been a day I looked back upon as one of the best I'd ever known.

Until that day, I lived in the small, bohemian ski town of Girdwood, a huddle of condos, log chateaus, hippie hovels, and crash pads with names like the Mushroom House, the Hobbit Hole, and Animal House, about forty miles southeast of Anchorage. Wedged between the Chugach Mountains and the silty, swirling waters of Turnagain Arm, the town was founded at the turn of the century as a gold mining supply camp, originally called Glacier City for the seven glaciers clinging to the mountains above. Girdwood was my kind of town, a place of artists and woods people and free-range dogs, worldly enough to have *Bon Appétit* noticing its restaurants, wild enough to have bears leaving nose prints on cabin windows.

In Girdwood, I found a community of kindred spirits, the kind who gathered regularly for potlucks and jam sessions, who lived to ski, kayak, hike, climb, and fish. The kind who launched paragliders off mountaintops at midnight on summer solstice, then soared, banked, and did pirouettes in the sky before landing in the backyard of my favorite watering hole in time for last call.

A college buddy and I had scored a sweet deal on a rental within walking distance of the Alyeska ski lifts. It was a funky (some would say derelict), rectangular, cedar-shake house that sagged like a hammock atop twelve-foot pilings. We joked how the floor was so bad in the kitchen, a minor earthquake, or even a passing gravel truck, might topple the refrigerator over like a drunk, sending it into a face-plant upon the patchwork linoleum floor. The carpet was a Pepto-Bismol pink muted by a series of previous tenants who apparently had an aversion to vacuum cleaners. On the upside, the place was cheap for a ski-resort town, and had a glacier view and a wraparound deck overlooking a creek. I could lie in bed in the morning, listen to howitzers being launched at avalanche chutes, and know without looking out my window a powder day was out there waiting for me. At the end of those powder days, I could ski past the lodge, across the road, down the street, and right up to my front steps.

After a series of miscellaneous jobs, from pounding nails to driving a shuttle for a whitewater rafting company, I'd finally landed one that gave my degree and sensibilities a workout. As an activity therapist for Alaska Children's Services, I was working with kids who'd been abused, addicted, abandoned, tossed out, and otherwise run through the wringer, kids who'd ended up in group homes and treatment programs rather than regular foster care. With a degree in natural history and a minor in environmental education from Arizona's Prescott College, I was a firm believer that the sanctity of nature could calm kids' troubled minds. I took them skiing, hiking, mountain biking, and climbing at the local rock gym. I explained how weather shapes the land and land shapes the weather. I had them spying on birds, peeking under rocks, and looking for pictures in the clouds. I had them kicking off their shoes and running barefooted along the shores of Cook Inlet and writing messages to pilots in the mudflats with sticks.

The job demanded creative thinking on the fly, the ability to shift into defuse mode when meltdowns were imminent, and to deal with them when they happened regardless, which was often the case. My boss at the time, Harlow Robinson, I later learned, referred to me as "the golden boy" and liked how well I connected with kids, including one of ACS's most challenging ones, a boy who'd blow up on an almost daily basis. I'd been at the job about six months, just long enough by a little over a week for my medical insurance to kick in.

Then there was Amber. I'd first noticed her the previous summer at my favorite hangout, Max's Mountain Bar and Grill, where she had a side job making pizzas and a crush on the house sound guy. Petite. Strawberry blonde. Freckles skittered across the bridge of her nose. Elegant arms. Curvy where it mattered.

As she tells it, she first noticed me, a six-foot-four, green-eyed, red-bearded, sun-streaked-blond ski bum, at the Aloha Alaska deli, which I walked or biked to nearly every morning with my dog, Maya, trotting alongside. Long before she and I knew each other's names, even longer before her dog, Hobbit, quit treating me like a burglar in my own house, our dogs had conducted full inspections, and approved.

They say opposites attract, and on the surface that may have seemed the case with us. I was the type who'd look at the highest peak in some mountain range and want to go there. Amber would glance up at the same peak, admire it from afar, and want to barbecue. Acquiring dreadlocks in high school and the nickname "Cedar" in college, I found even the vascular system of a blade of grass worthy of examination. Amber, a former high-school pom-pom girl and student-body president, once had to monitor a patch of land through the seasons for an ecology class, and just didn't get the point.

The worlds we grew up in, with courses set by our fathers, couldn't have been more different. My stepfather, "Dad" as far as my brother and I were concerned, was a senior manager in the chemicals division of Procter & Gamble, so my family lived life in the corporate lane of cocktail parties, BMWs, and world travel. He was a dapper, easygoing man who left the dirty work of discipline to my mother, and whose favorite sport was ensconcing himself in his easy chair with the *Wall Street Journal*, world affairs magazines, and something like the autobiography of Lee Iacocca all going at once. Plus CNN on TV in the background.

Amber's dad was a union pipe fitter with callused hands and a vise-grip view of his role in the family, who was either working long hours on overtime or waiting out the latest layoff. He had no use for travel at the time, preferring instead to tinker around the house, go walleye fishing, and watch football on the tube. As the disciplinarian in the family, he didn't just take Amber's car keys one time when she busted curfew so bad she barely made it home in time for breakfast, he took all four wheels off her car.

I grew up in California and Ohio, and spent my middle-school years in Malaysia, where my stepdad oversaw the building of a palm oil processing plant, and the family quarters came with a live-in housekeeper, a gardener, a driver, and barred windows to keep out monkeys. At the International School of Kuala Lumpur, class outings required leech-proof socks, and included kayaking down the Perak River and jungle trekking in the company of flying snakes, monitor lizards, and other fanged hazards.

Amber, whose family hadn't strayed far from the Boundary Waters area for three generations, grew up in the small town of Eveleth, Minnesota, home of the world's largest free-standing hockey stick, where blasts at the local open-pit mines sometimes rattled her school. Good times in Amber's childhood included cookouts, jet skiing, and attending an annual basketball match that pitted local firemen against the cops while riding on the backs of donkeys.

Besides that, I played guitar.

Amber played tuba.

For different reasons, we both rebelled against our upbringings, answered the call of the road, and found what we were looking for not far from where that road dead-ends at the northernmost edge of the continent. It wasn't long after I landed in Girdwood that Amber caught my attention. Once she did, I started keeping an eye out for her whenever I was out and about on the town. I took note of her on the sly, leaning behind a friend's back as she tossed horseshoes in the backyard at Max's. I checked her out from afar as she gyroscoped inside a purple hula-hoop to Grateful Dead tunes at the Jerry Garcia Pig Roast in Fairbanks. At that same festival, with me in a camp chair and her in a halter top and long, flowy skirt, I couldn't take my eyes off her as she cleaned and organized her Volkswagen van. She was a free spirit for sure, but not one of those cosmo-la-la types who think that if we all just embrace the magical power of crystals everything will work out fine. She struck me as the kind who could bake bread *and* change her own timing belt.

Amber may not have been up for skiing down chutes or hiking to the top of Max's Mountain at midnight, but as I'd later learn, she was actually ballsier than me. While pursuing a major in anthropology at the University of Minnesota, she'd boarded a plane to Kenya not long after a series of bombs at American Embassy buildings killed hundreds and wounded thousands. There, she lived with the Maasai, a semi-nomadic herding tribe that practiced polygamy and female circumcision, and traditionally offered its dead to the hyenas. While living in Malaysia in a gated house I'd felt brave eating shark-fin soup. While living in Kenya in a cow-dung hut, Amber ate what the Maasai ate and drank what the Maasai drank, which upon occasion meant taking a polite sip of blood from the throat of a slaughtered goat.

Once I learned through mutual friends that Amber had lived in one of the storied, off-the-grid cabins way up Girdwood's Crow Creek Road—in winter—she couldn't have been more appealing had she shown up on my doorstep in a nightie. The access alone, a gravel road winding its way up the valley along steep mountain slopes and across several avalanche paths, was enough of a moat to weed out most. Amber, her best friend, Rebecca "Bekkie" Volino, and their two dogs had moved into a tiny cabin up there in February, 2002. Although workers living at the gold mine above kept the road reasonably plowed, Amber was driving a low-rider Oldsmobile with summer tires that would sometimes lose traction and start sliding backward like a spooked horse. She'd have to back down, get a running start, and gun it. She'd then pull over at a spot a person might pick who wanted to wander off and never be found. She'd hoist her pack onto her back, walk into the woods, and head down a trail to a bluff so steep there were fixed ropes for lowering herself down.

The cabin, hunkered at the bottom next to Crow Creek, was about as spacious as a lunchbox, with as many amenities. No electricity. No phone. Not even cell phone coverage. Amber and Bekkie had to share the only sleeping space, a double mattress atop a sheet of plywood propped up off the floor on five-gallon buckets. They used a Coleman lantern for light and a woodstove for heat and cooking, hauling firewood down via zip line.

She was living elsewhere by the time we started exchanging greetings and opinions about the weather. Working as a high-school counselor for Cook Inlet Tribal Council in Anchorage, she was living halfway between Girdwood and the city in the small, woodsy community of Bird Creek. Tired of the commute, she'd heard about this oasis of mountain living above Anchorage called Bear Valley, considered by my crowd as the Girdwood annex, and was intrigued. I'd just put earnest money down on my cabin up there and was in a holding pattern waiting to close.

"You should talk to Dan," a friend told her.

Standing around the fire pit one night in the backyard at Max's, I saw her weaving around this person and that person and some other person's dog. In snug jeans, a maroon hoodie, and ankle-high Steger mukluks, she was headed my way as if on a mission. I plunged my hands deep into my front pockets and rocked back on my heels. She walked up. I grinned. She grinned. "Hey," I said. "Hey," she said. She hooked her straight, shoulder-length hair behind her ears and got down to business.

"I heard you got a place up Bear Valley. I'm actually looking to buy some land, and was hoping you might have some leads."

"Yeah, I do. I mean, I will once some property line issues get straightened out. I poked around up there for quite a while before finding my place, and have a pretty good handle on what's for sale. I could show you around if you want."

Amber stared at me a moment while the offer sunk in. She hadn't expected that. Maybe a nudge in the right direction, a number to call or something, but not a private tour. She started nodding her head in slow motion.

"Cool," she said as she fiddled with a dangly earring. "Great. Yeah. That would be awesome."

Her carpool partner dropped her off at Alaska Children's Services after work a couple of days later. Waiting for me in the lobby, she could have sworn that Barb Good, the motherly receptionist who'd more or less adopted me and kept me well stocked with her homemade wild-berry jams, was giving her the once-over. I finally rescued her, and we hopped into my truck, a tricked-out, tomato-red, extended cab Toyota Tacoma I'd bought at an Arizona pawn shop my senior year at Prescott—chrome runners, brush guards, custom rims, sweet struts, and a killer stereo with an amplifier built in under the seat. Banished to the backseat, my dog, Maya, who went everywhere with me including work, kept trying to reclaim her spot up front, pushing forward between the seats, panting over Amber's left shoulder, making her laugh and taking the edge off our mutual nervousness.

I drove south to the edge of the city, then up into the Chugach Mountains, taking a sharp turn at one side road, then another, and another. Amber, being the reticent type, seemed grateful that I was a talker. Born premature, I'd entered the world sickly and went deaf as a toddler, which seriously delayed my speech. Surgery fixed me, and I'd been making up for lost time ever since. We talked about my truck, about our dogs, about plans for the coming summer. The further up we went, the less hospitable the road. After several miles, we met the road-sign equivalent of a mean dog: "Restricted Road. Hazard. Ice conditions. Four-wheel drive, reinforced chains required. All vehicles travel at driver's own risk . . ." This was my kind of driveway.

On the final stretch, pavement finally gave up, and a contorted, grimacing guardrail made it clear the sign back there wasn't just for show. Halfway up the last mile of potholes and washboard came a nosebleed-steep pitch that had Amber clutching the oh-shit handle above the passenger door. At the top, I took a sharp right and the road narrowed, passing a cabin here and a cabin there before coming to one with a set of old wooden skis crossed above the porch, the one I was in the process of buying.

"Wow," Amber said as she climbed out of my truck in Birkenstock sandals, a short-sleeved blouse, and another of her long, flowy skirts. "It's pretty much heaven up here."

It was a gorgeous May evening, warm by springtime-in-Alaska standards, at least fifty-something degrees, although that high up, patches of stubborn, windblown snow still clung to the mountainside. We stood together in silence a moment.

"Obviously the place needs some work," I laughed.

Notorious Chugach Mountain gusts that can hit Category 1, even 2, hurricane strengths, had pried off a section of the cabin's weather-beaten plywood exterior, leaving Tyvek exposed and the place looking gap toothed. Its innards were about as refined, with an aluminum ladder connecting the first floor to the second via an opening just wide enough to shove through a mattress folded up like a taco. The kitchen counter was covered in a mishmash of salvaged linoleum, and the sink drained into a five-gallon bucket that demanded vigilance lest it overflow onto the floor. The bathroom was an outhouse with no frills, not even *Far Side* cartoons tacked to the walls, just a one-seater with a bucket of lime on the floor and a coffee can as a toilet paper holder. It didn't even have a door.

For me this place was all about the land. Out back was endless hiking and telemark-ski terrain, including a gully packed with snow that was skiable almost year-round. Out front was a view of Cook Inlet, Sleeping Lady mountain from her knees to her toes, and Denali, the highest peak in North America at 20,320 feet. Plus the next two stateliest peaks in the Alaska Range, Mount Foraker and Mount Hunter. Even the outhouse had a million-dollar view.

Three adjacent lots were among those for sale, so the three of us tromped over to check them out, brush and snow crunching beneath our feet. As Amber walked ahead, I noticed her skirt was the slightest bit see-through in the intense seasonal light, enough to imagine the shape of her legs. I watched as she moved across disheveled land as gracefully as a caribou floats across tussocks, except that her skirt kept getting caught on the shrubberies and she'd have to stop now and then and give a little tug. *Nope*, I thought, *I wouldn't mind having this woman as a neighbor one bit.*

"It's stunning up here," she said at the end of the tour. "I can't think of any place I'd rather live."

A silence settled over us as we stood side by side looking out at Denali, then down on the city, filling our lungs with the delicacy of mountain air. We turned to each other and locked eyes. I went all lightheaded. Time to go.

I got Maya loaded up, and we headed down the mountainside, then turned south toward Turnagain Arm, an alcove of Cook Inlet, with glistening mudflats and restless seawaters on one side, three-thousand-foot mountains on the other, Dall sheep poised like gargoyles on the cliffs above. About halfway to Girdwood, just a few miles from Amber's place in Bird Creek, I noticed a cluster of cars pulled off on the side of the road and people milling about the shoulder wielding binoculars and cameras. Out there in the arm the incoming tide was rising and rolling, rising and rolling like whitewater rapids. Only they weren't rapids. I checked my mirrors, braked, and pulled over.

"Sorry, girl," I told Maya, "but you gotta stay."

Amber and I scrambled out of my truck, and leaving the crowd behind, climbed over the guardrail, crossed the railroad tracks, slid down a short scree slope on our heels, then scrambled up a rocky outcropping that dropped off into saltwater the color of unpolished steel.

"Can you believe this?" I hollered over the din of water and wind. "They're right here! In-friggin'-credible."

Just beyond the water's edge, what looked to be at least a hundred beluga whales were riding the incoming tide in pursuit of a small, anadromous fish called hooligan. We sat spellbound at the edge of the outcropping, letting the scene before us sink in. The whales were so close we could not only hear the *poof . . . poof . . . poof* of their blowholes but could swear we felt the windblown mist of their breath upon our faces.

Amber shook her head over and over in disbelief. I scooted closer, until we were hip-to-hip and I could feel the warmth of her body.

"I had no idea they came this close to shore," I said. "We are so lucky."

"We are *so* lucky. This is unbelievable."

We sat then without talking, watching wave after wave of white whales, listening to the rhythm of their breath and of water lapping against the rocks below. Amber looked so fine, her wind-tossed hair the color of Scottish ale. I had to practically bite my shoulder to keep from putting my arm around her.

The belugas continued up Turnagain Arm, row after disorderly row of them. We saw them off until it was down to a handful of stragglers and the crowd along the highway had thinned. The wind picked up and the air got chilly. We needed to get moving, but neither of us was ready to call it a night.

We stopped for beers down the highway at the Brown Bear Saloon, a classic Alaska dive with dustbin decor, seam-sealed in cigarette smoke and wallpapered in business cards, autographed dollar bills, and bumper stickers like "Guns Don't Kill People; Guns Kill Dinner." The only ones in the place besides the bartender were two arthritic dogs, one of them missing a leg. We grabbed a table next to a window and, all hopped up from what we'd just witnessed, rattled on about the whales and Bear Valley and our respective jobs while Amber fiddled her cocktail napkin into shreds. One beer became another, and I found myself leaning into her words, unable to take my eyes off her. When she started describing her future ambitions, to live overseas so her children could experience things she never knew existed growing up in small-town Minnesota, I felt like the woman had been reading my mind.

"Exactly! That's exactly what I want for my kids."

Mid-laugh I kind of lunged across the table and grabbed both her hands in mine. Then, as if I'd snatched a pair of potatoes straight from the oven, I dropped them, jerked back, and continued to laugh, hoping she didn't notice. She noticed.

When our glasses were empty, I considered the possibilities of where another round might lead. Something between panic and euphoria balled up in my stomach, like fear dipped in syrup. I was falling for her, and when I fall, I fall like a sack of rocks. More beer, I decided, wasn't just a bad idea, it was a really bad idea.

I dropped her off at her house in Bird Creek, my engine left running. After an awkward and hasty goodbye, I sped the rest of the way home with Thievery Corporation's "The Richest Man in Babylon" blasting from my speakers, fingers drumming the steering wheel, wide-eyed and dumbstruck, as if Cupid had bashed me upside the head with a tire iron.

The next morning, recovered from the intensity of the evening, I decided not to push it. Things were too good in my life to risk falling in love. I'd been there, done that, and had sworn off girlfriends for a while after my last two relationships went up in smoke. As jerkish as it sounds, I didn't call her. Not the next day, nor the day after that. I'd had my heart broken twice, and wasn't ready to give it another try. Besides, I was still on this grand adventure and having too much fun answering to no one but my dog.

In the following weeks when I was out on the town, I found myself hoping to bump into her, and sometimes I would. We would hang out, drink some beers, shoot some pool, have some laughs, get a little cozy, and at the end of the night I'd chicken out and we'd go our separate ways. Not one for drama, Amber decided I really wasn't interested. The truth was, I couldn't get her out of my mind, especially during a trip I made to California for the High Sierra Music Festival over the Fourth of July weekend. There I was with my brother and some of my closest buddies from college, with music and theatrics and enticing women all around, and all I could think of was how much better it would be had Amber come along.

By the time I returned I'd decided to go for it. The New Orleans band Galactic was playing at the ski lodge that coming weekend, and I knew Amber would be there. I just hoped it wasn't too late.

The night of the show, I got home from work around seven. I grilled up some fresh salmon, tossed together a salad from my garden, and had a quiet dinner in the sun alone on my deck. I washed my dishes and stacked them in the drainer. I brought Maya inside, filled her water dish, poured kibble into her bowl, and topped it off with salmon skin peeled off the grill. While brushing my teeth in front of the mirror, I noticed my hair was a bit rowdier than usual. I pulled my favorite ball cap over the top of it, and headed out to the show.

Halfway through the first set I saw her up front near the stage. I watched her a while, then worked my way up, dodging dancers' elbows and toes. Our eyes met. We nodded at each other. If she was irritated with me for dropping the ball she didn't show it. I gave her a big hug, and she gave me a big grin.

"It's *really* good to see you," I shouted over the din.

We danced side by side facing the stage in a crush of bobbing bodies, and hung around each other off and on the rest of the night. But the place was so packed, by the time the show ended around midnight, I had lost track of her. I waited outside by the front door watching people pour out of the lodge, but didn't see her. I went back inside, looked around, went back out, waited some more. Then I noticed clusters of people milling about the parking lot, and there she was, sitting on the tailgate of her truck, talking to friends while Hobbit was off watering the shrubberies.

Everyone was heading to the bars, but Amber had been holding back, hoping I would show up. When she saw me strolling her way, hands in my pockets, acting all nonchalant as if I'd forgotten which way was home, she hopped off the tailgate to greet me.

"Yo, Amber! You coming?" someone shouted from across the way. She glanced in that direction, then back at me and shrugged. "Well?"

"I'm not feeling the whole bar thing right now," I said. "Could I talk you into a beer at my place?"

She paused a moment. "Yeah, sure, that sounds good to me."

Back at the house, I grabbed two IPAs from the refrigerator, popped them open, handed her one, and took a long draw from the other for courage. We took them out on the deck overlooking the creek, where, leaning side by side against the railing, I took a deep breath and finally said it.

"I thought about you a lot down in California. Actually, I couldn't stop thinking about you."

Amber stared down at the creek and felt her face grow hot. She turned to me with a crooked smile. "Oh, did ya now?"

I couldn't stand it any longer. I looked at Amber, and she looked at me, and for a moment we both forgot to breathe. I reached for her hand, and led her back into the house and down the hall to my bedroom, closing the door behind us.

My room had little to offer in terms of sitting options. So we sat cross-legged on my bed facing each other, the sound of the creek pouring in through my open window. I took Amber's hand and placed her palm against my heart, then put my own against hers. We sat without talking, without needing to.

"I feel like I've known you my whole life," I told her.

It wasn't anything either of us said that cinched it. We knew without saying that we would be making love. But not that night. Both of us were half-tanked, and we didn't want our first time to be that way. We lay snuggling on top of my comforter, talking in near whispers, soaking up the warmth of each other's bodies. We held each other until four in the morning before finally drifting off to sleep.

My buddy, John Duray, broke the spell when he showed up around 10:30 that morning. He knocked on the front door, and when no one answered, he let himself in. He shouted down the hallway. "Hey, Dan! You awake in there? Let's not keep those reds waiting!"

I awoke with a start. "Ah, yeah. Be right out."

When I wasn't, John walked down the road to the Aloha Alaska deli and returned a little later with my ritual morning elixir, a sixteen-ounce cup of Americano.

"Yo, Dan! Time to rally. I've got you some coffee out here."

A little embarrassed and more than a little groggy, Amber and I rolled out of bed and stumbled out to the kitchen. I didn't want to leave her, but like I've already admitted, fishing was my weakness. I liked to say that if I lost both arms, I'd figure out a way to fish. I considered inviting her along. But we'd had such an intense night I figured we could each use some space to let it percolate. So I didn't. I hugged and kissed her goodbye.

"I'll give you a call when I get back from fishing to see what you're up to," I told her.

It was a promise I would be unable to keep.

At Chilkoot Lake, 2001.

FAMILY PHOTO

CHAPTER 2

River of Bears

I was well aware I was heading into bear country. I could see that from my deck. In Girdwood, it wasn't unheard of for bears to bury their heads in garbage cans or dog-food sacks stored on people's porches. A friend of mine had his truck stolen by a bear. He was living up Crow Creek Road when he heard a commotion one morning, got up to investigate, and discovered his truck was gone. A black bear had climbed in through an open window and knocked it out of gear, sending truck and bewildered bear rolling down the driveway and off an embankment. (The bear was fine; the truck, not so much.) Even Anchorage, inhabited by Walmarts, Jiffy Lubes, and nearly half the population of Alaska, had bears in its backyard, and upon occasion, its front. Now and then a black bear or grizzly would forage its way into the land of car dealerships and mattress barns, crossing bike trails, lawns, sidewalks, parking lots, and busy roads before being stopped by the Alaska Department of Fish and Game's urban wildlife conflict-resolution team, with a tranquilizer dart if public safely allowed, with a slug if not. Bears have been hit by cars in Anchorage. They've been hit by bicycles. Just the day before, as I was getting a capture the flag game underway with a group of kids, a young grizzly popped out of the woods. The hair on the back of my neck went red-alert, but the situation ended the way nearly all encounters do, with the bear taking one look, wanting no part of us, and motoring off like its butt was on fire.

I had tremendous respect for bears, especially grizzlies—or brown bears as biologists refer to the larger, coastal dwellers—as powerful symbols of the wild lands I loved. I'd studied them as part of my senior project at Prescott College, and was convinced they were more tolerant of humans than the other way around. I also knew what they were capable of. Bears kill one or two people a year in this country. A person is much more likely to be killed by a dog, and even more likely to die of an allergic reaction to the sting of a bee. Although my parents would disagree, I wasn't much of a risk taker. I never felt the need to BASE jump off a cliff or kayak whitewater courses more waterfall than river. But for me to avoid the kinds of places large predators roam would be unthinkable.

Before a chance encounter with an indignant bear hijacked my dreams, my interactions with bears had ranged from amusing to annoying, and either way had left me with a good story to tell. Like the grizzly I came upon at Kluane Lake on my way up the Alaska Highway one summer. The bear was lying on its back on a rocky beach, tossing a driftwood log into the air, catching it, tossing it again, catching it, even giving it a little twirl, like a circus bear.

The fall before my freshman year at Prescott, I took a Sierra Institute wilderness field study course through the University of California Santa Cruz that had me living out of a backpack and sleeping outdoors for two months straight. One of those nights, sleeping under a full moon near Mammoth Lakes, I woke up to a black bear sniffing my face. Although my heart felt like it might make a run for it without me, I lay still as concrete as the bear sniffed its way on by—front leg beside my left temple, followed by sagging belly, then a hind leg, passing me by with hardly a sound. Once the bear cleared my head and became preoccupied with other campsite curiosities, I slowly sat up in my sleeping bag. The rustle of nylon gave me away. The bear stopped, turned, and glanced back at me. I held my breath. The bear swung its head back around and moseyed on. When it was about twenty feet away, I shimmied out of my bag, rose to my feet, and followed barefooted as it made its way to the edge of camp. Now and then the bear would stop, turn, and glance back. I would freeze. It would swing its head back around and take a few more steps. Then stop. Turn. Glance back. Freeze. We kept up this game of red light, green light until the bear strolled into a moonlit meadow, and I decided I'd pushed my luck far enough and stopped to watch. When the bear reached the far end of the clearing, it looked me over one last time, then ducked into the woods. I took that encounter as a gift.

Only once did I harbor malevolent thoughts toward a bear. Or, in this case, bears. As I remember it, on what was to have been a ten-day trip, a half-dozen or so of us Sierra Institute students and our instructor hiked deep into Sequoia National Park to set up a base camp. After choosing spots on a map, we all took off alone in various directions for three-day solos, leaving our instructor behind to hold down the fort and mind our food cache. While we were off communing with the redwoods, subsisting on gorp, oatmeal soaked overnight in cold water, and the writings of John Muir, our instructor spent those days and nights fighting off a black bear sow and her three cubs hell-bent on stealing our food. When we trickled back into camp three days later, we were met by this wild-haired, wild-eyed frazzle of a man. He turned camp security over to us, stumbled off to his tent, flopped inside, and was asleep before his head hit his Therm-a-Rest.

Sierra Nevada black bears are notorious for such single-mindedness, having long associated people with food. In Yosemite, some punks of the bear world have learned to think of cars as cookie jars, and have popped windows and peeled back doors going after goodies inside. Minivans seem to be a favorite, probably because they're built to haul kids, and where there are kids there are Happy Meal remnants and wayward Cheetos. Once inside, they've torn through backseats to get at food stored in the trunk. They don't just go for food; beer or toothpaste will do.

The bears we were up against on that Sequoia trip were just as determined and relentless. Our food bags were hung high in various trees, and the bears came at them from every angle. Mom would shake the trees, trying to get the bags to fall. The cubs would climb up the trunks and out onto branches to try to snag the bags from above and below. When one strategy didn't deliver, they would try   her. We took turns hollering, waving jackets, and pelting their butts with rocks. They'd scamper off, only to come trundling back fifteen or twenty minutes later. They kept this up all night long. The next day and night, as well.

Wiped out by then, we decided to abort mission, and hiked halfway back to the trailhead. The bears followed. We'd stop for quick lessons along the way, dropping our packs and huddling around, say, a pile of scat to debate its contents and determine its depositor. The bears would be on our gear in an instant. My pack got gnawed, but a classmate's got shredded to the point we had to divvy up his load among us. We finally ditched the bears after our fifth day under siege.

Of the hundreds of miles I'd hiked and climbed and biked and boated in bear country, I'd only been charged once and it wasn't by a bear. It happened when two friends and I and our three respective dogs were backpacking near Boulder, Colorado, and made camp in a clearing in the Ponderosa pines. This was not only black bear country, we'd been warned of mountain lions in the area. Late that night as we stared into a campfire our dogs suddenly went ballistic, barking, snapping, and lunging, with the one named Gimli dragging the backpack he was tethered to behind him. I leapt to my feet, spun around, and saw a large, shadowy figure at the edge of the flickering campfire light.

What the . . . ? Heart revving, I reached down and grabbed a flaming log poking partway out of the campfire to wield as a club. As I wound up to swing, with the creature now illuminated by the campfire, I found myself staring into the most menacing eyes I'd ever seen.

Normally when confronted with danger, a porcupine will pull an about-face, warn off its enemy by flashing a tail-load of quills, then hightail it out of there with a determined waddle. Instead, this thing charged. Having no idea porcupines were capable of such locomotion, I staggered backward, took a swing with my flaming club, then launched the whole log right at it and took off running. *Ahhhhhhh!* The campsite, only moments before as peaceful as a quilting bee, turned madhouse with three guys darting around chasing the three dogs that were chasing the porcupine that was chasing me. Realizing it was outnumbered, maybe, the porcupine finally slipped back into the shadows and scurried off into the woods.

Since coming to Alaska, the first time to work on an independent study project in the summer of 2001, I had crossed paths with several bears, both blacks and grizzlies. Alaska's bears are generally wilder than Lower-48 bears, especially compared to black bears in areas as heavily traveled as the Sierra Nevada, and are therefore much less inclined to associate people with food. By mid-July, 2003, I had fished Alaska rivers the better part of three summers, enough to know bears could pop out of the brush anytime, anywhere, especially in places I most loved to fish.

While remote fly-in fishing is the quintessential Alaska experience, it can make the price per pound comparable to precious metal. The Kenai and Russian rivers on the Kenai Peninsula are prolific, world-class rivers accessible by road in a state where roads are rare, offering between the two of them trophy-size Dolly Varden and rainbow trout, and runs of four species of Pacific salmon—Chinook, sockeye, coho, and humpback.

I was partial to the Russian, the narrower and shallower of the two rivers, with its water running clear, as opposed to the cyan-tinted Kenai, a liquid conveyor belt of glacial silt. The Kenai can be excellent salmon fishing, but the Russian can be phenomenal. To me, the Russian River was the fisherman's equivalent of a neighborhood bar. When the salmon were running, I'd be down there after work and on my days off three times a week, not giving the 140-mile round-trip drive from Girdwood a second thought, especially considering how hard the salmon work to get there.

Theirs is a pilgrimage of epic proportions, which increased my reverence and gratitude whenever one intercepted the business end of my fishing pole. After surviving the freshwater phase of their formative years, they go to sea, spending two to seven years, depending on the species, dodging whales, salmon sharks, and other ocean-dwelling predators, and evading commercial fishing nets, before returning to Cook Inlet, then the mouth of the Kenai River. Then they basically run a marathon while on a hunger strike as they bulldoze their way against the current more than seventy miles to the confluence of the Kenai and Russian rivers, where they rest up before pushing onward and upward—all to sacrifice themselves for the posterity of their species, or, with any luck, a spot in my cooler.

The confluence of the Russian and Kenai rivers is the mother lode of fishing holes known as The Sanctuary. This is ground zero for combat fishing, with anglers standing practically elbow to elbow along the banks during the most prized salmon runs. Although the fish we were after that day, sockeyes—or reds as we call them—are on a spawning mission and stop eating once they hit fresh water, they plow their way upriver with mouths open, closed, open, closed, forcing water through their gills. The only way to catch them, legally anyway, is to intercept them with fishing line at a mouth-open moment. As the current drags the line downriver, you hook them in the mouth. This is called flossing, and it isn't as hard as it sounds when the runs are so thick it would be just as easy, it seems, to wade out into the river and pounce on them.

A side effect of such great fishing is that, through the years, great fishing has drawn more and more fishermen, and more and more fishermen catching more and more fish means literally tons of guts and carcasses get left behind. That has drawn more and more bears. People like me come for the fillets. Bears come for the leftovers, the egg sacks and carcasses rich with brains and other delicacies that are winged back into the river after we've cleaned and filleted our catches. The US Forest Service, landlord of the Russian River Campground and its day-use parking lots, installed fish-cleaning stations to address, among other issues, the problem of fish being cleaned along riverbanks, which drew bears, and fish being cleaned at the campground, which drew bears. The cleaning stations were positioned so people could toss carcasses into the main current where they were more likely to disperse, providing nutrients for aquatic life rather than a buffet line for bears. Instead, carcasses piled up here and there, caught on snapped fishing line, on rocks, and in eddies—which drew bears.

The way it's been explained to me, anglers discarding an average of 114,000 pounds, or fifty-seven tons, of fish waste annually within what's now called the Kenai-Russian River Complex (a five-mile radius from the confluence of the two) have lured bears to an area where they normally wouldn't linger or congregate in such high numbers. It's not that bears don't fish. They do fish. But there are much better fishing spots for bears, including farther up the Russian River valley where the water is shallower, fish are easier to catch, and people are few. As one local biologist explained it, bears would normally fish later in the runs, at times much less appealing to fishermen, when salmon are closer to being spawned out and dying, and therefore easier to catch. So I'm not saying bears are lazy. I'm saying bears are smart.

By the time I started fishing down there, the fabulous fishing and ensuing carcass pileup were putting bears and humans in the same place at the same time, both in ridiculous numbers, making confrontations inevitable. Bear cubs were growing up learning carcass-grazing as a legitimate means of making a living. A handful of brazen juveniles were losing their fear of humans, learning that all it took was a stroll along the riverbanks looking all badass to clear people out, leaving coolers, backpacks, and fish on stringers theirs for the taking, a no-good situation for either species since people can get hurt and bears can get shot.

The situation at the Russian had been years in the making. "What we've done is create an artificial food source," Alaska Department of Fish and Game bear biologist Sean Farley told the *Anchorage Daily News* after a grizzly sow was gut-shot at the Russian two years after my attack. "I know I'm going to get in trouble for saying that. It's a very strange, bureaucratic, Byzantine mess."

Looking after one of the state's most heavily fished salmon streams, while at the same time protecting bears from the artillery-packing angling public, no doubt made for some management challenges for the various state and federal agencies overseeing the river, its banks, the campground, and the wild lands beyond. But it seemed to me that if the carcass problem could have been solved, over time the bears would have returned to behaving more like wild bears, much like the garbage bears of Yellowstone National Park did when the last of the dumps was shut down in 1970. They would do as their ancestors had done; they would go out of their way to avoid humans, leaving The Sanctuary and other hot spots to the possessed fishing hordes.

Nearly every plan for managing the convergence of the fish, bears, people, river, and land came with a downside, it seemed. The cleaning stations becoming bear magnets was one of them. Bank restoration was another. The thousands of anglers descending upon these rivers between May and September each year were trampling the riverbanks to death, prompting a huge and spendy restoration project. Boardwalks were built, gravel trails established, steps constructed, and fences erected. As a result, tall, lush grasses, and other thick vegetation once again thrived. Wonderful, particularly for the fish since unfettered trampling of riverbanks impacts habitat. Only one problem. All that lushness made it harder for bears to see fishermen and fishermen to see bears, and that could lead to nothing but trouble.

The already worrisome bear situation was even more so in July, 2003. Earlier that summer, the first of two annual red salmon runs had been weak. The second run in July, the one I was going for that day, was stronger, but salmon bound for the Russian were still holed up at The Sanctuary, resting before continuing on to spawning grounds upriver. Maybe it was just a fluke, but for whatever reason, black bears and grizzly sows with cubs were pacing up and down the riverbanks in even higher than the usual high numbers. Grizzly boars, which normally keep to the high country, were wandering down in search of food, which put sows on edge, since males will sometimes kill cubs.

In early July, a sow with cubs charged through a riverside fence trying to get at a fisherman, who shot and wounded her in self-defense. Two days later three cubs were reported up a tree at the Russian River Campground. Their mother's carcass was found nearby. Biologists captured the fifty-pound cubs, then made the difficult decision to euthanize them when no wildlife facility or zoo could take them.

Two days before he would play a role in my rescue, fisherman Tom Swiech witnessed a terrifying encounter at The Sanctuary between a young couple and a sow with three cubs. They hadn't seen the bears, and were crossing the river more or less between them when the sow came huffing and splashing across the river straight at them.

"Behind you, behind you! Watch out! Don't move! Hold your ground!"

They dropped their poles, grabbed a hold of each other, and froze. Swiech held his breath. The bear charged. *I'm going to see these kids get eaten right in front of me*, he thought. The bear stopped no less than twenty feet away, slapped the water with a front paw, clacked its jaw, turned, and huffed off.

Swiech was visiting from Pennsylvania at the time, but had fished the Russian for four summers while stationed at Elmendorf Air Force Base in Anchorage. Of all the previous trips he'd made to the Kenai and Russian rivers, he'd seen only one bear—a black one. This trip, fishing six days over the course of two weeks, he'd seen thirteen grizzlies, or brown bears as they're called in these parts.

The bear situation I was heading into that day was what some might consider off the charts. According to news accounts at the time, no one in the previous twenty-five years remembered seeing so many bears at one time near the confluence.

My buddy, John, and I had heard talk of bears in the area. But when fishing the Russian, there was always talk of bears in the area. Anyone dead-set against seeing bears should fish somewhere other than the Russian, somewhere other than Alaska, for that matter. So my bearanoia meter wasn't set any higher than usual that day.

I'd been in California the previous week for the High Sierra Music Festival, and was telling my friend Jeremy Grinkey my Alaska fishing stories, including how it's not uncommon during salmon runs to share the best fishing grounds with bears.

"Man, that would scare the hell out of me," he'd said.

"That's just part of fishing those rivers," I'd told him. "As long as you handle yourself correctly, keep your guard up, make noise, stay alert, and be respectful, you'll be fine. The bears pretty much mind their own business."

I was dead wrong about that. Because what awaited me down on the Russian that day was a pressure cooker about to blow its lid.

Brown bears at the Russian River.

A squabble over fishing rights.

CHAPTER 3

Last Light

THE LAST MORNING I WOULD EVER SEE, AFTER AMBER'S TRUCK disappeared around the corner, I went back inside to round up my gear while John organized the back of his car. I grabbed my tackle box, daypack, polarized shades, and trademark hat, a kiwi-green ball cap with "Bonfire" emblazoned across the front, a freebie I'd scored working as a ski tech at Dodge Ridge ski area in the Sierras. Although it made me a walking billboard for a snowboard apparel company, I'd latched onto it because I was drawn to bonfires like a skydiver to gravity. Bonfires drew people together. I'd made friends, swapped stories, played tunes, and conjured up some of my most epic adventures, plus a misadventure or two, around these tribal gatherings. Plans to show Amber around Bear Valley were made around a bonfire. I was so attached to that hat it had practically become part of my anatomy, enough that some started calling me "Bonfire Dan."

After slapping it on my head, I poured Maya a bowl of Eukanuba for breakfast, then rummaged through the cupboards for snacks to toss into my pack. I paused a moment and leaned against the kitchen counter as my night with Amber replayed in my head. It was out of character for me to look forward to a day of fishing being over before it had begun, but I couldn't wait to see her again.

"Hey, Dan, you about ready?" John shouted from below.

I washed down the thought with my last gulp of coffee, threw on my pack, and clomped down the steps in cargo pants, a T-shirt, and the Chaco sandals I wore everywhere, preferring them to boots on backpacking trips until moving to Alaska, where sandal-friendly terrain is in short supply. At the bottom of the stairs, I grabbed my chest waders and rod, which I kept hanging from hooks beneath the deck so they'd be ready to go at a moment's notice. I tossed it all into the back of John's Subaru next to the cooler and gave the hatch a slam. Swinging open the back passenger door, I called for Maya.

"Come on girl, let's load up."

A Lab mixed with whatever ran through the breeder's barnyard that day, Maya and I had hiked hundreds of miles together on countless trips, from the saguaros, jumping chollas, and prickly pears of the Sonoran Desert to Alaska's Chugach Mountains in terrain more suitable for goats. Although she'd tangled with a rattlesnake, a javelina, and several moose, Maya was a good listener and I could always call her off. Almost always, anyway. As my most loyal fishing partner, she had her etiquette down. She was content to sit back and watch, letting her tail express approval as a fish flopped on a riverbank, but staying out of the way until it had been whacked, and then just a quick inspection with her nose. Maya knew exactly what a car loaded with fishing paraphernalia meant. She got her wound-up hindquarters under control and jumped into the backseat. The front passenger door handle only worked from the inside, so John leaned over and opened it for me. I slid in, John cranked the engine, and off we went southbound on the Seward Highway with John Brown's Body reggae tunes booming from the speakers.

I had just twelve hours left, twelve hours before being plunged into darkness, twelve hours before the life I loved and assumed was mine for keeps would no longer exist.

Until then, the day couldn't have fit my mood better. Warm, cloudless, and ridiculously blue, that day in July was one of those classic Alaska summer days that induce winter amnesia, deleting from memory all those long dark months of icy roads, dead car batteries, and bitter winds that seep through windowsills and send backyard greenhouses flying like box kites. As we passed the turnoff to Portage Glacier, I glanced up the valley, a foyer of mountains with hanging glaciers all shimmery and mouthwash blue, and reminded myself yet again how blessed I was to have landed in such a place. Soon after, the highway bore right toward the Kenai Peninsula at the far end of Turnagain Arm—so named after a scouting crew in 1778 that included William Bligh of *Mutiny on the Bounty* fame, serving as sailing master on Captain James Cook's quest for the Northwest Passage, was forced to turn around again. I leaned forward in my seat and soaked up the glacier-sculpted landscape, with Chugach Mountain peaks dolloped with remnants of winter off in the distance, multiple variations on the theme of green sloshing up their mountainsides. To my left, trumpeter swans bobbed in a marsh. Up ahead, a lone raven surfed thermal waves high above the trees.

As the highway parted company with the Arm and started climbing toward Turnagain Pass, my mind wandered back to Amber. I debated whether to bring her up, but couldn't stop myself. I knew John had to be wondering.

"So, you know, Amber and I really hit it off last night. It's kind of crazy, but I think we're going to go for it."

"Oh yeah? Huh. That's cool." By that he meant, this better not interfere with our fishing.

John had actually met Amber before any of us had moved to Alaska, as mutual friends of the Minneapolis-based jam band the Sweet Potato Project. He didn't know much about her other than that, like me, she couldn't say no to live music shows. In fact, our paths may never have intersected if not for the Girdwood-based band the Photonz, which lured us both to town. Amber was at the end of a festival-hopping road trip from Minnesota to Alaska when someone urged her to check out the band, which was playing that night in Girdwood. I'd befriended band members while they were on tour and I was a senior at Prescott, and they had talked up the place. Although John and I had sworn off girlfriends, we both knew it was only a matter of time before one of us caved. Falling for someone during ski season would have been bad enough, but during salmon season?

John and I had been practically inseparable since the previous summer when we worked security for the Girdwood Forest Fair, keeping an eye out for drinking outside of the beer gardens and making sure freeloaders didn't sneak in through the back gate, even though, had the circumstances been different, we might have been the ones doing the sneaking. Over the course of the three-day festival, we discovered we shared a go-with-the-wind, howl-at-the-moon spirit, and during down times had long discussions about Aldo Leopold's *A Sand County Almanac*, which John carried around with him like a bible. Both of us were getting over heartbreaks that neither had seen coming. Both of us were more interested in fishing, even if we ended up getting hosed, or climbing some mountain in rinse-cycle weather than pursuing new girlfriends.

I had taught John how to roll a kayak, and had turned him on to the euphoria of skiing in deep, backcountry powder. John, who'd worked at the Russian River Campground for two summers, showed me all the sweetest fishing holes. What I appreciated most about John, a quiet and thoughtful Wisconsinite with a long red ponytail and a matching red beard, were his spiritual priorities, evident in his willingness to go fishing anytime, anywhere, day or night. Working the graveyard shift at the Alyeska Prince hotel, John could punch out at 7:00 in the morning, and be on the road for fishing by 7:15. I was always good to go, too, even if the urge hit at one in the morning. The way the two of us saw it, we'd catch up on our sleep come winter.

My grandfather had made a fisherman out of me. I'd become an instant convert upon catching my first fish before I'd outgrown the training wheels on my bike. During our grade-school years, my older brother, Brian, and I spent time each summer at our maternal grandparents' remote lakeside property in southwest Ontario, accessible only by boat or floatplane, a CB radio the only means of communication with the outside world. The place included a main cabin and a small guesthouse built of hand-hewn logs, a boathouse, and a dock on Clearwater Lake with water that lived up to its name. I could lie on my belly at the end of the dock, look down through water well over my head, and see the bottom as clearly as if looking through glass.

While our grandmother grumped about the rustic accommodations, particularly after chasing bats out of the rafters with a broom, our grandfather loved the place. A retired Purdue University professor and agricultural geneticist who normally kept himself creased, starched, and splashed with aftershave, he'd trade his dress shirt, beige trousers, and buffed shoes for blue jeans, lace-up boots, a denim jacket marinated in grime, and a ratty ball cap with a corncob emblem across the front, a fitting off-duty uniform for a man who went by the CB handle "Rusty Rooster." Every day that the weather was even halfway decent, he'd take us two boys fishing for walleye, lake trout, and bass. At the end of the day, he'd pull up a stool in the boathouse, fillet the fish, then hand me and Brian a bucket of heads and guts and let us take the boat over to an outcropping poking from the lake to make an offering to the gulls.

"Oh, you did good," our grandmother would say upon presentation of the day's catch. "Now go wash up."

She'd then tie on an apron, make a mountain of coleslaw or potato salad, heat up some Boston baked beans, mix up a pitcher of Tang, and set dishes atop the red-and-white checked tablecloth in front of the picture window overlooking the lake. If we brought home lake trout or bass, she would be in charge. If we brought home walleyes, my grandfather would take over, dipping the fillets in flour, then whisked eggs, then coating them in seasoned cornmeal, and sizzling them in peanut oil in a cast-iron skillet. After supper, I would join my grandfather in banishment to the screened-in porch where he'd smoke his Kools and I would listen to the loons wail and the old man's stories, animated by the comet of his cigarette doodling in the dark.

Under my grandfather's guidance, I learned how to speak in hushed tones and how to be still in a boat. I learned to catch my own bait, to tie a reverse clinch knot, to read the water, to drive a skiff. By example, I learned to love fishing as much as catching. My grandfather had high expectations for me, as a fisherman and as the man I would grow up to be. After his death in 1994, I never failed to bring him along beneath my shirt, up against my skin, whenever I was out on a river. My grandfather was always right there with me whenever some fish brought it on after taking my hook and arcing my rod, which was an extension of my arm, which was an extension of my heart, which was an extension of the old man who taught me patience and humility, as well as the fisherman's motto: "Early to bed, early to rise, fish like hell, and make up lies."

Since moving to Alaska, Chinooks, or "kings," had become my favorite among the state's five salmon species. They're finicky, aggressive, hard to outsmart, and harder to outfight. The Kenai River holds the world record for the largest king caught by rod and reel in fresh water at ninety-seven pounds, four ounces, which is about what a sixth-grader weighs and the upper end for a baby hippo. For me, there was no bigger thrill than playing a king, kind of like bull riding. But reds were a close second, appreciated for their attitude once hooked, for their rich flavor once filleted, marinated in Balsamic vinegar, minced garlic, fresh lemon, salt, and pepper and slapped on a grill. I loved the way they had this one-second delay after a hook had been set, followed by a turn of the head. I could imagine them going, "What the . . . Holy crap!" before going absolutely berserk, darting up river and down, this way and that, like a gazelle with a cheetah on its heels. I liked that reds made me work, and that just because I'd turned one's head didn't mean it would be coming home with me that night. I'd had them spit out my hooks in disgust. I'd had my lines "spooled" and my lines snapped. I'd seen others lose them after they were banked to the biggest con of all—a supposedly depleted fish suddenly leaping up and punching a fisherman in the face, then flip-flopping across the shore with stooped-over fishermen, arms outstretched, in hot pursuit. I'd seen reds make it back to the river, then swish away, their tails flipping the aquatic-vertebrate equivalent of an extended middle finger.

On that day in July, a couple of hours out of Girdwood, John pulled off the Sterling Highway and onto a gravel side road near one of my favorite Kenai River fishing holes. While not exactly secret, it was definitely not on the tourist radar, and with tricky access, not a place someone would happen upon. It was one John had shown me, a cramped hole on the inside of a bend with a steep embankment on one side and room for no more than fifteen to fish. Once a fish was hooked, the biggest challenge was denying it access to the spurt of rapids immediately downriver that if allowed to be reached, would funnel it into a sayonara zone before a single profanity could be spewed. So it needed to be banked pronto, before it had the opportunity.

The spot was a microcosm of the mob scene some thirty miles back up the highway at The Sanctuary. I had no idea combat fishing existed until a friend invited me along on a trip to the Russian River a day or two after I'd moved to Girdwood. We arrived around ten that midsummer night. I was floored. Here I was in a state more than twice the size of Texas with about a third as many inhabitants as Houston, and The Sanctuary looked more like rush hour than anything remotely resembling its name. For me, fishing was about being alone with the river, about stillness and meditation interrupted only by catching, not by some dude three feet off my right elbow discussing his preference in strip clubs with some other dude three feet off my left elbow. As turned off as I was, the mind-blowing number of fish had me salivating. It was the Serengeti of the freshwater world.

After my initiation, I usually made an effort to ditch the throngs by hiking into the Russian River's upper valley. Yet over time, as absurd as it was, I started getting a kick out of combat fishing. I grew to appreciate the social scene and sense of community, with the exception of the occasional dipshit, since cooperation was the only way chorus-line fishing could work without descending into a riverside mosh pit. I liked the etiquette of reeling in like your life depended on it and getting the hell out of the way the moment someone yelled, "Fish on!" I liked the synchronization, the casting and flipping of lines almost as a single entity: *Ker-plunk, ker-plunk, ker-plunk, flip, flip, flip, ker-plunk, ker-plunk, ker-plunk, flip, flip, flip,* all down the line, the same motion, the same rhythm, like the fishermen's version of the stadium wave.

Bears could crash the party at any moment. We all knew that. But given the hordes and close proximity, what worried me most was catching a bullet if some fisherman got spooked and started blasting. What was more likely was catching a wayward hook, since reds are famous for spitting them out, sending them flying backward, return-to-sender style, and keeping the local medical community busy removing them from various parts of angler anatomy. Not to mention the kind of damage a weight can do slamming into an eye. Emergency room personnel at Central Peninsula Hospital in Soldotna remove something like seventy-five fishhooks a year, some years closer to one hundred, from the cheeks, chins, noses, elbows, and eyebrows of anglers fishing various rivers along the Kenai Peninsula. I heard from a Cooper Landing emergency medical technician that one unfortunate was taking a leak when he caught one in his privates.

South of the madness, John and I climbed into our waders and loaded up our gear. With Maya trotting on ahead, we hiked the short distance from the car to a bluff, got down on our butts, dangled our feet over the edge, launched off, dropped onto a trail, and made our way down the steep, narrow path while leaning our shoulders into the embankment, steadying ourselves with our hands as we went. At the bottom, we set down our rods, pulled off our packs, and sat leaning against the embankment to wait our turn. In the meantime, we scoped out stringers for a fishing report, and it looked promising. When the first opening came up, John went for it, while I remained on the lookout for the next potential slot to drop into. After about fifteen minutes, another angler reeled in his line and gathered up his gear.

"Mind if I jump in there?" I asked. He didn't, so I did. My line ready, the drag set fairly tight to accommodate the current, I slid into his spot and waded in up to my knees. I glanced upriver, then down, taking note of the rhythm of those on either side of me. I merged into the cadence, casting in synch with the others to the ten o'clock position, then slowly pivoting as my line drifted downriver anchored by just the right amount of weight to keep my sinker skipping along the bottom, my coho fly dancing a few inches above, but not so much weight for it to get wedged between rocks. I felt the subtle bounce, bounce, bounce as it hopscotched along. When my rod reached two o'clock, I flipped the line fly-fishing fashion, pulling several feet free, then cast back upriver to ten o'clock. *Ker-plunk, bounce, bounce, bounce, flip. Ker-plunk, bounce, bounce, bounce, flip.* Over and over and over. After a few rounds, I zoned out as the river scurried by, circumnavigating my legs on its way to the sea. I couldn't have felt more at peace. My grandfather would have been proud at how firmly his lessons on the lake had taken hold. I'd grown up to love fishing as much as catching, and especially that day, warmed by the brilliance of the sun and the glow of new love.

I'd been at it maybe twenty minutes when I felt it: *bounce, bounce, bounce. Thud. Wait!* I held my breath. The jerk of a head. *There!* I yanked, setting the hook.

"Fish on!"

The sockeye hit the gas. Anglers on either side of me reeled in their lines full-tilt and backed out of the river to make room.

"Woo! Oooh, yeah. Yep, there's fish in there," I hollered.

"Damn! What are you messing around for, Bigley?" John shouted. "Bring that bad boy in!"

Adrenalin pumping, I reeled as fast as I could before my fish could bolt downriver into the current of no return. I reeled and reeled and reeled. Despite its vigorous protest, I dragged it closer and closer to shore, then steered it toward the bank with the tip of my rod. In one final, sweeping motion, I dragged it onto the riverbank, where, full of piss and vinegar, it thrashed about as if the stones were hot coals. I dropped my pole, pounced on it, trapped it between my knees, grabbed a rock, and brought it down hard between its eyes. It quivered. I whacked it again. The fish went still. Maya, perched on the bluff above, barked and wagged her entire hind end.

"Nice one, huh, Maya? You approve? I thought so. Good girl."

I rinsed my hands in the river, put my fish on a stringer, secured it with a rock, then rinsed my hands again, shook them off, picked up my rod, and stepped back into the current.

By early evening, between the two of us, we had three reds the size of canoe-paddle blades on ice in the cooler, all caught within the first forty-five minutes, after which it seemed the reds ended their shift and punched out for the day. Although the limit was three per angler per day, after more than two hours without a single intercept, we called it quits, loaded up our fish, hoofed it back to the car, peeled off our waders, and headed toward home.

Other than caffeine, granola bars, and a couple handfuls of gorp, we hadn't eaten all day, and our engines were sputtering like old Buick Skylarks with bad distributor caps. So on our way back to Girdwood, we stopped for dinner in Cooper Landing, a community of tidy log cabins and quaint fishing lodges along a winding stretch of highway that skirts the shore of Kenai Lake and the upper part of the Kenai River. A sleepy settlement of 370 in winter, the town triples in size and never sleeps in summer, during which locals and non are interested in two things and two things only: fishing and talking about fishing. As the launching pad for fishing trips on the Kenai and Russian rivers, key services at the time were open for business all day and night, including the bar at Gwin's Lodge, which on a hopping night back in the day would close at five in the morning and reopen in time for breakfast.

We pulled into Gwin's around 6:30 that evening. Burgers and beer at the half-century-old log roadhouse had become an end-of-the-day fishing tradition. We headed into the bar, parked ourselves at a table against a wall, and ordered without bothering to look at the menu since we knew it by heart. The place was abuzz with anglers comparing notes and guides dropping in for beers after work, several of whom we either knew or recognized, all of whom talked fish. Halfway through our burgers, we overheard a couple of guys talking about how the reds were holed up at The Sanctuary. From the sounds of it, they had limited out without much trouble.

John and I looked at each other, both thinking the same thing. I didn't have to be at work until ten the next morning, but John was due back at the hotel later that night for the graveyard shift. It was just after seven, it was a gorgeous evening, and the sun wouldn't be setting for about four hours, and even then "dark" would be relative. John threw it out there.

"What do you think about running down to the Russian real fast and trying to get those last three fish?"

"Hell yeah," I said. "Let's do it."

John, who had no problem keeping his priorities straight, called in sick.

"We should swing by and see if Jaha wants to wet a line," I said.

Jaha, short for Jeremy Anderson Hard Ass, a nickname earned in middle school for holding his ground against bullies half again his size, was the most natural-born fisherman I'd ever known, an angling genius who could practically talk a fish into skipping the drama and hopping straight into his cooler. My favorite image of him came from a day at that same fishing hole we'd just left down the highway. Standing atop a boulder at the water's edge, he'd cracked open a can of Coors Light, raised it toward the heavens, hollered out the motto, "Tap the Rockies!," tipped it straight back, chugged the whole thing down, crushed the can against his chest, tossed it over his shoulder next to his pack, cast into the river, and instantly nailed a fish. Everyone down there about died laughing.

"Do it again! Do it again!" we all chanted.

Jaha, a woolly Wisconsinite like John, was working as a river guide on the Kenai and had been living out of a tent pitched on his boss's property since the cabin he'd been renting got sold out from under him. It was his day off, and since too much fishing could never be enough, I had no doubt he'd be up for a quick jaunt to the Russian. I was right. His girlfriend, Emily, was game, too. We swung by, they tossed their gear into the back of John's Subaru and climbed into the backseat with Maya, and off we went to the Russian River with hopes of better luck.

During the height of the salmon runs, there isn't a spot to be had at the Russian River Campground or its day-use parking lots. Long lines of cars, pickups, and RVs wait at the entrance for hours, and sometimes an entire day, for an opening to come up. We were down there so much and were friends with so many of those who worked there, we had it wired. Sometimes we'd stash the car and go in on bikes. But mostly our strategy was way more obnoxious. We'd drive past the line of vehicles, turn into the "Exit Only" lane, pull up to the information booth, hand over a six pack of beer, and secure for ourselves the next available parking pass while those who'd been waiting their turn annihilated us with their glares.

On the night of July 14, our timing was such that there were only a couple of cars in line, so we entered the respectable, grown-up way, through the entrance. Around 8:30, we pulled into the campground's Grayling parking lot, built on a bluff above the river. Maya hopped out, put her nose to the ground, and started skimming back and forth like a minesweeper while everyone sorted out gear. I climbed back into my chest waders and dropped extra weights, spare coho flies, and a pair of pliers into my front pocket. I grabbed my pack, which was set to go with a fillet knife, a stringer, a few garbage bags, a thin gray sweater, and a green fleece jacket. Before closing it up, as was my fishing ritual, I tossed in a bomber-size bottle of Midnight Sun Brewery's Sockeye Red IPA for good luck.

In three hours I'd be blind.

Fishing rods in hand, we headed across the parking lot and down the long set of stairs leading to the Angler Trail that runs alongside the river. The four of us fished together at a spot called the Cottonwood Hole for a while without a single successful flossing. John and I decided to move on to The Sanctuary. New to Alaska, new to the notion of grizzlies being part of the landscape, Emily wasn't up for that, especially after hearing how many bears were out and about at the time. So she and Jaha stayed in an area where she felt less skittish—closer to the stairs. Given that everyone but John had to work in the morning, we all agreed to meet at the car around 10:30. John and I had hoped to stay longer, but knew it would be wise to wrap it up while there was still plenty of light since bears tend to move in at night, or what passes for night in the height of an Alaska summer. Night was when a lot of anglers preferred to be on the river. Salmon tended to be on the move then, and there were fewer people to contend with. I'd done my share of middle-of-the-night fishing.

John, Maya, and I made our way downriver. It was a Monday night, but when the reds are running, every night is a Friday night at the Russian. We waded across the mouth of the river just below its confluence with the Kenai, while Maya did her beaver impersonation, paddling across the current with just her head, ears, and nose poking out of the water. A little farther down, John and I found ourselves a couple of nice spots to slide into. We took note of the rhythm and joined in.

It took more than an hour to catch those last three fish, for both of us to limit out. There's nothing easier than to lose track of time when standing knee deep in a river. By the time we packed up, we were already behind schedule for meeting up with Jaha and Emily. We still had to clean our fish at the cleaning station across the mouth of the Russian and hike back to the car. Then we ran into some friends from Girdwood, Jaelyn Rockman and Carl Roesner, and stopped to swap fishing stories. At the cleaning station we ran into another Girdwoodian and chatted with him a spell.

"Hey, guys, be really careful," he said before turning the table over to us. "There are a ton of bears around."

"Thanks, man. We will."

I had thirty minutes left to see.

We filleted our fish, wrapped them in garbage bags, and slid them into John's pack. We loaded up and began hiking back to the parking lot, bantering back and forth, laughing, making ourselves well heard as one does in bear country, filling lulls in the conversation with an occasional "Hey, bear!" or a whistle or my signature bear-be-gone call, "Hootie-Hoo," inspired by a hip-hop song I was fond of as a teenager. About three-quarters of the way back, we passed four guys in camo and fatigue greens on their way to The Sanctuary, poles in one hand, cans of Pabst Blue Ribbon gripped in the other.

"Hey, how's it going?" I asked with a nod and a smile.

They tromped on by as if we didn't exist.

John and I stopped a second and looked at each other.

"That was weird," John said. "I wonder what the hell their problem is."

"They sure didn't seem to be having much fun. How can you not have fun going fishing? Maybe it's their taste in beer. I hear fish can smell PBR a mile away." We laughed and continued on.

I had five minutes left.

A little farther up we came upon a surprise in the trail—two cans of Pabst, one mostly empty, the other unopened. Both were dented.

"Score!" John shouted as he bent down to pick them up. As rude as those guys were, at least we would get a beer out of the deal. "Thanks, guys!" John slid the empty one into the top pocket of my pack, popped the other, took a swig, and passed it to me. We walked on.

Three minutes.

We reached the intersection where the riverside Angler Trail meets the path leading to the stairs and turned the corner. There, moments from the safety of the car, Maya glued herself to my side and let out a low, eerie growl.

CHAPTER 4

This Can't Be Happening

A BEAR.

We hit the brakes. Blocking the trail thirty feet ahead, just below the stairs to the Grayling parking lot, was the hind end of a grizzly. It glanced over its shoulder, then whipped around to face us in the midsummer twilight. I slowly reached down and grabbed Maya by the scruff of her neck. John took a couple of steps backward so we'd be standing side by side, making us look bigger, nothing to mess with.

"What do you want to do here?" I whispered without taking my eyes off the bear.

"Let's give it a second."

"I don't know, I don't like this."

Between the two of us, we'd encountered a lot of bears through the years. This one wasn't like any of the others. Instead of the typical bear behavior—the take-note-of-humans-and-trundle-along routine, or better yet, take note and run for the hills—this one held its ground, hackles raised. Then it began huffing and woofing and bouncing to and fro on its front paws. We needed to get out of there. Now.

We backpedaled slowly, calmly, keeping an eye on the bear while negotiating a right-hand turn in reverse at the corner where the path to the stairs intercepted the trail paralleling the river. We would continue upriver, we'd decided, and take a roundabout way to the car, giving that bear plenty of space. Once we made the corner, we were out of sight. We continued up the trail a ways, and I let go of Maya. She shook herself, then scampered on ahead. John and I relaxed our shoulders and picked up our pace.

"Whoa, that was kind of crazy," I said. "Something must have really pissed that thing off. I wonder if those guys we just passed . . . Oh shit!"

We screeched to a halt. Up ahead, the alders were shaking violently. John grabbed me by my shoulders and yanked me backward a step. My stomach plunged. My heart felt like a fist trying to pound its way out of my chest. Was that bear stalking us? Had it circled around to cut us off? Instantly, and without need for discussion, we about-faced and started hoofing it back the way we'd just come. We didn't get far.

In a flash, the bear we thought was now behind us came tearing around the corner in front of us so fast it had to dip its shoulder to make the turn. Head lowered, ears flattened against its neck, eyes on fire, it took a running swipe at Maya. Maya yelped and leapt sideways off the trail, avoiding the blow. Without breaking stride, it took a running swipe at John. John launched sideways into the alders with such propulsion he flew out of his wader shoes, leaving them behind on the trail. The bear blew by him like a missile, eyes locked on mine.

Those eyes, I remember them as yellow and burning like comets. Those eyes would be the last thing I would ever see.

In the nanoseconds I had to decide how to save myself, I whipped around, took two running steps, and dove headfirst off the trail into the brush. The bear slammed into me like a wrecking ball and had me before I hit the ground, snagging my left thigh midair with a powerful swing of its paw. Crashing through a barrage of snapping branches, I landed with a thud, the wind knocked from my lungs, in an explosion of pain.

Slow motion is cruel, the way it draws out the horror, each second crawling along, dragging its hindquarters. *This . . . can't . . . be . . . happening.*

With its claws embedded in my leg, the bear yanked me from a tangle of brush back out to the trail in short, jerky motions like a dog playing tug-of-war with a sock. Lying facedown, fingers interlaced around the back of my neck, elbows tucked tight around the sides of my head, I tried to play dead. From somewhere above, I heard sickening, primal screams that didn't sound human. It didn't register that they were coming from my own throat.

Lying ten feet away, stabbed and scraped by branches that had splintered on impact and made a sieve of his waders, John lay in dense brush, armed with nothing more than a fishing pole, listening to the roars and screams and thrashings of the bear killing me. Eyes wide, chest heaving, unable to see more than two feet in front of him, he rose onto his elbows and started a frantic belly crawl through a thicket of prickly branches and devil's club spines that bloodied his hands and face. Upon reaching the edge, he stood, stumbled, and started running, screaming for help. Remembering the fish on his back, thinking it bear bait, he wriggled out of the shoulder straps of his pack and winged it on the run as far as he could into the brush. He stopped a short distance later, at the Cottonwood Hole, where earlier we'd all been fishing together. Hyperventilating, he paced back and forth, back and forth on rubber legs. He felt sick about leaving me. About running. *What to do? What to do? What to do?* The urge to go back was overwhelming. But the bear . . . He whipped around toward the parking lot and cupped his hands to his mouth.

"HELP! SOMEBODY HELLLP!"

After dodging the bear, Maya had bolted downriver, but came charging back when she heard John's screams. "Get out of here!" he hollered, giving her a kick in the chest, partially for her own good, partially for fear a freaked-out dog would make matters worse. Maya yelped, turned around, and dashed back down the trail toward The Sanctuary. Still within earshot, John paused to listen. All he heard were dogs barking off in the distance and the river flowing by. I had passed out, and the bear had wandered off a few paces to wait and watch, as bears do when neutralizing a threat, real or perceived. Thinking the bear had gone, John called out.

"Dan! DAN! ARE YOU ALL RIGHT?"

He could barely make it out but he heard me moan. The bear heard me, too. It returned, and the roaring and thrashing and shrieking started all over again. Suddenly, I felt the ground rushing by beneath me, my head bouncing over jagged roots and rocks, one clocking me so hard I lost consciousness. The bear dragged me twenty-five feet off the trail and into tall, thick grass below the bluff. When I came to, it was standing over me, panting. I could feel the massive volume of its hot, rank breath heavy upon my face.

Oh shit! My face!

Somewhere between the bashing of my head and regaining consciousness, the bear had managed to flip me over. It stood over me now, straddling my body, claws sunk deep into my shoulders, pinning me to the ground with bone-crushing weight. My arms useless, I could do nothing to stop it as it cocked its head sideways and clamped its jaws across the middle of my face.

Crunch. Like a mouth full of eggshells. Crunch, crunch. Something inside my head went POP.

A flash, then an awakening in someplace new, suspended in luminous blue. I was floating, detached, as if gravity had given me up. No fear, no pain. So pleasant. So strange. I looked all around me. I was alone in a blue zephyr. I knew then that I was dying. How tempting it was not to resist. How tempting it was to continue drifting right out of this world.

An image of my mother formed in my head, like an old home movie from a time she was young and healthy. She was standing in a blue oscillating forest, smiling and waving, looking happier than I'd seen her in years. She was glowing. I was glowing, too. Pure mother-son connection—just me and the woman who brought me into this world. A surge of euphoria wrapped around me like silk. I felt the presence of family and friends holding onto me, infusing me with love. I felt my strength returning, and with it, my will to live.

I knew what I had to do. I had to fight to stay alive, no matter what it took. I remember this as a conscious decision. I remember promising myself that if I fought and lived, I would never look back and regret it. I didn't know the mauling had left me blind.

Once I'd made my decision, my mother vanished but I was not alone. A figure materialized off in the distance, showing itself as a silhouette backlit by a starburst of blue light. My long-dead grandfather. I recognized his lanky legs and the outline of his favorite ball cap. Grandfather nodded. I took that as his approval of my decision not to give up.

Then I found myself lying on a table, with those who loved me clustered around, not in human form, but in essence as shimmering waves of light. They held hands in a circle, infusing me with love and energy. My Prescott friends, Blair Carter and Martha McCord, were overseeing the session, speaking in an ancient language I couldn't understand and didn't feel the need to. The others spoke in garbled whispers, their lips not moving. Telepathically, they let me know they were pleased with my decision but worried, knowing I'd chosen the much more arduous of the two roads. They wanted me to rest a while before returning to my body at the river. To be still. To breathe. Just a little while longer. Rest. Just rest.

Then it was time. Blair gave the nod that I was ready to go. The circle of friends dropped hands, raised them, palms open, and let me go as though freeing a bird. I was no longer floating on my back then, but looking down into the bottom of a well at an undulating image reflected in the water—my own body, curled up in the fetal position on the forest floor. Slowly I descended into it. Darkness replaced blue light. I could hear leaves fluttering around me in a gentle breeze and the river ambling by on its way to rendezvous with the sea. The bear was gone. All was calm. I was alive.

Pain started crawling back into my body, slowly at first, then in a huge hurry, throbbing and digging deep into muscle and bone. I tasted blood. It was trickling down my throat. I gagged.

Where's John? Where's Maya? How long have I been lying here?

I tried shouting but what came out was a pathetic wheeze. I tried to sit up, thinking I should crawl out to the trail. My arms, like bags of sand, wouldn't respond. My legs felt shackled, as if roots had reached up from the soil and lashed them to the ground. I tried again to rise . . . and failed. I could hear blood dripping off my face and hitting the grass. Drip . . . drip . . . drip. I could feel blood pooling inside my waders. *God, it hurts. It hurts so bad.* My mind began racing with crazy, crazy thoughts.

Oh man, I have to work in the morning, and now I'm probably going to be late. Oh, and isn't this just great; I'm supposed to drive the kids to that compass course tomorrow, and the keys to the van are in my pocket. What a mess you've made of things, Bigley. Mom and Dad are going to be so pissed. And what about Amber? What's she going to think of you now that you've gotten yourself mauled by a bear?

Lying on my back, wet and sticky and too weak to move, my thoughts continued to spiral until I just wanted to sleep.

How long have I been lying here? A half hour? More? Does anyone even know I'm here?

I started to shiver, just a little at first, and then violently.

John, where are you? Please hurry. I'm cold. So cold.

CHAPTER 5

Hanging on in the Dark

IT WOULD BE YEARS BEFORE I WOULD PIECE TOGETHER WHAT HAPPENED in the minutes, hours, days, and weeks that followed my decision to fight for my life. I remember vividly, unfortunately, some of the most disturbing moments between me and the bear. But I recall only scraps of what happened after the blue place dissolved into darkness and I lay alone on the forest floor. The friends I fished with that day, as well as medics, law enforcement, forest service, and other officials called to the scene, plus others who were down at the river or up in the campground have filled in details of my rescue. I continue to run into people now and then who tell me more, most recently, eight years later, as I was emerging from a restroom.

"Hey, are you Dan Bigley?"

"I am. Who's that?"

"I'm Wes Masters. I was with you in the ambulance that night."

Medical records, doctors, surgeons, nurses, hospital staff, my family, my friends, and many others who passed through my life without me even knowing it have helped me reconstruct the times for which I have no memory. They've helped me make a bit of sense of the morphine-induced hallucinations—or dreams, I'm not sure what to call them—that occasionally intercepted reality while I was clinging to life in intensive care. Physical descriptions of people, places, and events I could not see, of the expressions, gestures, and body language of those around me, were provided by many along the way.

I know that memories, my own and those of others, can be fickle. They can fade, evolve, and distort in both the heat of the moment and with the passage of time. But as far as I can determine, what happened went something like this.

About the time John and I were packing up to leave The Sanctuary, Jaha and Emily were topping the stairs to the parking lot. Finding the doors locked, they leaned their poles against the side of John's car, slid out of their packs, and set them down next to their rods. Fifteen minutes came and went. Then thirty. Although the sun hadn't officially set, it had ducked behind the mountains a good while ago, so it had to be around eleven. It was a beautiful evening for killing time, but they both had to work in the morning and were getting antsy. More time went by. What the hell was taking us so long, they wondered.

They noticed people taking pictures on the bluff above the river, so they wandered over to see what was up. What was up was bears. Emily hadn't been in Alaska long, and she had yet to see one. Jaha, who'd worked at the Russian River Campground the previous summer and had since landed a job as a river guide on the Kenai, had seen a lot of them, especially lately, like fifteen the previous week, mostly at night. Seeing a bear was always a thrill, but something felt off this time. Upriver, a large grizzly sow with two cubs was bounding through the water, swinging her head from side to side, slapping the water with a paw, clearly worked up over something. To Jaha, it seemed her cubs weren't listening to her, and she was not taking it well. The cubs then wandered off toward shore and disappeared into the brush toward the Angler Trail paralleling the river. The mother bear veered off after them on a trajectory that gave Jaha a sick feeling in the pit of his stomach.

Moments later, four guys dressed in camo and fatigue greens started down the stairs, all amped up and ready to slay themselves some reds. Each clutched a pole in one hand and a can of Pabst Blue Ribbon in the other.

"Hey, guys," Jaha called out, "just so you know, I saw a mama bear with a couple of cubs down there, and that mama looked really pissed. There's been a lot of bear activity in the evenings lately, so you might want to be extra careful."

"Yeah, thanks. We're from here. We've got guns. We ain't worried about no bears."

"Okay," Jaha shrugged. *Jackasses*, he thought. "Well, good luck with the fishing, then."

He watched them tromp down the stairs and disappear on a potential collision course with a stressed-out sow. He and Emily lingered at the bluff a while, then wandered back toward the car. Emily pulled out a pack of rolling papers and a pouch of American Spirit tobacco, rolled herself a smoke, and lit up. Then came the screams. Horrid, hideous screams.

That sow got somebody; Jaha was sure of it. He shuddered, assuming it was one of the guys he'd just tried to warn. He and Emily dashed back to the bluff and leaned over the railing to see if they could see anything down below. They couldn't.

"Are you okay down there? HEY, you guys all right?"

More shrieking, flailing, and thrashing. A bear roaring. Then came a second voice a ways downriver screaming for help. Emily stayed put, while Jaha started down the stairs. He didn't get far. He whipped around with a crazed look in his eyes.

"Emily, RUN!"

The cubs were bounding up the stairs, and he knew that meant mama wouldn't be far behind. She wasn't, but she was charging straight up the bluff directly below where Emily was standing.

Running from a bear is almost always a bad idea, say those who study bear attacks for a living. Grizzlies may seem ungainly, but they can sprint like blasts of wind, up to thirty-five miles per hour. Jaha knew that, but instinct said to run, and there was no time to argue.

They sprinted for the restrooms. Concrete walls. Metal doors. Bear proof.

No time.

Emily, just a few paces ahead, altered course and made a beeline for a Chevy Blazer that had pulled into the parking lot fifteen minutes before. It was closer and the back window was missing, busted out with a baseball bat, as twisted karma would have it, by the guy's pissed-off girlfriend just the night before. Emily, still wearing her waders, tried to climb in, but her foot slipped off the bumper. Jaha had just enough time to hoist her up, shove her inside, and dive in after her. Glancing over his shoulder on his way in, he saw the sow's head closing in, her mouth smeared with blood.

They scrambled over the backseat and into the front, where they ducked down, Jaha covering Emily's body with his own. The sow, huffing and growling, circled the Blazer. Once, twice. Terrified it would climb in after them or come crashing through one of the windows, Emily reached over and laid on the horn.

Beeeeeep! Beeeeeep! Beeeeeep!

Jaha poked his head up in time to see the sow and cubs dash across the parking lot and disappear into the woods. With no time to think of dropping it, Emily still had a cigarette wedged between her fingers. Jaha, who didn't smoke, reached for it and took two long, hard drags before handing it back. Shaken to the bone, Emily kept blasting the horn, hoping it would bring help. Nobody came.

Meanwhile, two Alaska National Guard buddies, Sergeants David Roberson and Bryan Irby, were hiking up from The Sanctuary when Maya came bolting down the trail. How strange, they thought. While they were cleaning their fish, they'd seen that same dog trotting alongside two guys who'd started back not long before they did. They continued on with Maya on their heels, and five minutes later heard cries for help. They started running toward the voice and came upon John at the Cottonwood Hole. He was shaking and could barely keep it together.

"A bear . . . it got my friend! I don't know . . . what kind of shape he's in . . . or if he's even alive. We have to help him." John shook his head in disbelief, his hands balled into fists. "What if the bear is still there? You have a gun?"

"We don't. But don't worry, we'll help you find your friend. Now try taking some deep breaths."

The three of them put their faith in safety in numbers and cautiously made their way back to where John had last seen me. Upriver, just past the turnoff to the stairs, a grim story unfolded in the trail. A fishing pole here, a pair of wader shoes there, a dented can of Pabst Blue Ribbon, a green ball cap with a Bonfire logo across the front. Gouges in the trail where something heavy had been dragged through the dirt. A trail of blood.

"Dan!" John shouted as they drew near. "Dan! DAN!"

They heard moaning and found where I'd been dragged below the bluff about twenty-five feet off the trail. I lay curled on my side in a grassy area all matted down in a ten-foot radius. Blood was everywhere. John's mouth dropped open but no words came out. Roberson asked him to step back. He yanked off his T-shirt, covered my head, and applied pressure to stop the bleeding while Irby checked for other wounds.

"How old are you?" Roberson asked, knowing it was critical to keep me awake.

"Twenty-five," I slurred.

"Do you know what day it is?"

Silence. "No," I finally said.

"Can you move at all? Your arms or legs?"

No response. Afraid I was fading fast, they went for help while John stayed with me to keep applying pressure and prevent me from going to sleep. Once they were out of sight, John fell to his knees beside me.

"Oh, Dan," he said in practically a whisper, so relieved to find me alive that the devastation failed to register.

"I'm fucked up, man," I groaned. "I am *so* fucked up."

"No. No, you're all right, brother. You're going to be okay."

I was going to be anything but okay. My face was pulp, and with all the blood and grime, John didn't notice that my eyes weren't where they were supposed to be. All he saw was that I was breathing. A surreal calm came over him as he did what he could to keep me from going into shock, to keep himself from going into shock. Afraid of bleeding to death, and trained as a Wilderness First Responder, I tried to help him out.

"John," I wheezed, "I need more pressure on my head. Not too much. Just keep it steady. God, it hurts. It really fucking hurts."

John closed his eyes and leaned back. He called upon his dead great-grandmothers, who he believed watched over him, to pull some strings for me up there.

Back up top, with all the shouting, car-horn blasts, and cacophony of dogs barking in the campground, people were poking their heads out of their tents and RVs, trying to figure out what the hell was going on. In the front seat of the Blazer, once he was sure the bears were gone, Jaha started climbing toward the busted-out window to get help for whoever had run into that bear.

"Where are you *going*?" Emily demanded.

"Those folks down there need help."

"Are you kidding me? I am not getting out of this car."

"Well, I'm going."

Sprinting for the Blazer, the one thought in her head had been that this was it, she was dead. She was in no mood for heroics.

"Please don't go," she pleaded.

"You can stay here. You'll be okay, the bears are gone. I'll be back as soon as I can."

She didn't want him going alone so she climbed out after him. They scanned the parking lot, then dashed to the nearest rig in the campground.

Frank and Celeste Valentine, former Alaskans visiting from Georgia, had driven their RV up the Alaska Highway and were spending the summer bouncing between their favorite fishing spots up and down the Kenai Peninsula and visiting family in Anchorage. Colonel Valentine, a former US Army Ranger who'd fished Alaska rivers religiously the years he was stationed at Fort Richardson, had also fished The Sanctuary that night. He'd come up that same trail not long before we did, just long enough to put the three reds he'd caught into the RV's freezer, wash up, and get ready for bed. He and Celeste had just settled in when they heard all the commotion, first a lot of yelling from atop and below the bluff. Then, not much later, somebody blasting a car horn over and over and over.

Celeste raised her head off her pillow. "I wonder what that's all about."

Some kids having a party, they figured. Then they heard footsteps running through the woods getting closer and closer, then someone banging on their door.

"I don't know if we ought to answer that," Celeste whispered.

The colonel felt otherwise. He got up, climbed into a pair of jeans, grabbed the .44 Magnum he'd borrowed from his son-in-law, hid it behind his back, and slowly cracked the door. Jaha and Emily stood there wide eyed and out of breath.

"Please, can you help us? We just got charged by a sow with cubs, and that same bear got somebody down by the stairs."

Colonel Valentine left the door open as he set down the gun, slipped into a pair of tennis shoes, picked his cell phone up off the table, and dropped it into his pants pocket. He holstered the .44 and strapped it around his hips, then pulled a sweatshirt over his head. Although there was still enough light to read by if you had to, it would be darker down below the bluff, so he grabbed a flashlight on his way out. The three of them jogged over to the parking lot.

"No way am I going down there," Emily protested.

The men left her at the restroom; she locked herself in, and they headed down the stairs. John heard them coming and stepped out onto the trail to meet them.

"John!" Jaha gasped upon seeing him standing there in a daze. "John, where's Dan?"

John led them to the spot. "This *is* Dan." He lifted the T-shirt covering my head. Jaha reeled.

To Colonel Valentine, a combat veteran who'd pulled three tours in Vietnam, it looked as though a bomb had gone off in my face. *My god, this kid's had it. He's going to die right here.* He pulled the cell phone out of his pocket, dialed 9-1-1, and was surprised he was able to get through.

"Nine-one-one. What's your emergency?"

"My name is Frank Valentine. I'm at the Russian River at the bottom of the Grayling parking lot. I have a fella down here who's been attacked by a bear. We need a medevac down here right away. We're . . ."

He lost the connection before the operator could acknowledge she'd heard what he'd said. He tried to redial but reception was too sketchy. He tried again. The call failed. He tried again. No good. Several minutes later, his phone rang.

"I've got the troopers on their way from Soldotna, and EMTs coming from Cooper Landing. Can you tell . . ."

Again his phone went dead. But at least he knew help was on its way. By then, John was looking thoroughly spent.

"Hey, man, let me take over for you," Jaha said. They traded places. John stood by in silence, shoulders slumped, frozen in disbelief. "Why don't you go up and wait with Emily? She's hiding out in the restroom, and I'm sure she'd like to get out of there. Tell her what's going on down here. Let her know it wasn't one of those jackasses. Let her know it was Dan."

By then it was fairly dark down there. They say I was talking one minute—"Where's Maya? Where's my dog? Has anyone seen my dog?"—and silent the next. Talking, not talking, fading in and out. Jaha kept checking my pulse. It was erratic, then weak, then he couldn't feel it anymore. *Oh, Jesus.* On his knees leaning over me, he crossed his hands over my heart to begin CPR. Before he could make his first compression, I gasped for breath like someone yanked from the bottom of a pool.

As word got around, a posse began to assemble. Some stood guard with .44s and shotguns since there was no telling where that sow might be. Even if she was long gone there were still a lot of edgy bears out there. Others illuminated the scene with flashlights and headlamps, and offered jackets and space blankets to help keep me warm. Not all were helpful.

"Oh my god!" one man gasped, covering his mouth with his hands. "Is he dead?" Colonel Valentine got him out of there.

"You know what would be a big help? Why don't you go up to the road and wait for the ambulance to make sure they know how to find us."

Among the first responders called out of bed was Todd Wilson, chief of Cooper Landing's volunteer fire department, who lived just a few miles away. He tromped down the stairs with his medical kit and found a crowded, chaotic scene. I was lying on my right side, my head resting on my arm to keep blood from running down my throat.

"Why the shirt?" he asked.

"You don't want to know," Jaha said in a low voice so I wouldn't hear.

"Well, I'm going to have to move it so I can see what's going on."

"You don't want to see this."

"Well, I really have to."

Jaha shook his head. Together they carefully peeled back a corner of the shirt. That was enough. They laid it back down. In twenty years as a first responder, it was the worst injury Wilson had ever seen, and he wasn't about to touch it. He caught his breath, then checked my vitals. He dug scissors out of his medical kit and cut open my waders from my chest to my waist to look for other wounds. I was fully conscious at that point, fueled by surges of adrenalin. I asked over and over about Maya. Nobody could believe I could speak, let alone fret about my dog. But what really got them was when I kept asking, "I can hear you guys, why can't I see you?"

Carrie Williams, who lived just up the road from Wilson's place, was the next medic on the scene, and the most credentialed as a volunteer Level III Emergency Medical Technician. She'd been sound asleep when the emergency tone went off on the handheld radio on her nightstand. She awoke with a start, groaned, and turned to her husband, a retired US Marine who knew the routine so well she didn't have to ask: "Honey, would you warm up the truck for me—please?" She rolled out of bed, got dressed, headed downstairs, climbed into the jumpsuit hanging by the back door, and grabbed her gloves and hat on her way out to the idling truck. At the ambulance barn across from the post office, she met up with teammate Phil Weber. They jumped into the ambulance and, siren blaring, lights whirling, headed down the Sterling Highway, pulling into the Grayling parking around one in the morning. Bystanders led Williams down to the scene, while Phil stayed up top with a radio waiting for orders. She did a quick 360 to make sure that between the bears and firearms there wasn't some other accident waiting to happen. She then set down her medical kit and knelt down next to me in the grass.

"This is what we're dealing with," Colonel Valentine said as he lifted the T-shirt.

Breathe. Focus. "Okay. Got it."

She'd save her reaction for later. Off duty, guard down, that's when she'd let the things she saw hit her. Like the time she worked a car accident that injured a mother and several children and left the youngest, a baby strapped into a car seat, brain dead. The mother and grandmother in Carrie didn't come out until she got home. That's when the shaking started. That's when she doubled over and threw up.

In EMT mode now, she took charge of the scene, radioing up to Phil: "We need a backboard down here. We need a C-collar, IVs, heat packs, oxygen . . ."

Bystanders in the parking lot helped carry gear down, and everyone stood back as she and Phil worked on me, checking my airway, monitoring my vitals, sliding IVs into both arms, suctioning blood from my mouth. Oxygen was a problem. There was too much damage to strap on the mask, so it had to be hand held above my mouth.

"Massive blood loss," Carrie would later note in her run sheet. Phil would later say he'd never seen a scene so bloody.

EMTs are the finger in the dike in cases this extreme. They needed to get me out of there and into a surgeon's hands as quickly as possible. After placing a C-collar around my neck, they supported my spine, rolled me onto my side, slid a backboard beneath me, then laid me back down and strapped me in. Getting me up to the parking lot would take some serious muscle, negotiating the two-tiered stairway with a six-foot-four man who couldn't take much jostling.

"Okay, here's the plan," Carrie said. "I need two guys at the front, two at the back, a couple on each side. I'm going to squeeze in along the side to keep an eye on him and manage these IVs. If any of you start to get tired, I want you speak up and trade off with someone. Now on the count of three, we're going to lift together. Okay, ready? One, two, three."

It was slow and awkward going as they ascended the steep stairway up the bluff to the idling ambulance above. After the team had set the backboard down on a gurney, Jaha gave my hand a gentle squeeze.

"You're going to make it, buddy. We'll be fishing again before you know it." I managed a thumbs-up.

Carrie hopped in the back. Helpers on both sides peeled away as she guided my gurney into place and locked it down. With Phil at the wheel, she'd be alone back there. She glanced out at those clustered around the rear doors.

"Need any help?" one of them asked. "I used to be an EMT."

"You bet. That would be great. Hop in."

Eric Christian was one of four fishing buddies staying at the campground, two of whom John and I had had a friendly chat with earlier that evening along the trail, all of whom had helped carry me up from the bottom of the bluff. Due to Eric's EMT experience, Carrie assigned him to help monitor blood pressure and continue suctioning blood from my mouth.

"I could use one more," Carrie said. "Any volunteers?"

Wes Masters, another of the fishing buddies, stepped forward. His job would be to hand her bandages, saline, and other supplies while she tried to keep me alive. Tom Swiech, another from the group, who a couple of days earlier had watched a sow charge a young couple at The Sanctuary, went along as backup. With the ambulance crew assembled, Phil closed the rear doors, climbed into the driver's seat, and pulled out to meet the LifeGuard helicopter en route from Anchorage.

Left behind was Eric's brother, Marco Christian. State troopers, forest service and wildlife officials, and campground manager Butch Bishop had arrived by then and were patrolling the area, waking up campers with coolers left out and dogs chained to their vehicles and RVs.

"Do you have a firearm?" one of them asked Marco.

"I do."

"Are you afraid to use it?"

"After what I saw down there, nope."

"You could help us out, then. If you run into anyone, let them know there's been a bear attack. If you see coolers, tell people to get them inside. Dogs, too. We don't want to attract any more bears."

While word was getting around up top, armed wildlife and law enforcement officers headed down below to let those along the trail and river know there had been a mauling. Other officials gathered up bloody clothing and gear and dropped them into plastic bags. Marco helped pick up the bandage wrappers, IV packaging, and other medical supplies strewn about.

Meanwhile in the back of the ambulance, en route to rendezvous with the LifeGuard helicopter, I kept mumbling nonsense. "My girl-friend's going to be so mad at me. She's going to kill me." I kept asking the same questions over and over: "I can hear you guys, why can't I see you?"

Suddenly I began vomiting up swallowed blood. Carrie and her crew tipped the backboard onto its side to keep me from drowning.

"Hold on, man," Eric said. "Hold on."

Between the vomit and the blood, Carrie and Phil wouldn't get back to their respective beds until around 4:30 that morning. Before calling it a night, they'd back the ambulance up to Carrie's garage, hook her garden hose to the outdoor hot-water spigot, swab the ambulance out with a mop, and hose it down before returning it to the barn and signing off for the night.

It was a short ride to the roadside pullout near the Resurrection Trail that would serve as an improvised helipad. Troopers had closed the Sterling Highway on either end with flares and a roadblock of vehicles. A fire truck, lights whirling, had been parked beneath a set of power lines that crossed the road so they'd be easier to see from the air. Flares and headlights illuminated the landing zone. With the ambulance idling, we waited. And waited.

Back at the campground, Marco finished down at the site and headed back up the stairs. As exhausted as he was, he wasn't about to crawl into a tent with walls as thin as tissue paper, and both vehicles his group had driven down from Anchorage were locked. So he piled wood onto the campfire and sat up waiting for the others with a .44 Magnum in his lap.

Around 2:30, the womp-womp-womp of the helicopter filled the air. Phil talked the pilot down by radio, using a high-powered flashlight as a beacon. He had the pilot come straight down on top of the light, then ducked away as the chopper closed in on the ground. Once it settled, two critical-care flight nurses hopped out, and keeping their heads low, dashed over to the ambulance with a gurney. After a quick briefing, they transferred me to a medevac gurney, dashed back to the helicopter, loaded me inside, locked the gurney down, and closed the door.

Nearly three hours after the sow came tearing around the corner in the trail, the helicopter rose off the ground amid a blizzard of dust and swaying treetops and whisked me off to Providence Alaska Medical Center in Anchorage. The beeper on Dr. Kallman's beside table would soon yank him from his dreams.

CHAPTER 6

Little Red Riding Hood's Hood

WHILE I WAS FIGHTING TO HOLD ON DOWN AT THE RIVER, JOHN WAS fighting to hold on up in the parking lot. He'd been waiting with Emily and Maya, alternating between pacing and shaking his head, and sitting on the ground with his head in his hands. As I was being loaded into the ambulance, Marco and the others tried to console him.

"I should have done something," he kept saying. "I didn't know what to do. What should I have done?"

"You did the right thing, man," they told him. "You went for help. What the hell were you gonna do? Get mauled, too? How was that going to help your friend?"

Once John heard the helicopter approaching, he felt free to go. But he was in no shape to get behind the wheel of a car. The Girdwood friends we'd stopped to chat with earlier that night at The Sanctuary, Jaelyn and Carl, convinced him of that. Carl offered to drive his Subaru, with Jaelyn leading the way in her truck. While Jaha and Emily stuck around to answer investigators' questions and later bum a ride back home, they headed for Girdwood with Maya crashed out in the back of the Subaru and John in the front passenger seat staring at nothing, replaying the attack over and over and over in his head.

They made the turnoff to Girdwood about the time the pager went off on Dr. Kallman's bedside table. A few minutes later, John and Jaelyn's vehicles pulled up in front of my place. John clomped up the steps to the deck with Carl and Jaelyn behind him. My roommate, Jamie Berggren, and I rarely locked our doors but for whatever reason that night was an exception. So John knocked, and when Jamie didn't respond, he banged.

Still nothing. He walked along the deck to the back of the house and tapped on his bedroom window.

"Hey, Jamie, it's John," he called into the darkened room. "Hey, man, you need to get up."

"Wha . . . ? What's going on?"

"Throw on some clothes. I have something to tell you. It's not good."

"What? What time is it? What's up?"

"Just get dressed. I'll tell you inside."

Jamie rolled out of bed, stumbled down the hallway, unlocked the door, and let the three of them in. Carl and Jaelyn sank into the couch, while John grabbed a kitchen chair and swung it around to face the living room. Jamie, dressed in sweats and a T-shirt, stood on the shabby carpet in bare feet, hair all confused, rubbing his eyes with the bottom of his shirt.

"What's the deal, guys? Where's Dan?"

John sighed deeply, shook his head, and started to talk.

John and Jamie took off for Anchorage just as the sun began to rise. They arrived at Providence an hour later, while Dr. Kallman was still assessing the gravity of my injuries and setting surgery plans in motion. They were ushered into a waiting room, where they spent the next hour mindlessly flipping through magazines and staring into space, too wired to doze off, too heartsick to speak. Finally, the door opened and in walked Kallman with a look on his face that did nothing to boost their spirits.

"I'm not going to lie to you," he told them. "It's bad. I've never seen anything like this."

Kallman could have decided in the emergency room to have me medevaced to Harborview Medical Center in Seattle, the Level 1 trauma center for the region. It did cross his mind. He'd later become a partner in Dr. Dwight Ellerbe's ear, nose, and throat and plastic surgery practice in Anchorage, but at the time he was the new guy in town and more like Ellerbe's employee. Kallman had tremendous respect for the man and some proving up to do. A graduate of the Citadel with a degree from the Medical University of South Carolina, Ellerbe had done two residencies, one in pediatrics, the other in otolaryngology, plus a fellowship at Johns Hopkins before becoming head of surgery at Elmendorf Air Force Base, then starting his own practice in town. The way Kallman saw it, his own medical degree and two board certifications were just pieces of paper until he could prove he could do what they said he could do.

So there was his future to consider. But there was also the possibility I would be better served by someone with more experience. Trauma surgery can be a thankless job. Severely wrecked people who get pieced back together often spend the rest of their lives steeped in bitterness, and especially angry at their doctors for not allowing them to die. Just as I had chosen the more arduous of the two paths as I lay at the crossroads down by the river, Kallman did the same. He didn't ship me off to Harborview to become someone else's problem. He made a commitment to stick with me.

Later that morning, while John and Jamie were on their way back to Girdwood after a somber breakfast in town, Kallman stood in the operating room, staring down at the explosion of my face, feeling much like the emergency room doctor had sounded on the phone. Standing there frozen, head cocked to the side, he felt all eyes upon him, and then a hand upon his shoulder.

"Doctor, would you like to shave the hair?"

"Right. That's where we'll start; we'll start with shaving the hair."

First he needed to clean me up so he could see what was what. He scrubbed the blood, dirt, and bear saliva off my neck, face, and forehead with gauze and squirts of hydrogen-peroxide/sterile-saline solution. Then he took an electric razor to me. As he followed the contours of my misshaped head, my sun-streaked hair, matted with blood and forest debris, dropped off in clumps. Over the top and around the sides, he carefully navigated around my wounds. As Kallman worked up top, Dr. David Wrigley oversaw the cleaning of the multiple puncture wounds from my shoulders down, on my arms and legs mostly, some deep enough to bury a finger well past the first knuckle.

Kallman covered the disaster area across the middle of my face with moist gauze and, to ensure a clear airway, bathed my neck in Betadine in preparation for a tracheotomy, a procedure he could do practically blindfolded. Extend the neck. Find the solid ring around the trachea called the cricoid. Move a finger's width down in the soft spot below. Incise the skin horizontally. Then dissect vertically in the center down to the trachea. Enter the trachea with a horizontal incision. Insert the tracheotomy tube into the windpipe. Inflate the cuff. Confirm placement and secure to the skin. Done.

He then rotated the operating table away from the anesthesiologist 180 degrees so he could easily move from one side of my head to the other as he worked. He prepped my face with Betadine, covered the intact parts with sterile drapes, and began extensive exploration of my wounds. Starting at the top, he found that five of the six arteries to my forehead and scalp had been severed. From my mid-forehead down he found few recognizable landmarks. Where my forehead was split, the skin peeled back like an orange, he could see bone and bone fragments. It appeared to him that the bear had not only bitten me across the face, it had chewed. Some of the skin of my shattered nose was also torn back, leaving my nasal cavities open with brain tissue visible amid the ruins. Looking into the top of my mouth, he could see that my palate was split open.

He moved on to my eyes. The upper and lower eyelids were shredded. My left eye, hanging loosely from vascularized tissue, was detached from the optic nerve and lying on the right side of what had been my nose. My right eye, which didn't appear to be attached to much of anything viable, lay near the other.

Despite the initial washing, the wounds were still filthy. With a fiber-optic headlamp strapped to his forehead and wearing magnifying loupes that resembled Buddy Holly glasses fitted with miniature binoculars, he began to pick out every speck of dried blood, dirt, twig, grass, leaf, spruce needle, and bear hair, all of which were scrambled with tissue and bone shards and driven deep into my nasal passages, eye-socket rubble, and the base of my skull. This was going to be a marathon. He lowered the operating table and pulled up a stool.

～～

As I lay unconscious beneath a warming blanket and blazing lights, Amber and her best friend, Bekkie Volino, were on their way to Bear Valley in Amber's truck on one of the most gorgeous days of summer. Amber still had land on her mind, and wanted to show her friend some of the properties I'd shown her that spring, including my cabin and the piece of land she was interested in next door.

No one knew Amber better than Bekkie. They'd come to Alaska together on a festival-hopping road trip with a third girlfriend, two dogs, and all their gear crammed into Amber's car, an Oldsmobile with blown shocks and a rear end slathered in bumper stickers with slogans like "Not all who wander are lost." They had spent the remainder of that summer living out of a tent in Girdwood, using the trunk of Amber's car as a closet, before upgrading to that off-the-grid cabin up Crow Creek Road that wasn't much bigger than a chicken coop and had a zip line for hauling down firewood and gear.

Dressed in a gauzy shirt, a short skirt, and Birkenstocks, Amber had a daydreamy smile on her face as she drove up Turnagain Arm to the Rabbit Creek turnoff that would take them up to Bear Valley. She glanced over at Bekkie a second, then back at the road, then back at Bekkie, then back at the road.

"I've got to tell you, I had a truly amazing time with Dan Sunday night. He came looking for me after the Galactic show and invited me over for a beer. Well, actually, I was pretty much waiting for him to come find me. Anyway, we ended up spending the night together, just cuddling, but connecting in a way I've never felt before. It was really kind of magical."

This did not sound like the Amber Bekkie knew. The Amber she knew didn't do touchy-feely, "magical" talk. She was a certifiable book-smart left-brainer. Earthy, but the kind with both feet planted firmly on the same planet she lived on.

"You sound like you're in love or something."

Amber laughed. "Well, I don't know about that. I barely know him. I just know I'd like to go for it. He was supposed to call me last night when he got back from fishing, but he must have gotten in really late. I'm pretty sure he had to work this morning. Anyway, we'll see where things go from here."

Later, as they were ordering sandwiches and microbrews on the sunny deck of an Anchorage brew pub, Dr. Kallman was picking the last of the debris from the wreckage of my eye sockets. When the final speck was out, he pushed my eyes more or less back where they belonged and moved on.

Putting my bones back together, confining swollen brain tissue, could have cut off blood supply and left me a vegetable. Most critical at this stage was closing my skin to minimize the risk of infection and to give every piece a chance to survive. He began with the tears and punctures across my scalp, which required multiple layers of stitches topped off with staples. Then he began sorting out the shreds of my face.

He worked slowly, methodically, as he separated the tatters, pulling them apart like tangled fishing lines, one segment at a time, carefully studying each piece of the puzzle. Did it go here? Or there? When he was unsure, he put in a thinking-stitch to hold the skin in place until he was ready to commit. This took not only a steady hand and immense skill, but extraordinary patience. Growing up in a family that did jigsaw puzzles had to have helped. Kallman has fond memories of sitting in front of the fireplace at Christmas, putting jigsaws together with his father, the tougher the better, including a two-thousand-piece puzzle that was entirely red called "Little Red Riding Hood's Hood."

His mastery of shape recognition paid off as he searched for the remnants of my eyelids, and when located, reconstructed and reattached them with tiny stitches. He closed them over my eyes and sewed my eyelids shut.

Word gets around when cases this extraordinary come along. Over the course of the day, a couple of Kallman's colleagues, scrubbed and masked, poked their heads into the operating room to see how he was doing and offer words of encouragement.

"Nice job, Jim," they told him. "Impressive."

By the time he came up for air, it was late afternoon. Cleaning my face and stitching it back together had taken nine hours.

Remarkably, nothing was missing. With all the skin and soft tissue accounted for, my face more or less came together in a meander of staples and stitches. I looked like a guy who'd tangled with a chainsaw, but at least I looked human again.

After surgery, I went straight to intensive care, where a ventilator made sure I kept breathing, and hoses, tubes, and wires poked tentacle-like from various parts of my body. To keep me from thrashing about, I was put into a drug-induced coma with Propofol, or milk of amnesia as doctors call it. There was nothing more Kallman could do for me until the swelling went down enough to go back in and start repairs. If I survived.

Kallman had his doubts about that. Any of my cluster bomb of puncture wounds could have become infected. With the floor of my skull in pieces, my brain was sagging into my nose, not the cleanest place for a brain to be. As cerebrospinal fluid drained out of my nose, Kallman's biggest fear was that I'd contract meningitis or some other potentially lethal infection.

Thoroughly spent, he stumbled back to his office late that afternoon, unshaven and in the same jeans and sweatshirt he'd thrown on around 4:30 that morning. His colleagues and staff were waiting for him, anxious to hear all about it. He filled them in, then pulled out photographs of my face, one taken in the emergency room soon after he arrived, another after he'd cleaned me up and pieced me back together. That's when it hit him, what such devastating injuries would mean to a twenty-five-year-old man in the prime of his life. He knew nothing about me other than my name, but he did know that if I beat the odds and survived, I would wake up from my coma blind, disfigured, and possibly brain damaged.

Kallman was too fried to fight it. A lump rose in his throat and tears welled up in his eyes.

Dr. James Kallman and his wife, Sara Methratta, in Denali National Park.

CHAPTER 7

Circling the Wagons

WHILE DR. KALLMAN HOVERED OVER THE RUINS OF MY LIFE, DOWN IN California my brother Brian was waking up to a day that would morph into the unimaginable, and nothing in our family would ever be the same.

Off from his seasonal job at a ski resort in the Sierras, he was hanging out at the family getaway, a country home called Arboleda in the hills above San Juan Bautista, with our friend Jeremy Grinkey, who was caretaking the place. Growing up, my role in the family had been peacemaker, while Brian's had been warrior-protector. Our division of labor had mostly to do with him being two years older than me, but also my dicey start in life as a sickly preemie with pencil-thin legs.

I worked hard to outgrow my childhood frailties, including allergies to just about everything. By the fifth grade I had immersed myself in sports, especially swimming, and was proud of how long I could hold my breath. Too proud. Showing off for a group of girls one time, I held my breath so long I managed to pass out. By the time I was in middle school and living in Malaysia, on top of playing conventional sports, I was a member of a high-octane hip-hop dance group that had me twirling girls over my head, and was a devout practitioner of Taekwondo, earning my black belt at fifteen. Not only had I long outgrown my mom's nickname for me as a baby, "Bird Legs," but my gym teacher started calling me "D'animal." Still, Brian saw it as his job to shield me from harm, a duty that started on the playground and evolved as we got older into running interference when my mom got in my face or grounded me for stupid infractions, like putting my socks in the laundry hamper all wadded up after she'd repeatedly asked me not to.

The morning Dr. Kallman sewed up my face, Brian shuffled into the kitchen around ten to make coffee. He noticed the light flashing on the answering machine, pushed the "play" button, and wandered toward the coffeepot. The urgency in the man's voice stopped him in his tracks. An Alaska state trooper was trying to get in touch with the family of Dan Bigley. Something about a serious accident. Something about a medevac to Anchorage's Providence hospital.

"What? Jeremy!" he hollered down the hall. "I think something's happened to Dan! You've got to come hear this."

Jeremy hurried into the kitchen. Brian hit the play button again.

"Am I hearing this right? What the hell is this guy saying?"

Time didn't stand still, it swirled like a cyclone inside his head. He played the message one more time before, hands trembling, he dialed the number the trooper had left on the machine. The woman who answered put him on hold, then came back and said something about a bear. *A bear? What does she mean, a bear?* There's been a mauling, she said, and no, she didn't have any other details. She suggested he call Providence hospital right away. Brian jotted down the number. He shook his head, glanced up at the ceiling a moment, stared at the phone, then dialed.

He learned that I was in critical condition, that I was still in surgery, that I had severe trauma to the head, that doctors were hoping for the best. Brian understood the code: I might not make it.

"It's important for you to get here as soon as possible," the woman said.

Brian doubled over and dropped to his knees. "You've got to take me to the airport, Jeremy. I mean right now."

Brian, tall and bearded like me, stuffed his wallet into his pants pocket and threw his address book and a change of clothes into a daypack. He and Jeremy were out the door in minutes. They jumped into Brian's Jeep, and with Jeremy behind the wheel, drove down the winding canyon road to the highway leading to the San Jose airport, forty-five minutes away. As Jeremy concentrated on the road, Brian sat slumped in the passenger seat, his head in his hands. What if he didn't get there in time? What if he never got the chance to say goodbye?

I had just spent a week with Brian and Jeremy when I flew down for the High Sierra Music Festival over the Fourth of July. Hanging out at Arboleda before the festival, I'd been telling Jeremy my fishing stories, and how in certain places, you almost expect to see bears. Only days before, I had assured him that as long as you followed protocol in bear country, you'd be fine. I had just assured him there was no reason to worry about me.

Jeremy dropped Brian off at departures, parked the Jeep, then made his way into the terminal to see Brian off. Struggling to keep it together, Brian headed straight for the Alaska Airlines ticket counter.

"I need the first flight you've got to Anchorage," he told the agent, his voice cracking. "I don't care how much it costs. My brother's been mauled by a bear, and they don't know if he's going to make it."

The agent's eyes grew wide. As crazy a story as it sounded, especially in the asphalt-and-steel landscape of Silicon Valley, the look on Brian's face assured him that this was for real.

"Oh my god, that's horrid. Don't worry about a thing. We'll get you up there as soon as possible."

His finger clacked across the keyboard as he stared at the screen. Brian held onto the counter with both hands and stared at the floor. *Clack, clack, clack.*

"Okay, I've got you on a compassion fare on our next flight out, which boards right down that hallway past security in about twenty-five minutes."

"Oh, man, are you kidding me? Thank you *so* much," Brian said as he handed the agent his credit card.

"Glad I could help. Good luck. I'll be thinking of you and your brother."

Brian was anti–cell phone at the time and didn't own one. While waiting to board, he found a pay phone and made some calls, pacing as best he could, a step this way, a step that way, tethered by the phone's metal cord. First he called our stepfather, Doug Wilhelm, the pillar of our family and "Dad" to us since our biological father had slowly faded from our lives for reasons we'd been too young to understand at the time. Our parents lived in Carmel, about sixty miles south of the airport, but were away in two different states on opposite sides of the country. They'd attended a family wedding in Florida, and my stepdad had stayed on afterward to spend time with his daughter, Gretchen, and others while our mom, Ann, had gone to Atlanta to visit her sister. Brian caught Doug on his cell phone.

"Dad, where are you?"

"I'm on the highway. What do you need?"

"Dad, you need to pull over. I have something to tell you."

"Can't you just tell me? I'm following Gretchen, and I'll lose her if I do."

"I don't care what you're doing or where you are. You need to pull over now."

Always even keeled no matter what kind of chaos was going on around him, Doug flipped on his blinker, braked, and pulled onto the shoulder.

"Okay, what's going on?"

Brian took a deep breath, and then just said it. "Dad, Dan got mauled by a bear. He's alive, but he's in bad shape. He's got a severe head injury, and they're not sure he's going to pull through. I'm at the airport now. I'm on the next flight out of here. You and Mom need to get to Alaska as soon as you can."

He was silent a moment, absorbing the news. *Dan . . . A bear . . .* Once it registered, he was his usual composed self: "Okay, call us when you get there. I'll let everyone know what's going on and go straight to the airport."

Brian still had a few minutes before boarding. He debated whether to call our biological father, Steve Bigley. We'd grown up hearing only one side of the story of our family's demise, which had its final meltdown when I was still a toddler. There was so much we didn't know. We'd only seen Steve a couple of times since returning from Malaysia, but despite being virtual strangers, I was still his son. Brian had been carrying his phone number on a sticky note inside his wallet for years. He dug it out and dialed Steve's home in Salinas, California. Neither Steve nor his wife, Margaret, picked up. Brian left the news on their answering machine, then hung up, gave Jeremy a stiff hug goodbye, and headed toward security.

He spent the flight immersed in tunnel vision, hunched forward in his seat, elbows on his knees, head in hands, ball cap pulled down low, trying to think while at the same time trying not to. A car wreck he could imagine. A climbing accident. But a bear? What were the odds? As the first family member to arrive, he'd be the one asking all the questions and making all the decisions. But what questions and what decisions? There were so many unknowns.

The last time Brian was en route to Anchorage, he'd been so stoked he could hardly sit still. That was the previous summer when he and his dog, Ram, short for the Hindu classic, *Ramayana,* came to visit me and

Maya and see Alaska for the first time. He had so many great memories from that trip. Looking left for Dall sheep and right for beluga whales on the drive down Turnagain Arm. The all-night music bash with the Photonz in Talkeetna. Our two dogs romping like long-lost cousins along the banks of a glacial-fed creek. He'd been so impressed with all he saw he took long stretches of video as we drove down the Seward Highway with his recorder out the window.

The highlight, though, was our epic fly-in fishing trip to Lake Creek south of Denali. We were after silver salmon, but all we were catching were spawned-out kings that were so past their prime, we could hardly stand handling them long enough to retrieve our hooks. After fishing a couple days without much luck, we followed a tip from another angler we'd happened upon that entailed a hairy river crossing in hip-deep current that was so pushy, the rocks we dislodged as we shuffled along in our waders glanced off our ankles and went bowling off downriver. Bracing each other, we barely made it across, and once we did we just hoped we could make it back. But we found the mother lode, what seemed like thousands of silver salmon holed up in the calm waters of a channel not much wider than my Girdwood living room. We had never seen anything like it, not even on some fantasy fishing show. Not only were the waters choked with silvers, those silvers were chromers, so fresh from the ocean their scales were as shiny as polished steel. Three days later, Brian and I flew out with a humongous cooler stuffed with our daily limits.

This time, landing in Anchorage filled Brian with unprecedented dread. My roommate, Jamie, picked him up at the airport and drove him to the hospital in relative silence. Brian found his way to intensive care, and at the security doors picked up a phone that connected directly to the nurses' station. He told the answering nurse who he was and why he was there. She said she'd be right down.

While waiting, Brian walked in circles, stroking his beard, a nervous habit the two of us shared. After several minutes, the doors clicked open and the nurse introduced herself and let him inside. The doors locked behind them. Before escorting him down the hallway and into the unit, she tried to prepare him. I was out of surgery, she told him, but not out of the woods.

"He's heavily sedated, so he won't be able to respond. You're going to see a lot of equipment and a lot of tubes. He's had a tracheotomy so he's on a ventilator. He has a feeding tube and a catheter. There are puncture wounds on his back, shoulders, arms, wrists, and left thigh. His eyes were severely damaged so his eyelids have been sewn shut."

"His eyes?"

"His surgeon can tell you more. Do you think you're ready?"

Brian shook his head no but answered "Yes."

He caught his first glimpse of me through plate glass. From the bottom of my nose to the top of my head, nothing was familiar. My head— black and blue and snaked with stitches and staples—was elongated and swollen like a giant lightbulb. My stitched-up eyelids were bulging, and the eyes beneath them didn't seem to be in quite the right place. The walls and floor started swaying. Brian's knees began to buckle. The nurse helped him to a chair and brought him a glass of water. My room was directly across from the nurses' station, its front wall entirely glass, so he sat there a while staring at me, trying to register what he was seeing, the nurse's hand upon his shoulder. After several minutes and several deep breaths, he rose to his feet and walked into my room. He stood in silence, holding on to the side of my bed with both hands.

"Is it okay if I touch him?"

The nurse nodded. He took my hand in his.

"Dan, can you hear me? It's Brian. I'm here now. Mom and Dad should be here tomorrow. We're here for you, so keep fighting, man. Keep fighting."

—◆—

No one thought to call Amber. She and I were such a new item that she was the last person on anyone's mind. Except for one. The previous night, Amber had wandered over to Max's, where she ran into her friend Julia Dykstra, a Girdwood musician. Julia knew me through the bonfire crowd and the music scene—the open mikes at Max's and jams around town. About the time John and I were making our first casts at The Sanctuary, Amber, still on a high from our night together, was updating Julia on our status.

"Dan and I have decided to give this thing a try," Amber told her. "I'm pretty psyched about it."

"You should be. He's a great guy. I really hope it goes well for you two."

"Yeah, me too. I was pretty much convinced he wasn't interested so I'm kind of surprised. I guess we'll just have to see what happens."

The following night, while Brian's plane was still in the air, Julia was home watching the ten o'clock evening news. One of the top stories was about a bear mauling at the Russian River.

"The victim has been identified as twenty-five-year-old Dan Bigley ..."

"What!" Julia stiffened and leaned in to the TV. That couldn't be right.

"According to state troopers, the Girdwood man had been fishing with friends when ..."

Julia slumped into her couch and chewed on the inside of her cheek as the news sank in. Amber must be going through hell right now, she thought. But what if she didn't know? It was possible. Having her find out through the newspaper or waking up to radio coverage would be brutal. She did not want to be the one to tell her, but she felt she had to call. If Amber did know, at least she could offer to be there for her.

She dialed Amber's house. The phone rang and rang and rang. She hung up. She paced. She tried again. And again and again. With each failed call it became harder to sit still. Finally around eleven, Amber picked up. Julia took a deep breath.

"Hey, Amber, it's Julia. I'm just calling to see if you're okay."

"I'm fine, why?"

Oh god, she doesn't know. Julia closed her eyes and mustered up her courage. "You did hear about Dan, didn't you?"

"What are you talking about?"

"Oh, Amber, you'd better sit down." She told her what she'd heard on the news. When she finished, there was silence on the other end of the phone.

"They said he's at Providence. I'm sure they could tell you more about what's going on."

"I've gotta go," Amber said, and hung up the phone.

Amber's roommate, Lindsay Pickrell, who'd been rooting for Amber and I to get together since the night of the beluga convergence, walked in about then. She'd known Amber since college, and had never seen her unglued. Amber was talking gibberish, something about a bear. She was walking in circles around the kitchen, wringing the bottom of her shirt in her hands.

"I don't know what to do. I don't know what to do. I don't know what to do."

Amber got Bekkie on the phone and told her what had happened.

"I am freaking out, Bekkie. I have no idea what to do. Should I go to the hospital? Should I wait until tomorrow? Dan's family is probably there and they don't know me from Adam. I'm not sure of my place. I feel like I need to go, but it's so late I doubt they'd let me see him. But I can't just sit here. What should I do?"

"Hang up, get in your truck, and go," Bekkie said. "Now."

Amber arrived around midnight, not long after my brother. He had no idea who she was, but to show up that late she was obviously someone who cared a lot about me. He gave permission for her to see me. She stood outside my room a moment and stared at me through glass. Her face drained, she walked stiffly inside and gripped the side rail of my bed with both hands. She looked down at a face she no longer recognized. Her mouth opened but no words came out. She closed her eyes and hung her head. She had no frame of reference for this. Nobody did.

Over the next day or two, as I clung to life, the rest of my family arrived from the Lower 48. My biological father, Steve, showed up first. Returning from a cafeteria break, Brian was taken aback when he saw him waiting outside the ICU. Steve rose to his feet the moment he saw him, and wrapped him in a hug.

"Thank you so much for coming," Brian said.

"There's no way I could have stayed away."

My mom and stepdad arrived soon after. Our mother never had anything but vitriolic things to say about my father, so Brian braced himself for a scene. My three parents encountered each other in the ICU hallway. They all hugged.

Next to arrive were two friends living in Oregon who were like brothers to me: a Prescott College buddy, Chris Van Ness, and my best friend, Jay McCollum.

I'd met Chris my first day at Prescott during an orientation backpacking trip into the Grand Canyon, a trip that nearly made felons out of us. Poking around during a lunch break, Chris and I came upon some old rusty cans scattered about and wondered who would do such a thing. Being fine stewards of the land, we picked them up and tossed them into our packs with the intention of hauling them out to the nearest trash bin. We carried them several miles to the Bright Angel Campground, where we showed the ranger on duty the good deed we'd done, and he informed us that our rusty cans were mining artifacts and that by taking them, we'd committed a felony. He'd just begun writing us up when a medical emergency arose in the campground. He reprioritized, let us off the hook with a stiff warning, and made arrangements for our "artifacts" to be put back where we'd found them.

Chris and I had just reconnected at the High Sierra Music Festival, where my favorite guitarist, Steve Kimock, played an extraordinary set that didn't wrap up until nearly sunrise. Still, neither of us had been ready to call it a night. After the roadies had shut down the stage, Chris and I had hiked to the top of a hillside overlooking the festival, where we watched the sunrise and waxed philosophical on the meaning of life.

He was watering his garden when he got the call. Working as a groundskeeper at the time, he scrambled to get someone to cover for him, and got himself on a plane.

Jay and I went further back, back to the days my family lived in Cincinnati, headquarters for Procter & Gamble, which is where my stepdad's job took us upon returning from Malaysia. Jay and I met after I graduated from high school, which I pulled off a year early, and he was fresh out of the Army. We raised a little hell, did a lot of environmental work, and spent countless hours dreaming up ways to save the world. Reveling in our newfound freedoms, we'd explored philosophy, spirituality, and wild abandon together. We became brothers at a time when we were invincible and prone to spontaneous acts of stupidity, like rolling down a hill in sleeping bags in the dark.

One of our dumbest moves was nearly a reenactment of the final scene in *Thelma and Louise*. We were hanging out in the Red River Gorge in Kentucky's Daniel Boone National Forest when we leapt to our feet and started running, just running for no particular reason, hollering "Waa-hoo!" as we charged down a trail. Then we veered off-trail, and started down a steep hillside, hooting and hollering and paying zero attention as we ran full-tilt toward a cliff. Running side by side, we suddenly realized the error of our ways. We dropped down, skidding on our butts and the soles of our shoes, barely stopping in time to avoid plunging over the edge.

We didn't stop to think about what almost happened, but immediately popped up and started running in the opposite direction hooting and hollering even more. The only explanation I can offer is to quote John Muir, "We must risk our lives to save them," although I doubt he had this kind of nonsense in mind.

As soon as Jay heard what had happened in Alaska, he put his massage therapy practice in downtown Portland on hold and flew up to be with me.

Once my inner circle had assembled, Dr. Kallman called a meeting. Down a hallway in the ICU, in a windowless conference room flooded with incandescent light, Kallman said what no one wanted to hear.

"There's not a lot we can do right now. We need to let the swelling come down before we can go back in and put him back together."

"You mean you haven't already done that?"

"If you enclose a swelling brain in a confined space, you risk brain damage," he explained. "Tissue ultimately loses blood flow and dies. So first we take care of the skin. We try to cover all the bone, putting vascularized tissue over it, to keep as much of it alive as possible. And then there's the second stage of putting the skeleton back together."

"When will that happen?"

"It depends on how he does this week."

"Why the drug-induced coma?"

"With something like this, everything is kind of delicate and fragile so we like to avoid a patient thrashing around. And for obvious reasons, an injury this traumatic is very disorienting. He's going to have pain and discomfort. We don't mean to be cruel, but when we have a delicate situation like this, we typically keep the patient heavily sedated for a while. We don't want him to jeopardize his chances of healing by banging his head against the side of the bed."

"Do you know if there's been any damage to the brain?"

"As far as we can tell his brain function is good—with the exception of his vision. He could move his arms and legs in the ER, and he was talking so he seems to be wired up right."

"What about his vision?"

"I have to be honest. One of his eyes isn't going to make it. The other has just enough connective tissue that there's a chance it will survive. But I can tell you right now, there's no hope for his vision. Both optic nerves were severed."

"Are you saying he's blind?"

"I'm terribly sorry."

"Are you sure about that?"

"I'm afraid so."

My mother's eyes filled with tears. The men in the room were stiff-upper-lipped.

"Can't the optic nerves be reattached?"

"I am not aware of any technology in the world to fix that problem."

"Is there a possibility that could change in the future?"

"Dr. Carl Rosen is the eye expert here, and he can explain all this better than I can."

The questions kept coming. Kallman gave what answers he could. One of his mentors had been especially good at talking to heartbroken families. Kallman had learned from him the importance of working the word "devastating" into the conversation, of using it as many times as it takes until it sinks in that nobody on the planet has the ability to put their loved ones back the way they were before.

"Dan has a devastating injury," he emphasized, pausing to let the word percolate. "Devastating. His wounds were very dirty. Dan was not only bitten by the bear, he was chewed. His wounds were also open to the outside world for many hours before he got here and we were able to clean him up. These factors significantly increase a patient's risk of infection.

"The good news is he's young, he's in good shape. He's got a good heart and lungs, so he's got resources. But he could still get meningitis or some other life-ending infection. We've got him on antibiotics to try to prevent that, but this is a waiting game now."

Although there was little more medical science could do for me at this stage, there were things my family and friends could do, Kallman told them. He didn't care how conservative or close-minded certain doctors might be, they had all seen recoveries that couldn't be explained by science.

"Let's bring in some things that are familiar to him, to keep him connected to the world," he said. "Bring in his favorite music, anything to keep him with us. And, if you have any kind of faith, now would be a good time to pray."

CHAPTER 8

Armchair Quarterbacks

As I was clinging to life, the armchair quarterbacks were going at it, quick to offer opinions about how and why I got myself mauled and what I could have done to prevent it. Among those chiming in on news websites and online sportsmen's forums were self-proclaimed bear experts who'd never crossed paths with a bear, and supposed Alaska experts who'd never set foot in Alaska.

I should have blasted that bear with pepper spray, they wrote. I should have shot the damn thing before it had the chance to charge. I should have climbed a tree.

I barely had time for "bear charging" to register in my brain before I got slammed. A highly motivated grizzly can sprint up to thirty-five miles per hour, covering major ground not just in seconds, but split seconds. Maybe bear spray would have made a difference. But from my vantage point, even if I'd had the canister aimed at the bear with my finger on the trigger, it would have been like a fireman trying to stop a backdraft with a squirt gun.

In Scott McMillion's book *Mark of the Grizzly,* retired researcher Barrie Gilbert, who lost an eye and half his face to a grizzly in Yellowstone National Park in 1977, best sums up this kind of second-guessing: "When you've been on the ground with a bear, then you tell me."

Bear maulings are rare, even in Alaska, where if Alaska Department of Fish and Game population estimates for all three species are within the ballpark, there's a bear for every five residents in this state. So maulings always make big headlines. Mine was so chilling, it went out on the national wires and appeared in newspapers from Seattle to Miami. On the flight to Anchorage, my mother noticed the woman in the seat next to her reading about me in *USA Today*. She leaned over and pointed to the article: "That's my son." In Alaska, the headlines kept coming and people couldn't stop talking about it.

"Did you hear? Some poor bastard on his way back from the confluence got his face ripped off by a bear."

"They say the bear clawed out his eyes."

"I heard he left one of his eyeballs down by the river."

My mauling was exceptionally hard for people to take, not only because a bear had blinded some poor bastard, but because it happened not much more than a stone's throw from the often jam-packed Grayling parking lot at one of the state's most popular campgrounds. Armies of people go up and down that same trail day and night between May and September, somewhere in the neighborhood of a hundred thousand trips a year, according to Chugach National Forest figures. My mauling might have been more understandable had the situation been, say, some clueless tourist who'd come within swiping distance of a sow and cubs to snap a picture. This attack, however, seemed so random, and random was too frightening to consider, especially for people who regularly stock their freezers at that river and have walked that same trail more times than they can count.

"He must have done something stupid," they rationalized. "Or maybe he just *is* stupid. Since I'm not stupid, it could never happen to me." This belief made their world seem safer.

There were so many rumors flying around. I'd thrown rocks at the bear, and that's what set off the attack. Better yet, I'd thrown beer cans at the bear. Or I was carrying fish in my pack, so no wonder. Not only was I not carrying fish in my pack, John was carrying fish in his pack and the bear blew right by him. If carrying fish was enough to provoke a mauling, then anglers would be getting jumped by bears on a regular basis.

The anonymous, insensitive, misinformed online commentators had themselves a field day with me.

"I heard this a.m. that the attack occurred because the victim's dog chased the bear, then, of course, reversed itself and came back."

"Well, this actually sounds like one of those rare and unusual cases where they had plenty of warning that the bear was going to go 'off.' They watched it run up and down and work itself into a frenzy."

"Just like some people, the sow went postal."

"People want so much to be 'one with nature' that they don't understand what a wild animal can do to a human being if it gets in its way."

"I remember a day when a cute yuppie couple and their doggie went on a little canoe ride in Florida. Cute little doggie jumped out of the canoe and was immediately chowed by a big ol' gator. . . . The guy actually dove in and tried to get the doggie back, he had the claw marks to prove it. . . . This bear situation sounds similar."

All the misinformation, judgment, and self-righteousness was deeply upsetting to my family, and convinced them not to grant interviews to the press. They could have set some facts straight, but they were too distraught to engage and didn't see any good coming of it.

It didn't take long for the debate over what I had done to deserve this to morph into a gun battle.

"He should have been better prepared," someone posted. By "better prepared" I can only assume the person who posted that thought I should have been carrying a firearm. The closest I had to weaponry was a pair of pliers and a fillet knife. But is packing heat the best way to go in bear country?

"Yes and no, maybe and sometimes, for some people and not for others," writes the Canadian expert on bear behavior, Dr. Stephen Herrero, author of *Bear Attacks: Their Causes and Avoidance*, and considered the leading authority on the topic. Firearms can give people a false sense of security, maybe even make them less alert for signs that bears are near. And there's a big difference between packing a firearm and being proficient at using it.

"To kill a charging grizzly bear in order to defend yourself, you must be capable of shooting to kill an object hurtling at you, perhaps through dense brush, at speeds of up to forty-four feet per second," Herrero writes. "If you aren't expert enough to do this, then you may be better off without a firearm."

That would be me, better off without a firearm. Had I been carrying one, I would have been as likely to shoot John as the bear. But Alaskans love their guns, and so online discussions degenerated into the "knuckleheads" versus the "idiots" squabbling over whose firearm was bigger and badder for putting down a charging bear. A snub-nose S&W 629? A WWG Copilot 457? A twelve-gauge shotgun with three-inch magnum slugs? Clearly manhood was at stake.

"I've hunted bear many times and am well aware of how to kill one, having killed several," one poster boasted.

"This is *not* a urinating contest," someone finally pointed out.

Lost in all this chest-beating was me. The backcountry-wandering, ski-bumming, river-running fishing junkie who was never going to see another sunset, the newly in love guy who'd been in such high spirits about the way his life was going, about the only thing that could have cranked up his happy meter would have been the sudden ability to fly. Lost in all the bickering was that if I pulled through, I would emerge from a coma into a world of pain, loss, and darkness.

One who understood the blame-the-victim mentality better than most was Craig Medred, longtime outdoor writer for the *Anchorage Daily News*. He understood because he'd gotten a piece of that action himself after being mauled by a grizzly sow while moose hunting alone in 1992. Here was a fully armed, seasoned hunter with more than twenty-five years of experience with firearms who was so confused about exactly what he should do in the heat of the moment that by the time he heard the pounding of the sow's feet and decided he had to shoot, it was too late. In the subsequent confusion, he missed his first shot. Before he could get off another, the bear had the scope of his .454-caliber Casull in her teeth, with the barrel perpendicular to her mouth. The impact knocked Medred over, leaving tooth marks on the gun's scope and an S-shaped claw wound where she stepped on his face while bowling him over. Somehow he managed to hang onto the gun. He still had it in his hand when she grabbed him by the leg.

His first shot had clean missed this enormous moving target an arm's length away. He did better with his second. With the sow's teeth clamped down on his right leg just above the ankle, he pointed the gun again. *Jesus, don't shoot yourself in the foot.* He pulled the trigger.

The 260-grain slug stopped the attack. The bear lay two feet from his right foot, horribly wounded. When he went to put her out of her misery, he discovered his gun had jammed. The bear got up, fell, rolled downhill away from him, got up again, rolled further away, got up again, and staggered off into the brush presumably to die. Medred was grateful to be alive, but sick about having to shoot a mother bear, and even sicker about leaving her wounded. And did he ever catch hell for it, both online and through letters to the editor. For hunting alone. For his choice of weapon. For getting himself mauled by a bear. For surviving, as some seemed to be saying.

Eleven years later, Medred, along with Doug O'Harra, covered the story of my mauling, its aftermath, and the impact it had on management practices along the Russian River, where Medred himself had fished for twenty-some years. He'd heard the rumors and read the comments about me, and wrote a column taking on this blame-the-victim mentality.

"When bears attack, people want a reason for it," he wrote. "In our comfortable and protected society, bad things like this just aren't supposed to happen to good people. . . . In the absence of explanations, people start making them up. . . . True outdoor accidents—as opposed to bad decision-making—are rare. But this appears to be one of them."

As details of my mauling and dramatic rescue unfolded in the news, it became obvious something had to be done about the Russian River problem. The day after my mauling, for the first time in Alaska history, state and federal officials ordered access to the river, its trails, and banks, closed by emergency order to nighttime fishing in the vicinity of The Sanctuary, and it remained closed from 11 p.m. to 6 a.m. for more than a month. Many were happy to comply, while others griped considerably, seeing it as misguided, as doing nothing to solve the bear-people problem once and for all, as surrendering the river to the bears.

Medred was among those who thought the nighttime closure was not the answer: "Who's the lucky person who gets to kick the bears out at 6 a.m.?" he wrote.

Until a better, long-term solution could be worked out among the various agencies involved, the intention was to keep the two species from bumping into each other along the river in the dark. Maulings—even if a mother bear is just protecting her cubs—tend to stir up anti-bear hysteria. With so many nerves on edge after my mauling, it seemed likely that more people were going to be packing firearms whether they were proficient at using them or not. If bullets were going to fly, far better to be shooting in the daylight than in the dark.

No one can say for certain exactly what happened that night, what it was that set off the sow Jaha saw running down the river not long before he heard my screams, or whether that was even the same bear that got me. There were plenty of potential suspects out there.

"The US Fish and Wildlife Service advised there are approximately fourteen bears on the Kenai River (in the confluence area) at this time," read the trooper report regarding my mauling. "Also, about three sows with cubs in the immediate area of the Russian River Campground."

No one can say for certain why of all the encounters between people and bears that end in mutual agreement to go separate ways, this one went so wrong so fast. The only thing that makes any sense to me is that the shaking in the alders—the shaking that startled us as John and I were retreating from the bear at the bottom of the stairs—was made by that sow's cubs. Although neither of us saw any cubs, Jaha saw cubs before and after the mauling.

There's more than one theory, more than one version of the various stories that converged at that spot by the river where the bear left me to die. That's often the case when adrenaline and fear shift time, space, and perception into surreal alternate dimensions.

Those closest to ground zero, John and Jaha, have their version. They believed those "We ain't scared of no bears" guys that Jaha had tried to warn about the sketchy sow he'd seen running down the river did, in fact, bump into her. Or maybe they ran into her cubs, little things about the size of half-grown golden retrievers. They believe those guys threw beer cans at the bear, or her cubs, to shoo them off. That would explain the dented cans John and I found strewn on the ground after passing them along the trail. It doesn't explain why these guys gave us the cold shoulder. It makes no sense at all that they wouldn't have mentioned such an encounter, that they wouldn't have warned us. Maybe they were too proud. Maybe they were unwilling to let on that they'd been unnerved. Maybe it didn't happen that way at all. All of this is speculation. But John and Jaha are convinced that's what happened, that throwing beer cans pissed off an already stressed-out mother bear, separating her from her cubs. If what they believe is true, then John and I walked between them and right into a trap.

Once all the witnesses had been interviewed, officials consulted, and reports filed, the reason I got mauled became clear: I was unlucky. I was in the wrong place at the wrong time with the wrong bear.

CHAPTER 9

The Vigil

THE WAIT-AND-SEE PERIOD TICKED BY ONE MINUTE AT A TIME AS I LAY in limbo, attached to machines by an octopus of hoses, tubes, and wires, with a monitor tracking every heartbeat and a ventilator that channeled Darth Vader amplifying every breath. Although I was drugged into submission, those first critical days I was also in restraints, my wrists bound in white terrycloth bands tied to the rails on each side of my bed. As cruel as that sounds, I would later understand its importance to my survival. Nurses were lightening my sedation two or three times a day for neurological checks, to make sure I had just enough going on upstairs to wiggle my fingers and toes. If I'd become conscious enough during those checks to reach up to my face I could have undone Dr. Kallman's work. If I'd become conscious enough to remember the bear, I could have thrashed so hard it could have killed me.

To drown out the cold, antiseptic sounds of medical technology, to help keep me tethered to the world, my brother rigged my room for music, setting up a minidisc player on a cabinet behind my head, speakers on each side, so my favorite bands could join my bedside vigil in five-hour loops: the Photonz, the Denali Cooks, the Grateful Dead, Thievery Corporation, Michael Hedges, Michael Franti, and Steve Kimock. Especially Steve Kimock. While ICU patients are usually kept more sequestered, Kallman as my primary physician gave my inner circle license to do what they could to keep me with them, to create their own version of a laying on of hands.

They sat with me in shifts, making sure at least one of them was with me twenty-four hours a day, not only so I'd never be alone, but also to stand watch over my care as a procession of aides, nurses, doctors, surgeons, and specialists came and went from my room. They leaned forward in their chairs, hands folded at their knees, staring at me. They stood at the window staring out at the Alaska summer. They held my hand, caressing its back with their thumbs. They talked to me, assuring me over and over that I was safe, that I was going to get through this, that everything was going to be all right. They read to me, Brian from *The Hitchhiker's Guide to the Galaxy* for its humor, and Jay from *The Book of the Dun Cow* for its epic struggle with victorious ending. Licensed in one of the world's oldest healing arts, Jay would pull a chair to the foot of my bed and gently lift one of my feet, wrapping one hand around the bottom and the other around the top. Leaning into his work, focusing his energy, he'd massage one foot, then the other, slowly moving up each calf then down again, about the only part of my body he could work on without hurting me.

A tense situation got more so when three days after my mauling, with cerebrospinal fluid still leaking from my nose, my temperature spiked. My turn south, despite a bombardment of broad-spectrum antibiotics, had everyone in the room exchanging grim glances. An ICU doctor ordered a spinal tap to check for the meningitis Dr. Kallman feared was coming. While awaiting results, Brian and Jay launched into research mode, hoping they might discover some way to help doctors help me since the foulness of a bear's mouth had called into question what antibiotic might put up the best fight. They hit the Internet hard and talked to bear biologists, even to someone at the Alaska Zoo. It wasn't so much naïve as it was desperate.

My results came back negative. My brother and friends did high-fives and fist pumps. My mom glanced toward the ceiling and mouthed a silent "Thank you" to no one in particular. My father Steve, who'd been praying for me, as had his church back in Salinas, thanked God specifically. But I still had a fever, a persistent one, a reminder that my hold on life was still precarious.

Had I not been out cold I would have been aware of the gaping absence among those gathered around me—Amber's. She got in two visits before crossing paths with my mom. On her third trip to the ICU, my overwhelmed mother fixed her eyes upon her. She furled her brow and glanced at Brian with a who-the-heck-is-she look on her face. He shrugged; he didn't really know why she kept coming. My mother wiggled the tip of her index finger in Amber's direction: "Would you come out here with me a moment?"

Amber's face dropped as she felt all eyes upon her. She swallowed hard, lifted her purse off her lap, set it on the floor beside her chair, and followed my mom out into the hallway.

"Excuse me, but who *are* you? And how did you get into Daniel's room?"

Amber was momentarily speechless. She wasn't sure who she was. She didn't think she had the right to call herself my girlfriend. She explained as best she could.

"Well, we just started dating . . ."

"Oh, really? Then why haven't I heard of you?"

Amber felt her face grow hot. "I understand. I really do," she said, staring at the floor. "You and your family need space. I didn't mean to intrude. I'll stay away. But would it be okay if I called you now and then to see how he's doing? Or maybe you'd be willing to call me?"

"That would be fine. Here's the number for the hotel where we're staying. I'll take your number, too."

Amber left the hospital feeling as if she'd swallowed barbed wire.

My family had no way of knowing her place in my life. Apparently a couple of my female friends had already played the girlfriend card as a way of getting in to see me. With her textbook case of Midwestern stoicism, Amber did the only thing she could do: She put one foot in front of the other and carried on the best that she could. For the first time in her life, sleep was not her friend, and she'd always been talented in that regard. As a toddler, she'd slept through a chimney fire, sirens and all, as her dad carried her out of their smoke-filled house. As a teenager, staying at a lakeside cabin with her family, she'd slept through a tornado that uprooted grandfather trees and ripped the roof off a neighboring cabin. As an adult, she typically set two alarms beside her bed since it often took that kind of teamwork to convince her it really was time to wake up.

Banished to the sidelines, she'd lie at night beneath her patchwork quilt, her head a swirl of images. Once she drifted off to sleep, the dreams would be waiting. She'd dream of me waking up from my coma and asking, "What are *you* doing here?" She'd dream of me asking her to marry me. She'd dream of me not remembering who she was and wanting nothing to do with her. The dreams wore her threadbare. And not just dreams, but the continuous loop of thoughts along the same vein that nagged her throughout the day. She began wondering if she'd just imagined the whole thing, that the connection she'd felt between us had been the beer talking or her wishful mind playing tricks. It was all so confusing.

While Amber stayed away, get-well cards and letters poured in—from friends and acquaintances, from strangers who'd heard of me through the news, from kids I worked with at Alaska Children's Services, the younger ones illustrating their thoughts in crayon and colored pencil. Colonel Valentine, a couple of the guys who rode with me in the ambulance, and a few others who'd been at the river that night dropped by the hospital to see how I was doing. Church people brought casseroles and moose stew to my family. Folks set up donation jars at the Russian River ferry and on countertops of Cooper Landing businesses. Buddies organized fund-raisers, one at the Sunrise Inn in Cooper Landing with the Denali Cooks, another in Girdwood at Max's with the Photonz. The generosity was overwhelming, from the owner of Girdwood's Double Musky Inn writing a fat check, to children shaking out the contents of their piggy banks. A man from Talkeetna even offered to donate one of his eyes.

In Girdwood, my community of friends gathered at Jamie's and my place, leaving a pile of shoes and sandals outside our front door, as is Alaska etiquette. They hugged and cried and shook their heads in disbelief. In a house stocked with outdoor gear I would no longer have much use for, my friends tried to fathom what had happened to me, the let's-hike-to-the-top-of-Max's-Mountain-at-midnight Dan, the Dan who loved to throw his head back and howl at the moon. Knowing I was blind, some wondered in whispers if it would have been kinder had I died at the river.

John called in sick the first couple of days, and then to say he wouldn't be coming back. His graveyard shift at the ski resort's front desk meant spending long hours mostly by himself, and he was having a hard time being alone with his thoughts. Although his place was a two-minute stroll from mine, he took up residence on my couch. My mother worried about survivor's guilt and offered to pay for counseling. John thanked her but said he didn't need it.

Now and then, when they weren't on hospital duty, Jay, Chris, and my brother would drive to Girdwood for respite among my friends. They'd raise a glass to me. Or two or three. Then the gatherings would turn from glum to Irish wake, and the stories would come tumbling out. From my Malaysia days, from my dreadlocked-with-attitude days, from my days of living out of a backpack so long I'd go feral. Like the time a buddy and

I ditched our clothes, straddled a driftwood log, commandeered it down the Merced River high in the Sierras, then had to hike back up to get our things barefoot and naked.

And the best prank ever: A group of us were backpacking in the shadow of Mount Whitney, and had just come upon a meadow brimming with wildflowers when we heard a helicopter approaching. Hiding at the sidelines, we watched as it landed in front of the remote park service cabin at the edge of the meadow. The chopper settled onto the ground, powered down, and the pilot and two others got out and went inside. Our buddy "Monk" started belly-crawling toward it. The rest of us exchanged glances, then followed, slithering along on our bellies up to the chopper, where we grabbed a camera off the seat, snapped a picture of our bare butts, put the camera back where we found it, and crawled back across the meadow in hysterics at the thought of some park ranger finding a chorus line of moons sandwiched between his nature shots.

While my survival was still uncertain, the time came for John to deal with the fish he and I had caught that day. After the ambulance pulled out of the parking lot, two armed troopers had escorted him down the stairs to retrieve his gear, including his pack with our fish. The fillets had been on ice in his cooler ever since, haunting reminders of how quickly the day had gone from just about perfect to unfathomable. John knew me well enough to know I would have hated for them to go to waste. So between the Russian reds and the ones we'd caught earlier that day down the Kenai, he wrapped some for the freezer and brined some for the smoker. Others he kept fresh, which he intended to grill with purpose.

John invited my family and a handful of my closest friends, including Amber, to this sacramental feast. Amber felt awkward and out of place around not just my mother, but all these people who had so much more history with me. Everyone remembers her being withdrawn and having little to say.

While a gastric tube fed nutrients into my stomach, the core people in my life loaded one of my mismatched Salvation Army plates with grilled salmon, a salad made of greens and stubby carrots harvested from my garden, and various side-dish contributions. While I lay as still as a post, they found spots on the couch, on the floor, or in one of the red-and-green vinyl chairs that came with the place, pilfered, I'd always assumed, from the ski lodge by some previous renter. Amber went straight for the deck, where she settled into a camp chair and picked at the plate balanced on her knees. Down below, our dogs played chase around the yard and splashed about in the creek. Amber kept her head down and poked at her food with a fork. She heard footsteps approaching and snapped her head up.

My father Steve knew that Amber had been shooed away. He's a PhD psychologist; it was obvious to him she was hurting. He saw her out on the deck, sat down beside her, and introduced himself.

"Hi, I'm Steve Bigley, Dan's father."

"I'm Amber Takavitz." Right away she noticed the resemblance.

"Nice to meet you, Amber. So, how do you know Dan?"

"Well . . ." she shifted in her seat. "I really haven't known him all that long, but we've been, umm, spending time together lately. Actually, we had just started dating. We were together the night before this happened."

"Really. You holding up okay?"

"I guess. It still doesn't seem real."

"It's been such a shock for all of us, but I have faith that he's going to pull through. About all any of us can do now is pray."

The significance of he showing up at the hospital was monumental, although if Brian had known the full story, he wouldn't have been so surprised that he had dropped everything to be at my bedside. Steve's absence from our lives had nothing to do with lack of interest. He never stopped loving us. To not come would have been unthinkable.

Trouble in my family started soon after Steve came home from Vietnam a different man than the one my mom married. They grew apart, and when they divorced, things got so ugly over custody and child support that the poison between them created an unworkable situation. After my mom married my stepdad and our family moved to Ohio, Steve followed. This did not please her. By the time we moved to Malaysia, Steve was worn down enough to let go. One could argue that a father should never let go of his kids. One could also argue that when the effort to hang on is like pogo-sticking through a minefield, ultimately it's the kids who suffer most.

Steve never gave up wanting to be a father. After he remarried, he and his wife, Margaret, adopted a son, and through the years took in so many foster children they stopped counting at a hundred.

Back at the ICU, Dr. Kallman checked on me at least twice a day. He'd get up to speed on my status, silently reading through my chart at the nurses' station directly across from my room. He'd slide the chart back into its spot, nod at the nurses, and head in.

"Hi, how are you doing?" he'd ask whichever members of the Dan-watch team were parked in my room. He'd then lean over me and meticulously clean, inspect, and re-dress the stitches holding my face together to a soundtrack of Steve Kimock tunes.

One night Kallman showed up while most of the city slept. With Sara and the girls visiting family in Philadelphia, he had no burning desire to go home to an empty house. He dealt with my wounds and checked my tracheotomy site, then pulled up a chair and sat quietly with me studying my face, fingertips forming a pyramid at his chin like a chess master pondering a move, thinking about how he was going to fix me. A nurse padded in to check my IVs, and padded out again. Muffled voices floated down the hall. At the nurses' station, a phone beeped and a keyboard clacked. That time of night the unit was relatively quiet, a good time for Kallman to be alone with his thoughts. He leaned forward in the chair, thinking of the disarray beneath my skin and his role in the four-surgeon team it would take to put my skull back together. Having Sara and the girls away during on-call weeks was usually for the best. This time was different.

"I'm dealing with a really tough one," he'd told his wife over the phone. "I really wish you were here."

Seven days after I was mauled, with Brian and Jay on duty, one of my nurses was overseeing the routine lightening of my sedation. As Kimock riffs played behind my head, I'm told my feet started tapping to the beat. The nurse raised her eyebrows, caught Brian's eye, and nodded toward the foot of my bed.

"Hey, Dan, your feet are really going there," she said. "Are you dancing?"

They say I gave a weak smile and a slight nod of my head.

Brian and Jay locked eyes. They knew then that the wait-and-see period was over. They no longer had any doubt that I was going to make it.

"Well, you just keep on dancing, Dan," Brian said. "Keep on dancing."

CHAPTER 10

Opiate Dreams

THE POTENT "MILK OF AMNESIA" DRUGS, ALONG WITH MORPHINE FOR pain, helped keep me among the living but not in the same solar system as my body. The drugs put me into a psychotic orbit that now and then plunged me back to Earth just long enough to intercept reality, most likely when my sedation was reduced for those is-he-still-with-us neurological checks. While my feet were tapping in bed, my mind was stuck somewhere between semi-consciousness and Asteroid B-612.

> *Brian and I are at a Steve Kimock show in the Oak Savannah hill country of coastal California. People are dancing all around us. I'm dancing, too, but only from the ankles down. The rest of my body is lead. I concentrate on the music, and my mind drifts off like a runaway balloon. Higher and higher. A woman's voice grabs the string and yanks, pulling me down, down, down toward the ground. Her words sound far away, like she's standing on a chair, talking through an air vent. "Are . . . you . . . dancing?"*
>
> *Am I dancing? Who wouldn't be? I nod at her and smile.*

I don't know how or why I remember these episodes, but I do, and in Technicolor. The images and sensations that cluttered my subconscious alternated between ethereal bliss and cheesy horror-movie scenes, like evil nurses wielding needles the size of chopsticks and waiters carting trays heaped with food stepping over patients lying amid tangles of feeding tubes.

Although the drugs were for my own good, hearing certain things and feeling certain others while unable to move or speak was disturbing at times, terrifying at others. Latex hands poking and prodding. The picking, scraping, and packing of multiple claw and bite wounds. The suctioning of sludge from my tracheotomy tube that could rival water boarding.

I remember feeling a sting in my arm and looking down to see a fishhook embedded in my skin, then watching in horror as it multiplied like a fork-tongued amoeba and crawled upward until I had fishhooks embedded all over my face. I was frantic to get them off me, but my arms may as well have been stitched to my sides.

Helicopters were a recurring presence in my tripped-out state of mind, most likely due to the comings and goings at the hospital's helipad. Now and then I'd detect that faint, familiar sound out my hospital-room window—womp-womp-womp—and off I'd go.

Medics tuck blankets around me, raise my gurney above their heads, and strap it to the top of the chopper just below the whirling rotor blades. If I try to sit up, they'll take my head off, so I lie still and concentrate on breathing. The helicopter settles down in front of an office tower in a tornado of dust, its rotors nicking the side of the building with a sickening scrape that reverberates inside my skull. The pilot jumps out and climbs into the building through an open window. He returns with blankets and drugs. "Please don't," I beg. A needle punctures my skin. "Here," a voice says. "This will help you forget."

Womp-womp-womp-womp-womp.

I'm hovering above Pebble Beach, the gated golf community near my parents' home in Carmel. The chopper lands in front of a mansion perched atop rocky cliffs with Pacific Ocean breakers below. Gulls, pelicans, and egrets fill the sky. A blanket of fog hovers offshore. The pilot waves like a beauty queen and vanishes. I stagger inside, blankets draped over my shoulders, my face in tatters. What kind of hospital is this? Chandeliers. Upholstered, wing-backed chairs. Carpet the color of blood. Wait! That IS blood, my blood! I'm bleeding all over the carpet! Where is everybody? I'm so tired, so woozy. Must rest.

"Sir, you can't sleep here," says a man in a gold-brocade vest.

A nurse taps me on the shoulder and pulls me to my feet. She leads me into a side room, one with a front wall made entirely of glass. She's gentle and concerned. Thank you, kind woman. Maybe now someone will help me. What's this? In the back of the room is a display case, and now I'm staring down at a diorama of the Russian River, with The Sanctuary, the parking lot, the stairs, and the spot where the bear dragged me off the trail. Is this so the doctors will better understand how to help me? I don't want to see it! I turn my head to the left. A huge, stuffed and mounted grizzly stands on its hind legs, paws the size of dinner plates, claws like railroad spikes, eyes on fire. I scream, but my lips don't move and no sound comes out.

"It's okay, Daniel. It's okay, it's Mom. You're safe here. I love you. We all love you."

Escapes from the hospital were another ongoing theme—floating down a river in a gurney, flying away on a couch, tumbling backward out of a window into the snow, hitching a ride behind a ski-trail groomer.

The dreams weren't always disturbing. I dreamed my father, Steve, showed up, that he was standing outside looking into my hospital room, holding my hand through the window. And I loved all the Kimock shows, especially the one I traveled to on a gurney powered by orderlies on bicycles. The Buddhist monk session was one I never wanted to end. Thirteen of them in saffron robes sat lotus-style in three circles, each on a different tier of a three-tiered floor. With prayer beads in their hands, they began to chant. *Oooooohhhhmmmm.* I could feel the vibration in my solar plexus, and couldn't have felt more at peace. When a nurse appeared with another dose of drugs, in my dream, maybe in real time for all I know, I tried to fight her off. I wanted to stay in that spiritual place inhabited by monks. I was powerless to stop her. Paralysis and unconsciousness crawled through my veins. The monks faded into the crawl space of my brain as I drifted higher and higher until I was a speck in the sky. Going, going, gone.

Once I was able, I starting writing these dream sequences down, and found I couldn't stop. I have filled pages and pages with memories just as weird and even weirder. For a while it was almost an obsession. Maybe someday I'll gather them all up and feed them to a bonfire on winter solstice, a good day for casting darkness out of one's life.

———

As miraculous as surviving the attack in the first place, I made it through that first week without any major complications. The swelling subsided enough that reconstructive surgery was a go.

It would take the collective expertise of a four-surgeon team to put me back together. It would take an assortment of building materials, manmade and biological, and a whole pile of hardware: screws, miniplates, microplates, titanium mesh, bars, wires, stitches, staples, and tissue and fat harvested from various parts of my body.

As my medical records tell it, top priority was constructing a watertight barrier between my brain and nose by repairing the tear in the dura mater, the membrane that protects the brain and keeps cerebrospinal fluid where it belongs. Dr. Kallman assisted neurosurgeon Dr. Louis Kralick by harvesting patching materials—fat from my abdomen and fat and fascia from my thigh. Once these were stockpiled and ready to go, Kralick used existing lacerations to access my forehead, snipping through the stitches, folding the skin back like an open book and holding it in place with stainless steel clips.

With my forehead skin out of the way, Kralick peeled down the pericranium, the thin membrane that covers the outside of the skull, as a single sheet from my upper forehead down to the brow. Much of the rubble of my facial bones was now exposed. Kralick picked out the fragments and chunks, passing them to Kallman, who reassembled those big enough to salvage with tiny plates and screws. Kralick then used a surgical saw to cut an oval of bone the size of a goose egg from the intact middle of my forehead. He carefully removed it, exposing the dura directly beneath, and passed it to Kallman. He lifted the frontal lobes of my brain with a retractor to access the large, crescent-shaped tear. Kralick used fat and fascia to patch it, then tucked the folded-down sheet of pericranium underneath the lobes to reestablish a watertight seal and provide blood flow needed for healing. This he tacked into place with tiny sutures.

After much discussion between the two surgeons, Kralick repaired the hole in the anterior base of my skull by spanning the gap with titanium mesh. Kallman had pushed for this extra support to ensure my brain would not sag into my nose down the road. Afterward, if you were to look up my nose, you would have seen titanium, but that would change over time. Titanium is unique among metals in that tissue will eventually grow over it. Kralick then lowered the retractors, setting my brain back into place. He scrubbed out while Kallman replaced the oval of bone and secured it with additional plates and screws.

Oral surgeon Ray Holloway stepped in next to lock down my jaw with an arch bar and wires to assure that when my split palate healed, my upper and lower teeth would line up straight. Also, since my mandible had come through the mauling intact, locking my teeth together would serve as a template for putting my mid-face back together.

Once Holloway finished, Kallman teamed up with oculoplastic surgeon Dr. Carl Rosen to tackle the disaster area around my eyes. "One of the most severe multiple injuries I have seen," is how Rosen would later describe it.

Working together, they rebuilt my cheekbones first, anchoring them with miniplates to nearby bone that was either intact or had been pieced back together. Next Rosen opened up the sutures holding my eyelids closed to examine my dead and dying eyes. What he saw took him aback. The optic nerves seemed almost surgically severed, as though the bear had studied human anatomy and knew exactly how to blind me with precision. The right eye was cleanly sliced off the optic nerve and all but a thread of muscle, and was shriveled like a prune. That one he took out. The left eye, the cornea partially cloudy, had a long piece of severed optical nerve still attached and just enough remaining muscle and blood flow to possibly survive. This one he kept, despite there being no hope for vision. He left it not only to keep the new socket he'd be building from contracting, but for cosmetic reasons since, if it did somehow survive, it would move in a more natural way than a prosthetic. He also felt strongly that it wouldn't be right to remove both eyes without involving me in the decision. Once he'd taken it out, it wasn't like he could put it back. To take it without me understanding why it was necessary could have left me with lingering doubts.

Some of the bones making up my eye sockets were big enough to be reassembled with plates, but the sides toward the center of my face and the bones of my nose were too fragmented, some even pulverized, to hold even the tiniest of screws. So Rosen and Kallman patched the sockets and fashioned a bridge for my nose out of titanium mesh and harvested fat and tissue. Rosen then placed an orbital implant, a ball made of unpronounceable plastic—polymethylmethacrylate—deep into the right socket, and secured as much viable tissue and muscle as he could on top. The remaining eye went into the left socket topped by a conformer, like a giant contact lens, to help maintain the shape. He then stitched both eyelids shut.

Their work done for now, Kallman unclamped the skin of my forehead, laid it back down, and stitched it in place. The medical marathon had lasted fourteen hours.

My family, Chris, Jay, and others in the loop had spent those long, anxious hours running piled-up errands, checking in, researching eye injuries at the library, checking in, getting something other than hospital food to eat, checking in, going for long walks on nearby trails, checking in, pacing up and down the hallways, checking in, cat-napping in the waiting room.

After scrubbing out, Kallman and Rosen met my family members in the ICU conference room to let them know the surgery had gone well. Rosen told them he'd removed one eye and that hope for the other being viable had faded. Then he choked up.

"I'm sorry. I can't tell you how much I wish there was some way to restore Dan's vision, but the bear made that impossible."

As hard as it was telling my family, the part Rosen dreaded most lay ahead—telling me. As Alaska's only orbital and oculoplastic surgeon, he had seen people lose vision in countless ways, from macular degeneration, to flying lawnmower debris, to war. You'd think he would have been used to it. Not that it's ever easy to tell a person he'll never see again, but I didn't lose my eyes in a bar fight, or in a drug deal gone bad, or driving drunk into a tree. I was just a guy out doing what he loved who unwittingly stumbled onto the mother lode of bad luck. Experience had taught him that it's best to deliver such news in small bites rather than serving up the whole elephant. Even so, telling me I'd never see again—meaning I'd never again see my family and friends, or a breaching whale, or a falling star, or a mountain cast in alpenglow, or a beautiful woman, or words on the page of a book—was almost too much.

"This one's really getting to me," he told his wife at home that night after the kids had gone to bed. "Sometime in the next week, this twenty-five-year-old guy is going to regain consciousness, realize how lucky he is to be alive, and then I'm going to have to tell him he's blind. I'm trained to fix things, and when I can't, I feel so inadequate. This is one of those cases that makes me wish I was in some other profession, any other profession. I am so not looking forward to this."

Early on, my family had posted a sign in my room asking those who entered not to speak of my blindness in front of me. Although I was comatose, they had no way of knowing how much, if anything, was getting through to me. In preparation for informing me that I'd be spending the rest of my life in darkness, after a week of recovery from my reconstructive surgery, Kallman gave orders to start weaning me off Propofol.

I was still swimming in heavy pain medication the first time I heard the word "blind." In my morphine stupor, what I remember most about being told I'd never see again comes from my opiate dreams. In one, I tried making a break for it by rolling myself out of the hospital in a wheelchair, stealing some doctor's BMW, and driving it across the lawn while men in white coats sprinted after me. My escape failed when I drove into a river and started to drown. The orderlies yanked me out of the water, threw me back into the wheelchair, and pushed me back inside, where I got a scolding: "You have no business driving! You're blind!"

In another, I was sure there had been a mistake, that my doctors had the wrong guy.

This hospital looks more like a storage unit than a medical facility. A garage door clatters open. My gurney is wheeled inside. The door clatters closed behind me. Against the wall is a long line of La-Z-Boy recliners, each with a patient attached to a ventilator and an IV pole parked alongside. I'm soon propped up in a recliner of my own and handed a remote control. I raise my legs, lower them, then take my recliner for a spin around the room. But there are too many tubes and wires attached to me to try to escape. Then along comes a doctor.

"I'm sorry," he says, "but you're blind."

That's ridiculous. I've got bandages over my eyes is all. Can't he see that? "You're wrong," I tell him. "I can see perfectly fine. I can see you clear as day." As proof, I reach out to shake the doctor's hand. "If I'm blind, how come I can see you?"

"I'm sorry," he tells me, "but that's impossible."

I have vague memories of hearing that I was blind three different times. As I became a bit more lucid, reality started sinking in. "Exhausted" doesn't do justice to the way I felt after fighting for my life so hard and so long. I was still in a barely-living state. So I didn't have the energy to have a big emotional reaction. That would come later.

CHAPTER 11

Tribe of Two

BEFORE I'D EVEN STARTED TO DEAL WITH THE BLINDNESS PIECE OF MY injuries, six hundred miles southeast as the raven flies, a stranger was about to take a detour in his life that would profoundly impact my own.

Lee Hagmeier was in the final phase of shutting down his life in Juneau and moving out of state. He and his wife were retired, Lee after a career in vocational rehabilitation, and Christy mostly in disability services. They'd bought a condo in Lacey, Washington, where the winters were kinder, and had just returned from tending to details down there. As the taxi backed out of their Juneau driveway, they walked up to the front door. Lee set down his suitcase, slipped his key into the lock, and gave it a turn. The door of their gray, two-story house with a view of Auke Bay and its harbor seals, Steller sea lions, and occasional humpback whale, opened with a click. Although the place had been home for nearly twenty years, the house felt unfamiliar, its bare walls freshly patched and painted, its rooms now furnished in echoes.

In the process of downsizing, they'd parted ways with many of their belongings. Before the first of two garage sales, they'd invited some friends who'd lost everything in a house fire to come by and take whatever they could use. Strangers, for the most part, carted off the rest, with Christy's leftover Avon sales inventory tossed in as a bonus. They'd already sold their twenty-foot fishing boat, their Oldsmobile sedan, and most of their furniture. Lee had said goodbye to the city he was born in by climbing some of the mountains he'd grown up with—Mt. Jumbo, Mt. McGinnis, and Thunder Mountain.

Coming home that day, with their black lab, Ina, still with the dog sitter, only their cats were there to greet them. After hauling luggage upstairs, Lee knelt down and gave Magic and Midnight each a pat, then headed for the phone to check the answering machine. Several messages were waiting for him, from people he knew and people he didn't.

Had he heard? It had been all over the news. A young man had been attacked by a grizzly at the Russian River, and the mauling had left him blind. Lee's body stiffened. He listened to one message after another.

More calls came the following day, including an impassioned one from my mother, who'd heard about him in a roundabout way through Providence. Was there any way, she wondered, that he'd be willing to talk to me? Lee had only a few days before he'd be leaving Alaska for good, but there was no question he would come. He got on the phone with Alaska Airlines and booked himself a flight.

My mom picked him up at the airport and drove him to the hospital. "I can't thank you enough for this," she told him.

While my stepdad sat with me, the rest of the crew met with Lee in the cafeteria to give him some of my background and fill him in on my injuries and state of mind, which was anybody's guess. Still coming off Propofol, loopy on pain meds, I was still in survival mode and looking like I'd been run through a blender—swollen, bandaged, wired, stitched, stapled, and slathered in ointment, tubes protruding from my neck, arms, and stomach. Propped partway up in bed to keep the swelling down, I could manage thumbs-up/thumbs-down communication and the slightest nod of my head, but I couldn't lift my head off my pillow. I barely had the strength to lift my arms.

What I remember about that day is lying in darkness in this alien body, hearing voices in the hallway, then several sets of shoes enter my room and shuffle up to the side of my bed. Brian was the first to speak.

"Hey, Dan. There's someone here we'd like you to meet. This is Lee Hagmeier. He flew up from Juneau to meet you."

As Lee reached out to shake hands, Brian took hold of mine and guided the two together.

"There's no way we can really know what you're going through. Lee's probably the only person on the planet who can. Because he lost his sight exactly the way you lost yours."

Although other bear-mauling survivors have lost an eye or partial vision, Lee had spent forty-four years as the only person in North America, in the world as far as he knew, to be completely blinded by a bear.

"I never expected to get a brother," Lee told me. "You and I are a tribe of two."

It happened on July 27, 1959, only a few months after the Territory of Alaska became the country's forty-ninth state. Lee was barely seventeen and, like me, not one for sitting still. While his twin brother, John, was most at home with his head buried beneath the hood of a car, Lee's place was in the woods or atop some mountain looking down on the Mendenhall Glacier. His mother was always saying she could never get that boy to come in out of the rain. He'd shot his first deer at twelve, and by the time he was seventeen had divvied up the venison of twenty-one others among friends and family. The previous fall, after he and his dad failed to rally one rainy weekend during hunting season, his father noted their blunder with a ribbing scribbled on the chalkboard in the kitchen: "Don't let it happen again."

On that day in July, Lee and his buddy, Doug Dobyns, were fishing for Dolly Varden just north of Juneau. It was gray and a little chilly, but the rain clouds managed to hold tight. The two had fished their way about a mile up McGinnis Creek, a twenty-five-foot-wide stream of silvery water that skipped over rocks and under occasional windfalls, and disappeared around bend after bend. In some places they could walk along an old creek bed, in others, where willows, alders, and devil's club marched up to the banks, they were forced to wade in the creek. Chums and a few pink salmon on their way to spawning grounds splashed about in the riffles and eddies. The carcasses of those that had already spawned and died gave the air a heavy reek.

Between the two of them fishing catch-and-release, they had landed forty to fifty Dollies when Lee got it into his head to go look for a bear. Slung over his shoulder was a 30.06 Husqvarna with a four-power scope that he'd fallen for at Skinner's Gun Shop. He'd saved up for it through various part-time jobs, including a family scrap-metal recycling business, and grocery-store work that included hauling five-gallon buckets of herring up from the docks to be packaged and sold as bait. The boys had spooked a brown bear earlier that day. It had spooked them, too, as it went crashing off through the brush. Lee decided the area they were in would be a good place to cross paths with another.

"I'm going to go look around," Lee said, nodding toward the thicket.

"No, we don't need to go in there," his buddy told him.

Lee would not be dissuaded. He was just five-foot-two, 115 pounds, definitely on the small side compared to most his age. But he was a seventeen-year-old boy with a powerful rifle. In other words, immortal. He propped his fishing pole against the bank and disappeared into thick brush. Doug reluctantly followed at a distance. They got through the understory to where the forest opened up to lichen-draped Sitka spruce towering over a carpet of ferns and mosses. They made it about a hundred yards in from the creek. Doug saw it first.

"Lee, brownie!" he hollered.

Lee was caught mid-step in an awkward position as he spun around to face the bear. It was coming for him, and fast. He fumbled with the safety on his rifle, managed to get it off, but there was no time to aim. He shot from the hip, sending tree bark flying. He whirled away, and as he did, the bear grabbed the rifle in its teeth, leaving deep gouges in the stock. The bear yanked the gun from Lee's grip. The force spun him around and knocked him to the ground on his back. The bear bit into his left knee, then picked him up and shook him. It bit into his thigh, picked him up, and shook him again. Then again. At some point, Lee tried to sit up; the bear bit into his side. He then played dead, not making a sound.

For a moment everything was still as he lay there, eyes clenched shut, holding his breath. Then the bear cocked its head sideways and bit him across his face. Lee heard a sickening sound inside his head like a celery stick snapped in two.

He lay still a moment, until the sound of the bear crashing through the woods faded in the distance. Then he slowly raised a hand to his face. He felt a hot, sticky jumble of bone and flesh from the bridge of his nose to the middle of his forehead. He felt his left eye hanging down his cheek. His right eye was gone.

"Lee, are you all right!? Lee! Lee!"

Moments later he heard Doug drop to his knees in front of him.

After a futile effort to walk out, Doug went for help, blazing a trail to the creek and marking the way in by plunging his knife into a tree. Nearly three hours would pass before Lee would be loaded into an ambulance and the siren would begin its high-pitched wail.

"Youth Attacked, Critically Injured by Raging Brown Bear," screamed the headline in the *Juneau Empire*. "Lee Hagmeier, 17, Loses Sight as Bear Gashes Face."

Now here he was, standing beside my hospital bed forty-four years practically to the day since his attack. My tribal brother.

"I have something for you," he said as he reached into his pocket. "This is a talking watch. That was a big issue for me after my accident, waking up disoriented, not knowing whether it was day or night. Is it okay if I put it on you?"

I gave a thumbs-up. Lee reached for my hand, slipped the watch over my wrist, and pushed the button: "The time is 2:52 p.m." I managed a smile.

"When something this traumatic happens, you can feel awfully alone," he told me. "I want you to know you are not alone. I also want you to know there's still a lot of life worth living. It may not seem like it right now, but you have a great deal to look forward to."

Lee was the only person on Earth who could have told me that, and I believed him. I pointed to my chest, pointed toward him, fumbled for his hand and gave it a squeeze. Then, for the first time, I lost it. With my tear ducts obliterated, I couldn't cry tears, but my chest heaved until I thought my ribs would break.

My father Steve first heard of Lee while staying at the Hickel House, low-cost housing for Providence outpatients and hospitalized patients' out-of-town families. The volunteer at the front desk recognized the name Bigley from the news.

"Are you the father of the young man who was mauled?" she asked.

Steve nodded.

"I know someone who might be able to help your son."

She knew Lee's story well. She told Steve she'd gone to high school with him in Juneau before his accident, and was in touch with his twin brother, John Hagmeier, an award-winning Anchorage homebuilder. She offered to track down Lee's number.

As excited as everyone was about his visit, all were a little nervous. None of them had ever met a blind person, and had no idea what to expect. Jay in particular envisioned some grizzled, hard-boiled character, not a five-foot-eight, soft-spoken, sixty-one-year-old grandfatherly type who collected bear T-shirts, especially ones with *Far Side*–type humor, like a picture of bears throwing people at each other with the caption, "Food Fight." He had a patch over his left eye and a prosthetic in his right that looked so real they wondered if he was really completely blind, especially after seeing the ease with which he moved through a room and the way he spun around to face whomever was speaking. His face didn't look "partially torn away," as reported in the *Juneau Empire* at the time of his attack. He looked good and completely at home in the world. They hoped they were seeing me in the future.

Lee stayed the weekend in Anchorage, and over the course of several visits told my family and I a little of what became of that seventeen-year-old boy he was before his bear. I've learned a lot more in our many conversations since.

If ever there was a guy who beat the odds, he's the one. Limited by the medical advances of the day, in a town of ten thousand accessible only by boat or plane, his chance of survival was one in fifty, he would later hear. The doctor who saved him, Dr. C. C. Carter, was the same doctor who had delivered him and his twin brother in 1942.

The people of Juneau also helped save him. The town's Territorial Sportsmen group launched a fund-raising campaign for his medical and educational expenses that went the day's version of viral, with donations coming from in and out of state. For one event, residents gathered around their radios and television sets for a three-hour, phone-in auction with such donated items as 150 yards of gravel, a full-day's labor with a chain saw, a banty rooster and three hens, and frozen herring that Lee had hauled up from the docks and packaged himself. One bidder even paid twenty-five dollars for the shirt off the auctioneer's back.

After seven weeks in the hospital, Lee and his mother boarded a plane for the East Coast, where he got his first round of plastic surgery at Massachusetts General Hospital in Boston. He went from there to Helen Keller's alma mater, the Perkins School for the Blind. Until then, as he puts it, he was the first blind person he'd ever met. He went from sharing a room with his twin brother to living in a cottage-style dorm with twenty blind strangers, and everything familiar as far away as it gets without leaving the country. At Perkins, he had to learn from square one how to live in the dark. This during an era in which appearing blind, even using a cane, was discouraged at the school.

At first his fingertips could barely feel Braille, let alone decipher it. Eight years later, he graduated summa cum laude from Chico College with a degree in psychology. He then earned his master's degree in vocational rehabilitation, followed by a doctorate in educational psychology from the University of Washington. In those days, recording lectures meant reel to reel, and writing papers meant using a Braille-writing machine, then having the document translated and retyped by a sighted assistant. He managed all this nearly two decades before the Americans with Disabilities Act.

Lee never gave up being an outdoorsman. He took up running at Perkins, teaming up with a legally blind student with just enough travel vision to make it work. The two of them set the East Coast record among blind and visually impaired athletes for the two-mile run at eleven minutes, twenty-seven seconds that the last time he checked, some forty years later, still held. He runs to this day, sometimes by teaming up with a sighted partner, sometimes with just his guide dog leading the way on trails he knows by heart.

Lee told me stories of floating the Yukon River and hiking the Chilkoot Trail. Of taking up sea kayaking. Of traveling the country and the world. He never did give up fishing. He'd even had his own fishing boat. That got my attention.

He didn't just help me get through my first raw days of darkness, he helped my friends and family get through theirs.

"Don't alter your language," he told them. "It just makes it awkward and brings more attention to the fact that he's blind. Just have a normal conversation. It's okay to say, 'Nice to see you.' It's okay to say, 'Have you seen so-and-so lately?'"

He taught them how to guide me without trampling my dignity.

"The instinct is to grab a person's arm and push them along in front of you, which is awkward and intrusive. It works much better to go first and have the blind person take hold of your elbow."

Most importantly, he taught us all that I was still capable of great things, that I was in charge of my own destiny.

"Dan still has vision," he told my family. "He just can't see."

Lee Hagmeier with a hefty silver salmon.

CHAPTER 12

Flailing Through the Fog

LONG BEFORE I COULD BEGIN TO PROCESS MY BLINDNESS, BEFORE I'D slam my face into a doorjamb for the first time, before I'd burn myself pouring a cup of coffee, before I'd cut myself grabbing the wrong end of a knife, I had to muster enough strength to fight my way off the alternate-universe drugs. I had the strength of a mouse to do it.

When I was first being weaned off Propofol, there wasn't a single thing I was capable of doing for myself. I was an incontinent twenty-five-year-old who didn't have the strength or coordination to scratch an itch. Strangers with chirpy voices were rolling me onto my side like a spruce log, changing the sheets out from under me, and rolling me back. They were wiping my nose and washing my privates.

I needed pain relief, no question; I had so much augering, bone-deep pain. If the pain-med peaks weren't in synch with my wound-care sessions, it felt like my face was being picked off one tweezer-full at a time, and the puncture wounds on my arms, legs, and elsewhere were being cleaned with battery acid and a wire brush. I wanted to scream bloody murder and shove whoever was working on me hard enough to bounce off the wall, but I was so debilitated all I could do was lie there and take it. These procedures were critical to my recovery, but from my perspective and twisted state of mind, the pain, fear, and helplessness didn't feel all that different from being mauled by a bear.

No one wanted me to suffer, least of all those whose job it was to tend my wounds. But being drugged all the time got to be too much. During windows when the morphine was wearing off, the meandering delirium in my head would fade and I'd become aware of my surroundings, of muffled voices down the hall, of curtains being yanked closed around some other patient's bed, of the occasional sharp laugh at the nurse's station across from my room. I'd hear my stepdad's voice. I'd hear my brother's. I'd hear Jamie's and John's and Jaha's. I'd just start to feel connected to the world when along would come the dreaded padding of soft-soled shoes. "Good evening, Mr. Bigley. I have something here to make you a little more comfortable." I'd hear the flick of a thumb and index finger against the side of a plastic syringe before the plunging of La-La Land into my IV line.

During my more cognizant times, an awareness seeped in through the cracks that the drugs of good intention, to calm me and shield me from pain, were holding me back, and I had no desire to stay where I was—out of my gourd much of the time, half out of it the rest, bewildered one moment, terrified the next, unable to cry out, barely able to move. I'd made my decision back at the river to live, not just continue to draw breath. Lee Hagmeier had shown me what was possible. During my more lucid moments, I sensed I had a major battle ahead of me beyond the mending of skin and bone. I could feel the enormity of its weight pressing me into my mattress. Before I could inch my way toward the surface I needed the ability to think.

I'm not sure where the energy came from but my first effort to let it be known that I wanted off the heavy drugs was noted in my medical charts just hours after Lee Hagmeier's first visit: "Patient agitated, flailing arms, refusing sedation med." Once I'd gained enough strength and clarity to progress from thumbs-up/thumbs-down communication to scribbling on a notepad, one of the first things I wrote was, "No more drugs."

Although I wouldn't know this until later, my muddled state of mind had made Amber's worst-case scenario come true. Still banned from my inner circle, she'd been checking in on a regular basis, and when my mother finally mentioned her, I had no clue who she was talking about.

"This girl, Amber, has been asking to see you. What should I tell her?"

Amber? Amber . . . Who's Amber? The only Amber I could think of was one of my brother's old girlfriends. *What is she doing here? Why would she want to see me? Why would I want to see her?*

Thumbs-down.

My mother spared Amber the rejection; she just kept her involvement as it had been since giving her the boot—at bay and by phone.

Amber was not the crying type, especially at times it would have done her the most good. When overwhelmed, her emotions would go into full lockdown. It was when she least expected it that they'd sneak up on her from behind. She'd be driving down the highway alone in her truck and— wham. Or something on the radio that had nothing to do with her life, a killer heat wave in Europe, for instance, would have her gripping the steering wheel in tears. But slumping down in her seat and breaking into sobs at a Dar Williams concert soon after my mauling, when the singer threw "Fishing in the Morning" into the mix, that time made sense.

> *Let's go fishing in the morning*
> *Just like we've always gone*
> *You can come inside and wake me up*
> *We'll pack and leave by dawn*
> *We'll pack and leave by dawn.*

The intensity of our attraction to each other being so new catapulted Amber into a head-on collision between longing and mourning. She'd never felt so confused. She did what she had to do to get through the days, the weeks, she was exiled from my inner circle. She'd drag herself out of bed each morning, tossing her quilt to the side. She'd plod through her morning chores, go for long walks with Hobbit, and curl up with him afterward on the floor. When evening came around, she'd go to her closet, put on her black pants, white blouse, and clip-on bowtie, pull her hair into a tight ponytail, and go through the motions at her summer job as a banquet server, delivering plates of pan-seared halibut and overcooked vegetables to people who barely noticed her.

Amber had told her parents that a "friend" had been blinded by a bear. How absolutely horrid, they thought. Can't imagine such a thing. But when they came from Minnesota for a visit in late July, they were bewildered by how distracted Amber was, by how this friend's mother was calling her with updates from the hospital, how whenever she ran into someone from Girdwood, this friend was the first topic to come up. When her parents took off on their own to do a road trip down the Kenai Peninsula, they kept seeing this friend's name along the way, especially in Cooper Landing, on flyers for a local fund-raiser and on collection jars on roadhouse countertops. Over breakfast one morning, they overheard some guy on the phone drumming up donations for the Dan Bigley benefit. This friend of Amber's sure has a lot of people pulling for him, they thought.

While Amber was struggling to accept her place in my life, or lack of one, I was inching my way back into the world of the living. I was weaned off the ventilator, my tracheotomy tube switched from cuffed to cuffless. With the help of physical therapists, I was starting to move again, which required breaking down into multiple steps simple maneuvers I'd done on my own since I was old enough to crawl. Like sitting up in bed. With a lot of help, I progressed from that to sitting on the side of my bed, first with a logroll onto my side, then the lowering of the side rail, the rolling of my legs over the edge, the pushing up onto an elbow, and finally, after a rest, the final push upright. Then just sitting, nothing more, just sitting there feeling dizzy and nauseous, my neck trying to support this humongous, foreign object that was my head. At first, I could stand it for only a couple of minutes, then five, then ten. Afterward, I'd be so fried I'd want to sleep for a week. Slowly, I built up enough strength and stamina to sit in a chair, then stand, then take a few steps behind a walker.

Two weeks after my reconstructive surgery, a week after being told I was blind, I graduated from ICU to the Progressive Care Unit, a sort of halfway house between intensive care and the outside world. I felt way too lousy to celebrate.

I'd developed a disturbing problem by then, a wound that was refusing to heal where the bear had split open my forehead, where the oval of bone had been temporarily removed during my reconstructive surgery. With five of the six arteries to my scalp severed in the mauling, the wound lacked blood supply, tissue had died, and the suture lines were pulling apart. Coughing not only felt like a Molotov cocktail hitting the roof of my mouth, but air leaked from the fissure in my forehead. Plus, I'd contracted MRSA (methicillin-resistant *Staphylococcus aureus*), a drug-resistant and potentially fatal staph infection.

I also had a constant headache, dull mostly with occasional shooting shards of pain. I had abdominal pain from my feeding tube, and endless irritation from the tube in my trachea. I had nausea, vertigo, nosebleeds, coughing fits so bad I'd puke, and a rash all over my body, a side effect of the heavy-duty IV antibiotics for managing the MRSA. These drugs also left me so itchy I wanted to tear off my own skin. Plus my mouth was as dry as yesterday's toast. Early on, I could have only a wet sponge under my lips, then ice cubes to suck on. I felt so thirsty, I dreamed of medics backing a water truck up to my hospital bed and blasting me with a fire hose.

Since I could have nothing by mouth, I fantasized constantly about food, comfort food. Cheeseburgers and fries. Pizza. Chips and guacamole. I so craved solid food, I dreamed of people tossing Doritos back and forth over my head while I tried and failed to intercept them. I dreamed of my family loading me into the bed of a pickup truck, driving to a restaurant, and leaving me behind while they went inside to eat. I dreamed of trying to shove burritos and bratwursts into my stomach tube.

Experiencing a depth of misery I never knew existed was a huge distraction from mourning the loss of my eyes. Instead, I focused what little energy I had on just getting stronger. Among those pushing me in that direction was my acute-care occupational therapist, Will Berry, who would later become one of my closest friends.

Will knew nothing about me until picking up my chart at the nurses' station prior to our first session. His chest tightened as he read. He slid my chart back into its slot, took a deep breath, gave a quick knock, opened the door to my room, and stepped inside. If he was stunned to see what a mess the bear had made of me he didn't let on.

"Hi, I'm Will. I'm from occupational therapy. Hey, Dan, you ready to get started? Here's what we're going to do today . . ."

Before the end of our first session, given the music playing in my room, he knew we had something in common. Between helping me build enough upper-body strength to get myself out of bed and enough dexterity to button buttons and zip zippers, he talked of some of the live shows he'd been to and new jam bands he'd discovered. He even brought me a bootleg recording he'd picked up of a Les Claypool show.

He also helped me realize I'd lost something besides my eyes to the bear when, during one of our sessions, he waved essential oils under my nose.

Lavender, cinnamon, peppermint.

I shook my head no.

Sandalwood, patchouli, eucalyptus.

No, nothing.

The bear had ripped out my olfactory wiring, too. I'm sure Dr. Kallman had explained this to me at some point, but that was the first time it sank in that I had lost my sense of smell. At the time, I lacked the presence of mind to ponder what it meant to be left with only three senses, or to consider how intrinsically connected smell was to one of my remaining ones—the taste of food. I would realize only later that I would never again take pleasure in the smell of wood smoke, or of wild geraniums blooming in the spring, or of freshly minced garlic sizzling in a pan. A sense of smell could keep a blind man from drinking milk that had gone sour, or from mistaking a dry cleaner for a pastry shop, or from striking a match around a leaky gas line. I hadn't even begun dealing with the blindness part yet; mourning the loss of smell would have to take a number and stand in line.

—◆—

As the days went by and I became more present, my circle of visitors grew wider. Some brought me recordings, others showed up with their guitars. One played a didgeridoo, which had every pair of shoes going up and down the hallway applying the brakes at my door. Whenever someone new came to see me, I was grateful I couldn't speak; not only was my jaw wired shut, I was under doctor's orders not to talk since everything from the roof of my mouth up had a long way to go to be healed. I was grateful because I didn't have the energy for talking, much less caretaking, a tendency of mine. When one-sided talk stalled and silence turned the room into an itchy sweater, I felt no pressure to fill the gaps. When people broke into sobs, I didn't have to think of what to say to make them feel better.

Even Maya came to visit. Everyone was excited for me to reunite with my Maya Bird, so named because when she got excited she chirped like a bird. I couldn't wait to hear the whack of her tail against everything within a two-foot radius, and feel her nose against my skin. When the day came, Brian brought her in on a leash, closed the door, unhooked her, and patted the foot of my bed.

"Up, Maya. Come on, up." She got all slinky and wouldn't budge. "Maya, up girl, up. Up!"

Finally she jumped. A dog famous for her full body wag and toothy grin, she stood trembling at the foot of my bed with her tail between her legs. She jumped to the floor. Brian's chest fell. He lifted her back up again.

"Stay, Maya. Sit. Now stay. Stay."

She stayed about three seconds, then jumped back down again. She wanted nothing to do with whatever that thing was in that bed. Or maybe seeing me brought back the bear; I'll never know. I would have been heartbroken, but it's hard to break something that's already in so many pieces.

～–～

Maya's reaction got me thinking about the last time I'd seen her, the last time I would ever see her, as she leapt off the trail, dodging the bear's blow. The next time Jaha came to visit, the time had come for me to face up to that day. By then I was communicating on a dry-erase board.

"What happened?" I wrote.

Jaha sighed deeply. He had not been looking forward to this. He wished he didn't remember, that he never had to tell the story again, that what he had seen beneath the T-shirt wasn't branded into his memory.

"Are you sure you're up for this, buddy?"

I nodded. I needed to hear it.

He shifted in his chair, hung his head a moment, then slowly raised it back up. Leaning forward, he reached for my hand and held on tight. He took a long, slow, deep breath, held it, let it go, then started in.

"We were waiting for you guys to show up when we saw this mama bear running down the middle of the river looking really pissed . . ."

He didn't get far before my whole body tensed up.

"Want me to stop?"

I shook my head no.

"Dan, really, you don't need to hear this right now."

I did. I needed to know.

"Do you really want me to go on?"

I nodded my head yes. So he told me, minus the gory details. If anybody knew those it was me. It zapped all our strength getting through it, reliving what was the worst day of both of our lives. When Jaha finished, he hung his head without letting go of my hand. We held on to each other long after my lips stopped trembling and the heaving of my chest settled down.

Later, feeling more clear headed than I had so far, I allowed my mind to visit the good times, the before times. I was thinking of the kids I'd worked with, the bonfires at Max's, the trip to the High Sierra Music Festival, the Galactic concert at the ski lodge, when it suddenly hit me like a needle screeching across a record. The night came rushing back to me in one gale-force, emotional gust. I fumbled for my dry-erase board:

"Where is Amber?" I wrote.

My mom furled her brow. "But Daniel, you said you didn't want to see her."

What!? Why would I say that? I would never say that.

"I do!" I scribbled.

"So you're saying you do want to see her, is that right?"

I nodded and gave a thumbs-up.

My mom gave Amber a call. "Dan's been asking for you. Would you like to come by?"

Amber's eyes grew wide as she clutched the phone to her ear. She closed her eyes tight, then asked, "Would it be okay to come this afternoon?"

Amber kept a stranglehold on the steering wheel the entire thirty-minute drive from her place in Bird Creek to visitor parking at Providence. She got out of her truck, smoothed her skirt, and walked across the parking lot on wobbly legs. Inside the lobby she hesitated. She looked around, noticed a coffee booth, and made straight for it. She ordered a twelve-ounce Americano, not because she needed to be any more wired; she needed something to hold on to. She paid, turned, and walked through the lobby, past the volunteer at the information booth, past a frail, elderly woman pushing her skeletal husband in a wheelchair, past a high-heeled teenager with a baby on her hip, past other visitors on their way to and from the joys and heartbreaks of visiting loved ones in various beds. When she reached the elevators, she stared a moment at the buttons before pushing the one with an arrow pointing up. Inside, she pushed "2." The doors closed. The elevator announced its arrival with a *bing*.

She stepped out and glanced up at the signs showing the way to the Progressive Care Unit. Light-headed, heart pounding, she gave herself a moment, then took a sip of her coffee, hooked her hair behind her ears, and headed down the hallway, her pace slowing the closer she got to the room number my mother had given her, which she'd scribbled on the back of a grocery receipt. She stopped outside my open door and glanced in, her eyes bouncing from my mom to my brother to me. Her heart seized up. I was sitting in a recliner next to my bed all bandaged and swollen and unrecognizable. She forced a smile and walked in.

"Hi. Nice to see all of you. Brian. Ann. Thanks for the call. Hey, Dan . . . it's Amber."

I turned my head toward her voice and mustered a small, dismal smile. She stared at the bulging bandages covering my eyes, or what had been my eyes. Brian cleared his throat. "Dan, we'll be down the hall," he said as he and my mother stood to leave. "We'll be back in about ten minutes."

Amber watched them go. She set down her coffee and walked up to me.

"Dan, I have no idea where to begin . . ."

I picked up the dry-erase board off my lap, scribbled on it, and turned it to show her. "Crazy," it said.

Amber shut her eyes tight and bit her lower lip. She stared at the floor, then flung her head back up. "Yeah, seriously crazy." She knelt down, facing me, and put a hand on my knee. I picked up my dry-erase board, erased it with a cloth, and wrote: "I am blind."

Amber shook her head. "I know," she said. "I know. I am . . . so . . . incredibly . . . sorry." She rested her head against my leg and closed her eyes.

I turned my board back around, erased it, and scribbled another message:

"I'm scared."

CHAPTER 13

Binoculars Are a Terrible Thing to Waste

It couldn't have been more obvious that I was in no shape to be in a relationship. I wasn't even capable of going to the bathroom by myself. I was the bombed-out shell of the man I'd been, and had a long, long way to go before I'd have the wherewithal to start figuring out who the new one was going to be.

Amber had been grappling with that bitter reality pill since she first saw me in the ICU. Day after day she'd been dealing with the emotional vertigo of mourning the death of a person who was still alive. Emotionally strong enough to bench-press an entire city block's worth of troubles, she accepted that this was the way it had to be. She stepped aside from her role as the new girlfriend and joined the ranks of others in my concerned circle of friends. She was just grateful to be back in my life.

My own emotions, other than bouts of paralyzing sadness, were still in a coma. I had so many overwhelming losses yet to confront that losing my relationship with Amber was just another added to the heap. Still, her presence comforted me.

I remember vividly the first time a glint of joy hacked its way through the cobwebs in my brain. A little bird smaller than a kiwi fruit did what pharmaceuticals couldn't do. It came the day I received permission to go outside for the first time. My eyes and forehead were in bandages, and I was wearing my own clothes for the first time, too, when my brother and Jay busted me out of there. (My father, Steve, had gone home to his work and family in California, and Chris had returned to Oregon, but would soon be back.) With Jay leading the charge, Brian pushed me out of my room in a wheelchair with a rattling IV pole attached to the back. Out of the Progressive Care Unit we went, into the elevator, down to the main floor, and out a side door leading to a courtyard. Brian parked me next to a bench by a tree, set the brake, and sat down beside me, resting an arm on the back of my chair. As I lifted my face to the sun I heard footsteps approaching.

"Hey, guys, they told me I'd find you out here." Amber knelt down in front of me and put a hand on my knee. "I didn't want to miss this."

Brian and Jay gave each other the look, and stood up.

"Hey, Dan, we're going to go for a little walk. Need anything? You good?"

I gave a thumbs-up.

They left, and Amber sat next to me on the bench with her hand atop my shoulder. Then I heard a song coming from the tree above me. Out of instinct, I looked up. I lowered my head, picked up my dry-erase board, and wrote, "Chickadee." I showed it to Amber, put the board back down on my lap, and held my hand over my heart.

A black-capped chickadee—*chick-a-dee-dee-dee*—is one of the easiest birds to identify by ear, but the ability to do so held huge significance to me. It was the first thing I accomplished on my own as a blind person. It was something I could do; I could identify a chickadee. I could still enjoy this little fluff of a bird that weighs barely half an ounce, with its black stocking cap and matching bib beneath its beak. I could still admire its ability to tolerate Alaska winters better than most people. Sitting in the sun, I could hear not only its song, but the flutter of its tiny wings as it flitted from branch to branch above my head. I had no idea whether it was true, but someone had told me they could see a tree outside my hospital-room window, and I had visualized that tree many times when I was feeling disoriented and lost, which was most of the time. It grounded me, believing it was there, peeking into my room, watching over me. That day, I knew the chickadee I was hearing was for real. Sharing its company was my first step back to the natural world.

~━━⌒━━~

By mid-August the time had come for my remaining eye to go. Although my doctors had known from day one that I would never see again, my family had clung to the hope that my left eye would survive and that medical advances might someday develop a way of hooking it back up to its optic nerve and restoring my sight. My stepdad had spent many hours researching the possibility. But the fact was, the eye was dead. It had to go.

The nights leading up to the surgery, I dreamed of my mother smuggling me out of the hospital. I dreamed of running out the hospital door and straight into the hands of white-coated orderlies.

In surgery number three, Dr. Rosen took out my necrotic left eye and filled the socket the same as he had the other, with an orbital implant covered with tissue and muscle and a conformer over the top, a place-holder for the prosthetics I'd be getting down the road—way down, as it turned out, on account of persistent swelling.

Some of the skin Dr. Kallman had tried so hard to save didn't make it, either, including the upper left corner of my nose and the corner of the adjoining eyelid, leaving the titanium of my nose bridge exposed. He removed the dead skin and patched the area with a small skin graft harvested from a spot in front of my ear. He also closed up the worrisome wound in the middle of my forehead.

Kallman made it his mission to spring me from the hospital before my twenty-sixth birthday, which was coming up on August 23. I wouldn't be going far. After a series of meetings with those in charge of various parts of my inner and outer anatomy, the plan was for me to move with my family into a nearby hotel for outpatient care, with regular visits from home-healthcare nurses and wound-care specialists. I worked hard to make that happen, doing strengthening exercises and sucking high-calorie Ensure protein drinks through a straw to supplement the nutrients flowing in through my feeding tube. I progressed from shuffling behind a walker to ditching the walker and using a long pole with a tennis ball on the end and my right hand to tap along the wall, always with training wheels—a heavy strap around my chest, gripped by a physical therapist, to break any falls.

The long-term plan was for me to go with my family back to California to continue healing and, at some point, enroll in a school for the blind. While I focused on what I needed to accomplish to be released from the hospital, a sorting of my stuff was underway at my place in Girdwood. Friends would have been happy to store things for me, but in order to move on in my life, I needed to let go of the one I'd had before.

I put Brian in charge of giving away or selling things I could no longer use. My camera, my video recorder, my TV set, my whitewater kayak, and some of my other outdoor gear. My birding binoculars were already gone. Soon after my mauling, a Girdwood friend I knew mostly from jam sessions had asked my roommate if he could borrow them to use as a portal for healing the wounded energy in my eyes. Or something like that. His intentions were good, but then he just kept them.

I held onto my skis and, I'm not sure why, my mountain bike. I could not bear to part with my truck. I loved that truck. That truck had taken me to so many incredible places, on pavement, gravel, dirt, sand, and mud. I thought of it as my partner in crime given all we'd done together. Even though, obviously, I would never again drive it, I was thinking that if I paid for insurance and upkeep, I wouldn't feel so bad hitting people up for rides since I could supply the wheels. It made sense at the time, anyway. Of my remaining possessions, what wasn't sold, given away, or dropped off at the Salvation Army was loaded into the back of my truck for my stepdad to drive to California.

As eager as I was to get out of the hospital, I was equally anxious. I still had a stomach tube, a trach, and my jaw wired shut, although I'd been okayed to attempt a little speaking by covering the trach with my fingers. I knew I'd be banging my head on a regular basis, and worried about the damage I might do. Since I was nauseous more often than not, I worried about puking, never a pleasant experience, but taken to a whole new level when you can't open your mouth. I worried about asphyxiating. I worried about it so much I asked for a pair of wire cutters to keep in my pocket.

On August 19, four days before my birthday, I was cleared to go. I dressed that morning in clothes that hung from my now-skinny frame, and settled into the recliner to wait. While Jay was getting my hotel room set up, my family loaded up the sound system, books on tape, and the cards and letters that had been tacked in layers to a corkboard in my room. Doctors, nurses, therapists, aides, and others who'd helped me pull through dropped by to wish me well. When it was time, Brian pushed me in a wheelchair out the front door and into the sounds of traffic, other people's chatter, and a small plane passing overhead. He helped me into my family's rental car, waited patiently while I fumbled to buckle my seatbelt, and off we drove into a world far different than the one I'd lived in before.

When we pulled up in front of the hotel, I reached for the door handle with one hand, the top of the doorframe with the other, and climbed out of the car. I took hold of Brian's elbow and he guided me inside. Slowly.

Walking was still wooden, exhausting, and painful. By the time I reached my room, I needed to lie down.

Everyone had made a pact not to mention the furnishings I'd passed on my way to the elevator, in a sitting room off the hotel lobby. In one corner was a stuffed grizzly posed in stalk mode, in the other, a Kodiak brown bear standing on its hind legs that was so enormous its head nearly touched the ceiling. We had permission for Maya to stay with me. After what she'd seen that day in July, my family thought it wise to bypass the bears and bring her in through the back door.

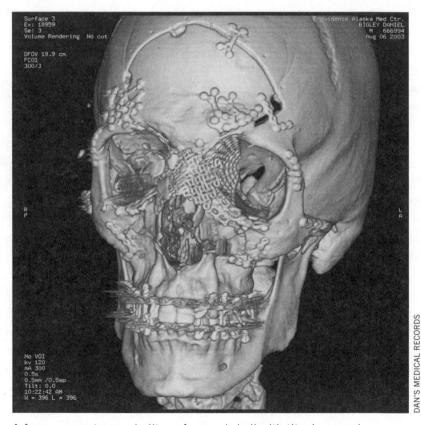

A four-surgeon team rebuilt my face and skull with titanium mesh, screws, mini-plates, and other materials. The surgery lasted 14 hours.

CHAPTER 14

Diving with Captain Nemo

SINCE I WAS A TEENAGER, I'D THOUGHT OF BIRTHDAYS AS MORE THAN an excuse to party. To me, they were a time to reflect upon the gift of being alive. Among my most memorable celebrations was sitting at the edge of Half-Moon Rock, arms wrapped around my knees, watching the rising sun spread a golden glow across Kentucky's Red River Gorge the day I turned nineteen. I spent my twenty-first in red-rock country near Sedona, Arizona, in a canyon of sandstone walls and emerald-green waters, camped out with friends, Maya, Maya's friends, and a bottle of Bushmills.

My twenty-sixth came and went at the Hampton Inn with bears in the lobby, my mother in the adjoining room, my brother across the hall, and a mini-fridge stocked with Ensure. The closet, windowsill, and dresser-top were cluttered with medications, hand sanitizer, Bacitracin, saline, gauze, bandages, and a goulash of other medical supplies. Friends showed up with music, books on tape, and a chocolate cake concocted in a blender. Propped up with pillows on the couch, dressed in bandages, pajama bottoms, and a sleeveless undershirt to keep from irritating the wounds on my upper arms, I could have been turning ninety-six as lousy as I felt. Still, I felt grateful to be alive, more grateful than I knew possible. Amber and about eight others were there that night, sitting beside me on the couch, on my bed, and cross-legged on the floor. My friends worked it hard, trying to keep things upbeat, telling stories, cracking jokes, and teasing me about my mullet, a tuft of hair along the base of my skull, the one Dr. Kallman left me with when he went at me with the electric razor. The man's a gifted surgeon but a lousy barber.

"Nice do, dude," was the general consensus.

As an outpatient camped out in a hotel room, I had even more visitors and fewer rules, which did not please my mother, who kept our adjoining door open more often than not. Her protective instincts on overdrive, she'd tell me when it was time for friends to leave and for me to go to bed, which made me feel like I was back in middle school. On the up side, I no longer had people I couldn't see or talk to poking me with needles or taking my blood pressure at all hours of the day and night. I no longer had people micromanaging my bowels and bladder. I finally got a little privacy, although that's hard to trust when you can't see those you're hoping aren't there.

Left alone to rest one afternoon, I began for the first time to confront my new reality, taking stock first of what I could "see." In a Malaysian jungle after sundown, I'd experienced blackness so thick I couldn't detect my hand in front of my nose. But this was not that. It was more like I was looking at distant galaxies through the Hubble Space Telescope. Billions of specks of light of various size and intensity, superimposed upon clouds of light from neon pink to iridescent blue, faded into infinity. It reminded me of stars being born.

I then started exploring my wounds, all in various stages of healing. I sat up in bed, leaned forward, reached up under the back of my shirt, and let my index finger linger a moment at the puncture wound on the side of my lower back. My fingers then crawled upward to another that was so near my spine I wondered how close I'd come to being paralyzed. I paused a moment to feel lucky, to wonder if the daypack I was wearing had saved me, before bringing my hand back down to my side.

I pushed back the covers, reached down the left leg of my pajama bottoms, and lightly ran my fingers over the buckshot pattern of wounds on my thigh where the bear first nailed me in midair, then apparently re-sank her claws a few times as she yanked me out of the brush. They were the most painful of the lot, especially when being cleaned and packed, an experience sometimes so excruciating my whole body would transform into a clenched fist. I have no memory of how or when I got the wounds on my wrists. I'm fairly certain how and when I got the ones on my upper arms and shoulders. They came when the bear had me pinned to the ground in the final moments that I could see.

I hung my head a moment and focused on breathing. After several long, slow, gut-deep breaths, I slowly lifted my head, then raised a shaky hand to my face to let my fingers have a look around. Starting at my left cheekbone, they paused a moment in a place that felt vaguely familiar, then inched their way toward my nose. Exploring gingerly with my fingertips, I encountered so much swelling I could find no discernable bridge. With fingers getting goopy from Bacitracin, I followed suture lines up to the middle of my forehead, pausing at the trouble spot just left of center. *Ugh. Is this thing ever going to heal?* I continued on toward the top of my skull and into the stubble of my rebounding hairline. I then lifted my other hand and, with one on each side, tried to comprehend the new shape of my head. Swollen here, dented there. Whatever that was atop my neck felt like it had bounced off the tailgate of a truck doing sixty. Upon further inspection of my right temple, I could feel a metal plate just beneath my skin. Too much. I dropped my hands in disgust.

I slumped back down into bed and pulled the covers up under my chin. I lay there ten, fifteen, twenty minutes begging for sleep. No chance. *I may as well get this over with.* Lying on my back, I slowly raised my hands to the epicenter of my injuries. What I found there were the oozing, crusty, swollen bulges of what had been my eyes. *God, this is sick.* My head started spinning. I leaned over the side of the bed, certain I was going to throw up. At that moment I was glad I was blind so I'd never have to see myself in a mirror.

My fourth surgery was an effort to sort out my scrambled sinuses, which had scarred closed and were not draining correctly, making me cough and inviting infection. It was also one more attempt to close up my forehead after the edges of the wound went from red to brown to black. Dr. Kallman was trying every trick in the book to get my forehead to heal. He had consulted the head of his practice, Dr. Dwight Ellerbe, and several other specialists, when one of them recommended a hyperbaric chamber. Breathing 100 percent oxygen under pressure delivers up to twenty times as much oxygen to damaged tissues, which stimulates new blood-vessel growth and revs up the process of healing. It may not help, Kallman told me, but it sure couldn't hurt.

First step—ear tubes. Like when diving, only inside a giant steel canister instead of water, eardrums must be equalized to keep air pressure in the inner ear in synch with the atmospheric pressure. Otherwise eardrums can burst. Equalizing isn't possible when you're breathing through a trach. Getting tubes put in my ears by a doctor was so painful I wondered how ruptured eardrums could possibly hurt any worse.

Inside the chamber, it's standard practice for patients to wear a breathing apparatus similar to the ones worn by F-15 fighter pilots. But nothing about my case was standard. The facility was new, and I was its first patient with a trach. Ray Barrett, the technician overseeing my treatments, adapted tubing to fit over it, which at first felt like trying to breathe through a garden hose. With a little more fiddling and a shorter length of tube between my trach and the regulator, I was set to go. Dress code was 100 percent cotton. No synthetic clothing, no petroleum products of any kind, were allowed inside. One does not enter a hyperbaric chamber without some risk, the least appealing of which is spontaneous combustion.

Ray, who dove with me to keep an eye on my vitals and talk me through in case I panicked, remembered me from Girdwood. He'd seen me taking tickets at a showcase of Alaska bands at the ski resort's Sitzmark Bar & Grill. He'd also been to those bonfires at Max's. For moral support, Brian dove with me as well. That made accommodations a bit tight, with me propped up lengthwise on one side, and those two sitting side by side across from me on a bench. Two hours a day, seven days a week for a month, Brian and I would duck inside our little submarine with the man we called Captain Nemo.

A sort of cross between Steve McQueen and a conservative version of George Carlin, the captain told raunchy jokes and regaled us with stories of his commercial diving days, mostly from the Chukchi and Beaufort Seas, but also of underwater welding in Cook Inlet in zero visibility in tides so strong he had to be tethered to the oil rig to keep from washing away. The chamber was monitored by colleagues on the outside, and when the captain didn't want them to hear certain things, he'd pass Brian a note; Brian would laugh, lean over and whisper into my ear, then I'd laugh, as well as one can laugh through clenched teeth and a hose in his neck.

He did his best to amuse me, or at least keep my mind off my body's ravaged state of affairs. He brought in a wooden Tic-Tac-Toe set, which was fun until I kept beating him, and then he was done with it. As a group project, the three of us decided to learn Morse Code, and passed away the hours tapping on the sides of the chamber.

A month of hyperbaric sessions did wonders for Brian. After all those accumulative doses of 100 percent oxygen, he'd never felt so good. Practically giddy. This must be what athletic blood-doping is all about, he joked. The same could not be said of me. My forehead did not respond.

It would take the swapping of body parts to finally fix that mess. Dr. Kallman made arrangements through one of his medical-school mentors for me to have highly specialized, free-flap microsurgery in San Francisco. This fifth surgery would involve harvesting a rectangular graft of skin and blood vessels from my forearm as a patch, and covering the donor site with skin from my thigh. Then the forearm skin, along with its blood supply, would be relocated to my forehead, its vessels connected to the arteries and veins in my neck by tunneling beneath the tissues of my face. The texture and color wouldn't match the landscape up there; I'd look like I'd been patched with a slab of rubber roughly the shape of Georgia. I didn't care; I just wanted my body healed.

———

In mid-September, two months after the bear, I made my first journey in public that didn't involve some kind of medical appointment. Brian and some of my friends arranged a coming-out gathering to hear reggae man Clinton Fearon at one of Anchorage's top music venues named, unfortunately, the Bear Tooth. I was ready, despite my constant headache and queasiness, despite still hurting like hell, my pains both real and phantom. Due to nerve damage, I had a lot of numbness from my upper lip to the top of my skull, as well as most of my left thigh. Between the numbness there and the stiffness most everywhere else, I walked like a rickety old man with lead in his pockets.

One of the managers at the Bear Tooth, who was in my circle of friends, cordoned off a section of the balcony and made arrangements for me and my entourage to come in a side door and through the kitchen. I made my debut in my favorite Photonz T-shirt, thrift-store linen pants, a loose-fitting trucker's hat, bandages across my forehead, and oversized shades to cover my eyes. Cooks, dishwashers, and other staff stepped out of the way and cheered as I shuffled by latched onto my Oregon friend Chris Van Ness's elbow.

"Hey, Dan."

"So glad to have you."

"Great to see you out and about."

"Hey, man, enjoy the show."

I smiled and bowed my head in gratitude. I took the stairs very seriously, holding onto Chris's elbow with one hand, gripping the railing with the other. By the time I reached the balcony I was ready for a nap. I was so damn tired of being tired.

The music and huddle of friends, including Amber, recharged my spirits to some degree. But it was a little too much reality for me, especially when Amber, after sitting with me a while, told me she'd be back in a bit, and headed down the stairs to do some dancing. I tried not to think about it, but it was there like a dull ache. If it hadn't been for the bear, I would have been down there with her. I would have been down at the stage front and center, grin slathered across my face, swaying on the balls of my feet, watching Fearon channel his soul through a microphone. Being unable to see music being made was profoundly upsetting. Being unable to see the crowd interacting with music being made was just as brutal. If I still had eyes, I would have known or recognized many of the people down there. Unless someone was talking to me or had a hand on my shoulder, I felt completely alone, isolated in a place throbbing with people. At the end of the show, I was so physically and emotionally drained I could barely make it down the stairs and out the door.

Amber continued her effort to blend into the background. The last thing she wanted was to put pressure on me to respond to her in a way I was incapable of responding. She just did what she could to be there for me and my family. She took Maya on walks and drove my mother up to see my place in Bear Valley, my dream of mountain living in a funky little cabin with a million-dollar view and skiing out my front door. She helped guide my mom through the maze of bills, insurance, and other paperwork hoops one climbs through when doing hard time in this country's health-care system. About the only piece of my tragedy that had any resemblance to good luck was the timing. I'd been at my job six months; my insurance had kicked in just a few days before.

A fondness for Amber quickly spread within my family.

"No wonder you two got together," said my mom, who'd heard the whole story by then. "That girl's a gem."

I just nodded, then changed the subject. There was no way in hell Amber would be interested in me now. I was deformed, scarred, and disabled, hardly boyfriend material. Living any kind of fulfilling life was not something I could imagine at the time. It was best for me not to dwell on what I no longer had.

Then one night, as my time in Alaska was winding down, Amber and I unexpectedly found ourselves alone in my room. I can't say we got to talking because I couldn't do much of that, just a few words here and there with fingers covering my trach. We were sitting on my king-size bed with Amber sitting behind me, facing my good side, massaging my neck. When she finished, she wrapped her arms around my waist and laid her head against the back of my shoulders.

"I still have a lot of feelings for you, Dan."

I leaned into her and felt a wave of sadness wash over me. We stayed like that for an entire Bebel Gilberto song. I then scooted down onto my back, and she lay down next to me, our legs interlocked like pretzels. As we held onto each other, she ran her hand under my shirt and stroked my chest until I wanted to cry. I covered my trach and rasped into her ear, "I wish you could stay the night."

"Me, too," she said. "I really do."

That was not going to happen with my mother in the adjoining room and my brother across the hall, although if he'd known, he would have figured out a way to keep my mom distracted.

"I've . . . missed you."

"I've missed you, so much."

I could not believe she still cared for me in this way. I mean, I really could not believe it. Maybe the lights were out, I didn't know. The chemistry was still there; we both felt it. But there was nothing at all we could do about it.

❧

As committed as Dr. Kallman was to getting me out of the hospital in time for my birthday, he was equally determined to get me to California in time for the Monterey Jazz Festival. The week after my coming-out party at the Bear Tooth, in preparation for leaving Alaska, I got my jaw unwired, my trach tube removed, and my stoma stitched up. My stomach tube had already been yanked out, not unlike how one yanks a lawn-mower cord, it turned out. So I was good to go. That left finding some way to thank the rescuers, doctors, nurses, friends, and strangers whose collective efforts were the only reason I was still among the living. Although it would never feel like enough, I gave it a shot through an open letter.

"If it were not for the wonderful treatment provided by Dr. Kallman and Dr. Ellerbe's office and the amazing care of Providence hospital, I would not have survived. The members of this community really came together in my family's time of need to extend their thoughts, services, financial aid, and most of all their prayers. I have been healing quickly and I attribute this to those Alaskans who have extended themselves and their thoughts to my recovery. I thank you more than words can express. Keep on fishing, and I'll see you out there next summer."

Excerpts of my letter, and an update on my recovery, were published on the front page of the *Anchorage Daily News*.

My mother, brother, and I, and Maya in her dog carrier, had an early morning flight to California. Amber showed up before work to see me off. The mutual understanding was that I was setting her free. I didn't know when or really if I'd be back.

"Just because my life has ended doesn't mean yours has to," I told her.

Amber, who doesn't have a single drama-queen cell in her body, accepted what had to be. We didn't know if we'd ever see each other again. We did know we both needed to move on. There was no choice, and so we hugged, said goodbye, and promised to keep in touch. And that was that.

The manager of the hotel, who was coming along to help with luggage and see us off at the airport, said it was time to go. I climbed into the shuttle and settled into my seat, and the van pulled away from the curb.

I was off to begin the daunting task of learning to live as a blind man. My indoctrination came sooner than I expected, before our plane backed out of the gate. As passengers were settling in and fastening their seat belts, a flight attendant came up to me.

"Excuse me, sir, are you Mr. Bigley?"

"That's me," I said in my hoarse, newly restored voice.

"Mr. Bigley, just so you know, the emergency exits are located three rows in front of you. In the event of an emergency, just remain seated until one of us can assist you. You'll need to be the last one off the plane."

This was my welcome to the world of the blind.

CHAPTER 15

Arboleda Sessions

I BOLTED UPRIGHT IN BED, CRYING OUT, ARMS WINDMILLING AT NOTHING but the night. Again. I'd had this same nightmare so many times I'd lost count. I dropped my arms, grabbed fistfuls of sweat-soaked sheets, and waited for my heartbeat to return to idle. I pushed the button on the side of my talking watch to get my bearings.

The time is 3:12 a.m.

What else was new? For whatever reason I'd developed a habit of waking up at 3:12, if not exactly, then close to it. The precision timing was eerie, and I could make no sense of it. The nightmare responsible played out in chops, its images more like a series of snapshots than a movie rolling inside my head. The final moments I could see would come to me in a freeze-frame replay of the seconds between John diving off the trail and me getting slammed, just me and the bear, its huge head getting closer and closer, its eyes locked on mine.

Typically, I'd bust from sleep just as the sow made contact. But I'd dreamt every aspect of my mauling and from every possible angle—up, down, and sideways. In some dreams I could feel the bear's weight upon my chest, my lungs deflating like punctured inner tubes. In others I could hear the scraping of teeth against my skull. Traumatic memory can be kind or cruel that way. People remember either too much or too little. I remembered too much. On nightmare nights, which were most nights, falling back to sleep was out the window. Even if I could, chances were high the bear would be waiting for me.

My dreams weren't always about bears. I'd dream of being chased by thugs with Glocks, or militia with assault rifles, and me with nothing to defend myself. I'd run and run through city streets and alleyways, through shopping malls, through jungles. In one version, the militia would catch up with me, throw me to the ground, and spray me with lead. I'd feel the bullets hit one after another before finally lunging up in bed and gasping for breath.

Over time, with the help of distance and coping strategies prescribed by a trauma therapist, the dreams became less frequent and less terrifying with infinitely better outcomes. The bears, almost always a sow with cubs, would appear farther way, then off in the distance, then no longer in the woods but in a fields of flowers, then in the outfield of a neighborhood ballpark grazing on dandelions, the sow as docile as a Holstein cow. My role would shift from being eaten alive to being to startled to being wary to admiring them the way I had before. In one scenario, I would see the bears in the outfield from atop the ballpark's chain-link backstop, watching from above with no fear at all. But those dreams didn't come until much further down the road.

I hadn't been in California long, and was still adjusting to a new landscape of sounds. I was still adjusting to the walls and corners and tables and chairs and sleeping dogs not used to being stepped on. I was still getting acquainted with the doors and their jambs, sometimes finding them abruptly with my face, feeling at times like a pinball, bouncing off one thing into another.

As much as it smarted learning the lay of the land, I loved the place, my family's second home called Arboleda, Spanish for "grove of trees." After my grandparents passed away, my mother, aunt, and uncle sold the lakeside cabin in Ontario, and for years my mom had dreamed of buying another getaway closer to home. The two places were the antithesis of each other, but the moment she pulled into the circular driveway she knew Arboleda was it. While my grandparents' home away from home had been a hand-hewn log cabin with bats in its rafters, Arboleda was a two-story, passive-solar, Mediterranean-style country house on five acres in the hills above San Juan Bautista, an hour's drive from Carmel, where my mom and stepdad lived. With its gardens, manicured lawns, grape arbors, and old-growth sycamore trees, the place had operated as a bed and breakfast and retreat house for small groups, family reunions, and weddings. Trails meandering through the property came upon benches tucked between live oaks dripping with Spanish moss. A pathway lined with grapevines led to a lower lawn with a meditation labyrinth made of white pebbles and ringed in abalone shells. Behind the house was a lawn terraced down to a small pond fed by a trickle of a creek that I could hear out my bedroom window, along with the owls and frogs and crickets of the night. The property even came with a dog, a mutt named Cloey, short for Inspector Clouseau of *The Pink Panther* series, who showed up when the construction crew was building the place and never left.

As a teenager, I was self-conscious of my family's financial resources, and would get embarrassed when my mom picked me up in her snow-white BMW. In college, I'd prided myself on being a minimalist, on my plastic milk-crate bedside table, my freebie dresser, and my second-hand and Dumpster-dive household scores. If I could have, I would have awarded myself a merit badge for being able to fit everything I owned into the back of my pickup. Of course, my pickup wasn't exactly a handcart. The pretense wasn't lost on me. I couldn't have been more appreciative to have a wonderland like Arboleda to do my healing, or the resources to get the extraordinary help I got along the way.

As Dr. Kallman had hoped, I made it back in time for the Monterey Jazz Festival in late September, and was able to rally for a few hours each day. It was my first time in a crowd, and this festival drew a massive one, forty thousand people over three days, nearly ten thousand more than Alaska's third largest city. With all the swelling and bandages, my left leg stiff as a baseball bat, I looked like an escapee from *Night of the Living Dead*. If people stared I didn't know it.

The festival did my spirits good, especially when the funk-jazz trio, Soulive, heard my story, then gave me, my brother, and Jeremy, our friend and caretaker at Arboleda, the VIP treatment by setting up chairs for us on the side of the stage, then coming over after the show dripping with sweat to give me full-body hugs and wish me well. But one day I overdid it, walking farther than I had since the night of the bear. Fearing my leg wounds were opening up, I asked Brian to check me out. We opted against inspection in the men's restroom. Two guys in a stall? Pants hitting the floor? Ah, no. So we went to one of the festival's medical tents and asked for a spot where I could drop my drawers and Brian could take a look at my leg. It seemed like such a simple request, but there was that liability thing and paperwork to fill out. We tried to explain that we just needed some privacy where we could do this one little deal and be on our way. No paperwork, no service, the attendants insisted.

Paperwork. What was I going to put on the form? That I'd been mauled by a bear? It just seemed ludicrous. Out of context, a couple thousand miles from Alaska, I felt even more like a freak.

Even in Alaska, people had no idea what to say to me. I heard some of the strangest things. "I know just how you feel. I had a friend who had an eye shot out by a BB gun," was one of my favorites. And I loved this: When I signed in as an outpatient for my fourth surgery, the woman behind the computer at patient check-in asked the purpose of my visit.

"I'm here for surgery with Dr. Kallman and Dr. Ellerbe."

"And the nature of the surgery?"

"Closing up the wound in my forehead."

"And the cause of the injury?"

"I got mauled by a bear."

The woman paused, studied her computer screen a moment, then asked: "Was it an accident?"

~~~

At Arboleda, I devoted myself to healing inside and out. Brian took a leave of absence from his ski-area job to be with me. Jay again put his Portland massage therapy practice on hold and arrived soon after I did. Jeremy added looking after me to his list of caretaker duties.

He and I had met as neighbors in Prescott, Arizona, my junior year of college. He'd see me driving by and would nod and raise a beer from his porch, until one day I stopped to join him. We'd been friends ever since. He also befriended my brother, and was visiting him at Arboleda when my mom offered him the job caretaking the place. Studying to be a winemaker, he'd planned to tend to the house and grounds for just a semester or two, but once I arrived he stayed on indefinitely. Among other alterations, he set up a system of ropes so I could find my way alone across the driveway to the vegetable garden, and from there across a little creek to a lawn lined with fruit trees and lavender bushes that I called the Secret Garden.

Many others helped out here and there, but those three had my back. They did wound care, drove me to and from appointments, cooked for me, and cleaned up my messes. When I would throw up, sometimes without warning, from the ongoing antibiotic warfare against MRSA, I'd try to deal with it myself, but sometimes I needed a little help.

"Man, I hate to ask you this. I did it again. I cleaned up the best I could but I don't know if I got it all. Would you mind taking a look?"

They also kept me from spending too much time alone with my thoughts. We went for walks on the beach and to as many music shows as I could handle. When people made comments like, "Cool glasses, dude," because I was wearing sunglasses at night, they set them straight. When people raised their voices and spoke slowly, they reminded them that I was blind, not hard of hearing. When servers at restaurants asked, "What does he want?" they'd say, "Why don't you ask him? He's sitting right here."

Mornings were my favorite time of day. I'd rise at five with the roosters, pour coffee into a cup as big as a cereal bowl, and sit in the sun listening to the pickup chorus of birds and the roosters harassing the chickens. Jeremy was another early riser, and we spent many a morning out there together, greeting the sun as it peeked over the ridge, talking about pretty much anything and everything except what had happened to me. Jeremy didn't know the details, didn't want to know them, and would walk away when others asked.

Throughout the fall I had a steady stream of Prescott and Alaska friends coming and going, to help out and play music—artists and musicians and grad students and ski bums and a freeloader or two. In addition to the conventional route, my healing path included acupuncture, meditation, massage, homeopathic remedies, craniosacral therapy, and a couple of sessions with an "intuitive healer," which was where I drew the line—too woo-woo for me. I also did a little time at Esalen, a 120-acre healing and retreat center founded in Big Sur in the sixties, called the birthplace of the New Age movement, a term I've heard is now despised at the place. Those who've led workshops there include such literary, philosophical, and spiritual heavyweights as Aldous Huxley, Buckminster Fuller, Joseph Campbell, Deepak Chopra, Timothy Leary, Jack Kerouac, Ken Kesey, Allen Ginsberg, Carlos Castaneda, Moshe Feldenkrais, and Andrew Weil. Although many would agree with the graffiti artist who once spray-painted at the entryway, "Jive shit for rich white folk," I was in dire need of nourishment for my body and soul, and I got it there through massage, soaking in spring-fed hot tubs perched above the Pacific, and just absorbing the restorative energy that permeated the place.

My massage therapist at Esalen, Ilene Connelly, mother of Academy Award–winning actress Jennifer Connelly, it turned out, took one look at me our first session and said, "Okay, we need to talk." She ended up becoming a great source of support and a great friend who would work on me at Arboleda and then refuse to take my money. She talked me through my first panic attack, when my heart rate went ballistic and I was convinced I was dying. She helped keep me present rather than off on some distant walkabout in my head. She gave me healing beads blessed by the Dalai Lama. I've kept them close to me ever since.

Staving off dark thoughts took vigilance and a concerted act of will. I was tested hard and often, beginning soon after arriving at Arboleda when I came within a heartbeat of getting my brains tenderized. Jeremy and I were hanging out in my favorite nook called Bella's Garden, a circular clearing ten feet in diameter tucked away in a thicket, with wooden benches and chairs and a table with a stone top. Jeremy was telling me about some of the improvements he wanted to make around the property.

"Those fruits trees need a lot of work. The nectarines, I'm pretty sure, are toast and . . ."

An ominous commotion cracked above our heads. I leapt to my feet; he grabbed my arm and yanked me aside just as a huge branch off a willow tree came crashing down onto our chairs with a BOOM.

"Dude, you're not going to believe this," he said.

He led me back over to inspect the impact zone. I ran my hands over the bark and up the length of the huge branch. The thing would have creamed us both. I had a constant headache back then, and just thinking about the closeness of that call added another on top of it. Back in my previous life, I'd often felt the universe was looking out for me. I had many reasons to feel that way. After the bear and the branch, I really had to wonder.

My efforts not to go to the dark side began back in the hospital, or even back at the river when I promised never to regret my decision to live. When my mother gave me the book on tape *There's a Spiritual Solution to Every Problem*, by Dr. Wayne W. Dyer, I listened. But listening to a spiritual tape doesn't make a person spiritual any more than swimming in a lake makes him a trout. While the book is not particularly profound, at the time it was exactly what I needed, and not so much the spiritual part; I'd believed in forces beyond the tangible long before the bear, confirmed every time I stood on a mountaintop or watched a sunrise.

More than one well-meaning friend tried to put a spiritual spin on my mauling, about me being some sort of chosen one, about how I now had the spirit of the bear residing within me. Right. So if you get mugged in an alley does the mugger's spirit get to move in, too? The natural sciences, from the microbes in the soil beneath my feet to the Arctic tern's annual migration from one hemisphere to the other—the equivalent in its potential thirty-year lifespan of one and a half roundtrip journeys to the moon—provided all the evidence I needed that there was magic in the air without resorting to making stuff up.

"Everything happens for a reason," people would say. *Is that right? And the reason a bear ripped my face off is what, exactly?* What happened to me was sociobiology in its rawest form. The bear thought I was a threat to her cubs and did what any good mother would do; she put a stop to me. Nothing personal. It wasn't fate that brought us together. It wasn't my destiny to become Lee Hagmeier's tribal brother. It was nothing more cosmic than at that particular moment having shit for luck.

Coming so close to dying has a way of flipping what you thought was important on its head. Even if I hadn't lost my sight, I had been to the blue place and had returned profoundly altered. So the spirituality part was not so much what drew me to Dr. Dyer's message. It was the solution part. Dyer's case for the power of intention resonated with me, that we have the power to control how we respond to the tragedies in our lives. He spoke of turning adversity into something meaningful, and how our traumas can become our strengths. That gave me something to focus on. It gave me hope.

As best as I can remember, Harlow Robinson, who'd been my boss at Alaska Children's Services, was the first person to whom I expressed this. During one of his visits to me in the hospital, I wrote on my dry-erase board: "Something good will come of this."

"It was probably the single most inspiring moment of my life," Harlow later told an *Anchorage Daily News* reporter following up on my story. "Dan's the kind of guy you'd name your kid after." And he did a year later with the birth of his first son, Eli Daniel Robinson.

All through this time of healing and grieving and soul searching and dreaming, Amber and I were staying in touch by phone. Not much at first, maybe once every couple of weeks, then gradually more often. Amber was still working as a school counselor for Cook Inlet Tribal Council, so we talked about her work with kids. We talked of mutual friends and music shows we'd been to. We talked about our dogs and we talked about the weather. Our chats were friendly, but guarded. That worked for me until my brother dropped the bomb.

Brian had acquired a girlfriend during his time in Alaska, had flown up to see her, and had bumped into Amber at the Bear Tooth at a David Grisman show. She was with a guy, and it was obvious to him that they had something going. Not that anyone blamed her, least of all me. I didn't want her waiting for me out of any sense of charity or obligation. Amber was doing what she needed to do, what I had expected her to do, what I pretty much told her to do. She was moving on.

"Huh. Okay," I said, when Brian let me know. "I'm good with that. Amber and I are just friends. Really, we'd only been together a day—not even. I've put her through a lot, and she deserves to be happy."

Ouch, that hurts, is how I really felt about it. Surprised by how conflicted I was, I brought it up the next time she called.

"There's something I want to talk to you about. Brian says you're dating somebody. I just want you to know that's totally cool with me. I want you to live your life, to move on. I would hate to think you didn't feel you could do that. But I've got to say, he's a lucky guy."

Pause.

"I appreciate that," Amber said. "But you don't have to worry about him. I don't see this going anywhere. He's already annoyed with me because I talk about you so much."

Pause—my turn this time.

Our phone calls became more frequent after that. She continued to be guarded, assuming I meant what I said when I left for California, that I was too messed up to be in a relationship. On my end, I got to where I couldn't stop thinking about her. That started chipping away at the wall I'd built between how I thought I should feel and how I really did.

❦

I had my free-flap surgery to repair my forehead in early November at the University of California San Francisco School of Medicine. This fifth surgery was exceptionally tough on me in terms of pain and anxiety. Nothing else had worked; what if this was a bust, too? Once the surgeons got inside my head, they discovered that the oval of bone that had been temporarily removed during my reconstructive surgery in July not only wasn't viable due to lack of blood supply, it was harboring MRSA. It had to be tossed, leaving my brain beneath that spot without armor. One wayward softball to the forehead and game over, is how Dr. Kallman put it. There was talk of me having to wear a helmet the rest of my life—a helmet!—to which my sentiment was, screw that.

Because of the MRSA, I had to ramp up the antibiotics, back to the heavy-duty IV kind, so heavy they turned my sweat orange. Twice a day, no matter whether I was on the couch or out in public, Brian, Jay, or Jeremy would hook me up through a PICC line on the inside of my upper right arm, first flushing the port with a syringe of saline, then attaching a bag of antibiotics that took a half hour to drain, followed by another flushing of the port. This, I was told, drew some dirty looks and turned heads at festivals and music shows. At one, some space princess was convinced I was mainlining heroin and kept hinting that I should share.

After the free-flap, I had a lot of healing to do, and I had every intention of doing it well enough to celebrate the end of that year and beginning of a new one in spectacular fashion. Steve Kimock was playing three shows in Colorado around then, including one on New Year's Eve. That was my carrot. Recovering enough to make those shows felt hugely symbolic since his music had been the soundtrack of my bedside vigil. A mutual friend of his, one of my former housemates from Prescott, told him about me and was keeping him posted on my progress. I threw it out there to Amber the next time she called.

"So, I have this plan that I've been kind of dreaming up. I've set a goal for myself to work on healing and get back on my feet in time to make it to the Kimock New Year's shows in Colorado. Being well enough to go would be a milestone for me, making it past all the surgeries. So I'm asking some of my closest friends to meet me out there. I'm wondering if you would be interested in joining us. Jeremy and his girlfriend, Paige, are coming. Brian's on for sure, and there are several other definite maybes. If you could make it, I would love it if you'd let me buy your plane ticket."

"Wow, that's really tempting. School doesn't start again until the fifth so that part works. I don't have anything else planned so, yeah, I'd be up for that. But you don't have to buy my ticket."

"I insist."

"If you're going to put it that way, I guess I could let you. It really would help. I've been a little strapped. I should probably get right on making a reservation."

That we'd be sharing a hotel room was a given. At the end of December, Amber and I met up in Colorado, and I had every intention of picking things up where we'd left off in Girdwood. The first night, at the Fox Theater in Boulder, at the front of the stage with Amber beside me and my buddies all around, I couldn't have felt more grateful, or more deeply moved by what we die-hard Kimock fans call the K-waves. The notes he doesn't play are just as important as the ones he does, and the ones he does play, he dances circles around. I was already flying when he gave me a shout-out.

"I don't usually do this sort of thing but this song goes out to Big Dan Bigley, who came a long way to be here today."

I was floored. Amber put her arm around my waist and gave me a squeeze. Kimock then launched into one of my favorites, "Tongue n' Groove." I grinned so hard my jaw hurt.

It was an epic night on many levels, a high-spirited celebration of better times to come. The free-flap surgery had worked; my forehead was finally fixed. I was back in my natural habitat. I was back with Amber. Only, for some reason, I felt more skittish than romantic.

When the show ended, she and I made our way back to the hotel. She disappeared into the bathroom. I sat on the couch with a thorn in my stomach and a bad case of sewing-machine leg. She came out in a silk nightie with a fresh dab of Egyptian Goddess on her wrists and neck, although that detail was lost on me since I had no sense of smell. She pulled back the covers and slid into bed. My hands out in front of me sleepwalker style, I groped my way to the bathroom, bounced slightly off the doorframe, rebounded, went inside, and closed the door. I dropped my clothes on the floor and climbed into my pajama bottoms. I came out and shuffled toward the bed, finding it first with my left shin. I climbed between the cool, cotton sheets still wearing my sunglasses. Once I heard Amber reach over and switch off the reading lamp, it felt safe to take them off and set them on the beside table close enough to grab in a hurry. Amber snuggled up next to me. I turned toward her, wrapped my arms around her, and drew her close. She rested her head against my shoulder, her body pressing against me, a leg draped over mine, a hand on my chest.

And then . . . nothing. I could not move. I could barely breathe. *What is WRONG with me?*

We lay there wide awake, each wondering what the hell was going on. We lay like that, not talking, not moving, until finally drifting off to sleep.

My behavior was even more puzzling the second night. When Amber put an arm around me at the show, I'd take it for a while, then turn to the side and slide out of it. When she would sit down next to me on the couch in our room, I'd sit there a few minutes, then get up to do something bogus, grab a beer, whatever, then sit back down on the opposite side of the couch. In bed, after about fifteen awkward minutes of nothing happening, Amber rolled over and went to sleep.

By the third night, New Year's Eve, she wasn't even trying anymore. Even the kiss at midnight was more like how I'd kiss my aunt. In bed that night, lying side by side, I was actually feeling claustrophobic, like my skin wanted to crawl off my bones and hide under the bed. It was so awkward and upsetting to us both.

To my brother and friends, who'd had high hopes for the two of us, it was obvious I was blowing it. *What the hell is Dan's problem?* they wondered. *Amber's awesome. Has he lost his mind?*

No one was more bewildered by my behavior than me. That fireworks show we'd had between us, where did it go? Here I was blind and disfigured, not exactly a dream catch, and here was this beautiful woman who obviously wanted me in spite of it all. The chemistry was no longer there, I assumed. Nothing else made any sense.

At the airport two days later, we stood around waiting for our planes, not talking about much. Brian, Jeremy, Paige Howarth, and I were all on the same flight. Amber's wouldn't leave for another couple of hours. When ours was called, she and I hugged goodbye once again. This time, it really was over between us. I just hoped I hadn't blown it so bad we couldn't be friends.

"It was a lot of fun," I said, not the least bit convincing. "I'll be in touch."

"Yeah, okay. Thanks for everything. Take care."

I felt entirely empty, like a pocket turned inside out. The agent called our rows and we all headed toward the plane. Amber watched us go, then turned and walked away.

CHAPTER 16

Victory Lap

A WEEK AFTER RETURNING FROM COLORADO, JEREMY DROVE ME DOWN the winding canyon road from Arboleda to San Juan Bautista, then worked his way northwest toward the seaside town of Capitola to deliver me to the one person who seemed to know me better than I knew myself at the time. My mother had lined me up with therapist Joanne Young before I'd left Alaska to help with nightmares, post-traumatic stress, and my staggering sense of loss. Jeremy and I stopped as usual to grab coffee and breakfast sandwiches along the way. With my ongoing struggle with antibiotic-inspired nausea, I needed something in my stomach before swallowing my weekly dose of reality, which at times was not unlike swallowing bleach.

"Thanks for bringing him in, Jeremy," Joanne said as she met us in the waiting room that day. "We'll see you in a couple of hours. Dan, you ready to head back?"

"Ohhh yeah," I said as I rose to my feet. I took hold of her elbow, and we walked out the waiting-room door, through a commons area, and into her office, a room of bookcases, pillows, and plants, with lighting as soft as cotton and walls infused with troubles, some of which could peel paint.

Jeremy would kill the time picking up my prescriptions at a nearby pharmacy, reading the newspaper at a bakery down the road, or sitting in my truck listening to Howard Stern on the radio. He never knew which version of me he'd be picking up at the end of these sessions—the one who'd psychobabble the whole way back, telling him more than he wanted to know, or the one who'd sit slumped in the front seat, mindlessly fiddling with his beard, thoughts lost in the exosphere, the one who'd crawl back into bed for the rest of the day as soon as we got back home.

That day, after I faced up to how I'd treated Amber, he'd be getting the solemn, beard-fiddling one.

Back in Joanne's office, I settled onto a leather couch, kicked off my flip-flops, and tucked my legs up beside me. She handed me a cup of lemon zinger tea. I heard the brush of fabric as she sank into her chair.

"So Dan, tell me, how was Colorado? How did it go with Amber?"

"Well, actually . . . I'm pretty disappointed. It was so strange and awkward, the opposite of what I expected. The chemistry, the energy, I just wasn't feeling it. So I guess that's pretty much the end of that."

"Um-hmm. Is that so?" Joanne wasn't buying it. "This is not about Amber," she said. "I doubt what you were feeling had anything to do with a lack of chemistry. I'm wondering if it was more the opposite."

I paused a moment. "Okay," I said. "I'm listening."

Two hours later, I walked out of there painfully aware of how little progress I'd made on the emotional frontlines of my recovery. Since I'd first gathered my wits about me in the hospital, I'd focused all my strength and energy on physical healing, but was still white-knuckling the internal kind. I didn't feel connected to my own misshapen head, let alone this amorphous being I was inside. My own heart was a stranger to me.

I wasn't interested in having a casual relationship with Amber. Had I been, things would have been much different in Colorado. Falling in love means making yourself vulnerable, risky under the best of circumstances. And there I was, a blind man with no blind-man skills whose curb appeal was in the tank. Why would Amber want me? Charity? Although I had a primordial fear of living alone in the dark, I preferred that to a relationship based on pity. Combine my post-bear insecurities with the standard ones that come with the territory in any new relationship, then pile on the squirrely highs and lows of that raging cocktail of love chemicals, and what you get doesn't feel all that different from an anxiety attack. Joanne's theory was that sensory overload had tripped my emergency shutdown breaker, and the more we talked, the more I could see that she was right.

I'd been mulling this over for a few days when Jeremy and Paige brought it up over dinner.

"Amber seems really cool, the kind who's down for just about anything," Jeremy said. "You didn't seem all that into it. We were all wondering if you'd lost your mind. Have you even talked to her since we got back?"

"Yeah, she's great. And no, I haven't."

"Seriously? What a dumbass you are."

"I couldn't agree more."

I got up my courage to call her later that night. I took the phone from the kitchen, felt my way down the hallway trailing my hand along the wall, went into my room, and closed the door. I sat on the edge of my bed thinking about what I was going to say to her. Before I could lose my nerve, I dialed her number. She answered on the third ring. I could sense her stiffening when she heard my voice, so I jumped right in.

"I've got something I need to tell you. I think you know, I'm sure you know, it was pretty weird between us in Colorado. I don't want you to think you had anything to do with the way I acted. You didn't do anything wrong, you didn't say the wrong thing. You were completely stunning and beautiful. I don't know how to make sense of it. I just thought that somehow the chemistry wasn't happening. I know now that wasn't the case. I think my emotions just got all haywire and I pretty much wigged out."

It was a good thing Amber was a great listener because I had a lot of explaining to do. I just hoped it wasn't too late.

"I'm sure I hurt your feelings, and for that I am truly sorry. If there's any way you'd be willing to give me another chance, I would really, really love that."

Amber was silent long enough for me to wonder if I'd managed to make things worse. After all, I'd pretty much just told her I was an emotional nutcase.

"Amber? You still there?"

"Yeah, I'm here. It was a tough trip," she finally said. "Thank you for the apology. I'm willing to keep talking and see what happens. No promises."

"Amber, thank you. I feel like such a jerk. The good news is, I'm aware that I bring a lot of baggage into this. The bad news is I have a lot of baggage. But I'm going to work really hard to make sure it no longer gets between us."

After that, I launched into full-steam-ahead, hot-pursuit mode. I started calling her most every night, and sometimes we'd talk for well over an hour. I'd talk for well over an hour, anyway. I was eager to share with her what I was learning in my sessions with Joanne. I wanted to show her the progress I was making, and the commitment I had to making it.

I would talk and talk about my fears, insecurities, and revelations, and Amber would listen without drama or judgment. Some nights, most nights, she'd listen herself right to sleep. I'd hear the shift in her voice, then in her breathing, heavy and rhythmic.

"Hey, Amber? You still with me? Amber?"

I'd smile and imagine her curled up on her futon with Hobbit, her head resting on her arm, mouth slightly open, phone lying abandoned on its back. I'd imagine myself lying next to her, brushing the hair from her face with my fingers.

All winter and spring we had our late-night talks, speaking in soft tones, getting to know each other by sharing our stories. Courtship by phone put us on equal footing. With blindness irrelevant, we were just two voices in the night. Without the distraction of trails to follow, rivers to run, and fish to catch, Amber, I came to realize, was the best thing to come my way. Ever.

I'd known all along that at some point I needed to return to Alaska to visit my former life, to wrap things up in a way I was incapable of when I left in the fall. I could still hear Jaha's voice from the Russian River just before the ambulance doors closed between us. "We'll be fishing again before you know it," he'd said. It was time for me to get back on the horse, and so I booked a flight for July. After six months of working with Joanne, I felt ready to audition once again for boyfriend status with Amber. Visiting her in Alaska would be my comeback. Fishing again with John and Jaha would be my victory lap.

Once my plane touched down in Anchorage, I had to sit tight until everyone else was off and a flight attendant came to assist me. I was halfway decent with a cane by then, but didn't feel like pushing it. So I took her elbow and we headed up the aisle, through the jetway, and into the waiting area at the gate, where she handed me off to a passenger-assist associate with a big, beefy voice that suggested she was a woman used to getting her way.

"Hello Mr. Bigley. I've got a wheelchair here for you."

"No thanks, I'm good."

"It's no problem, sir. It's all ready to go. Wouldn't you like to take a load off and go for a little ride?"

"No, not at all. I don't need a wheelchair. If you don't mind, I'll just take your arm and we can walk together."

She sighed and cleared her throat. "You're sure?"

"I am *so* sure."

"Well, o-kay then."

Once we passed the security exit and entered the main terminal, I heard Amber's signature, "Heeey, there."

"Thanks," I told my escort. "I'm good here."

I felt Amber's arms wrap around me. I wrapped mine around her. We held onto each other almost long enough to qualify as a scene.

⌁

Amber never did buy land in Bear Valley, but she did find a cabin to rent not far from my own. We pulled up to her place around one that afternoon. I stood in her driveway a couple of minutes taking in the familiar Chugach Mountain air and calls of the ravens, then took hold of her arm and went inside. I kicked off my sandals, slipped out of my backpack, and set it down in a corner. She took off her jacket and hung it over the back of a chair.

Her cabin was nearly as Alaska-ghetto as mine, only with indoor plumbing. More than once while she was away at work, the freight-train winds of winter had blown her front door open, frozen the pipes, and deposited snowdrifts upon her bed. It wasn't the smallest place she'd lived in but it was close, so small her twin bed, draped with her patchwork quilt, doubled as a couch. How convenient. How awkward. While she busied herself making tea, that's where I sat, cross-legged on Amber's bed, fiddling with my beard. There was a lot to fiddle with. A remnant of my former self, my beard was one thing I felt I had control over, and I hadn't let anyone trim it since the hospital. Down in California, having feral facial hair that reached my chest, along with my hefty sunglasses, brought a steady stream of ZZ Top wisecracks.

As I twirled it between my fingers, familiar clouds of doubt formed inside my head. Seriously, why would Amber want me? Half the time I couldn't even find my own shoes. A year after my accident, there was still a little too much swelling for prosthetic eyes. In the meantime, I was stuck with these green plastic placeholders. The lids of my right eye were swollen shut, and the lids on the left were stuck slightly open, exposing the space-alien green of my conformer. What a turn on. And here I was in Alaska in July. At least in Colorado it got dark at night. Amber handed me my tea, and I jumped off that train of thought.

We sipped our tea. I ripped the tab off the string and rolled it into a ball between my fingers. We sipped our tea some more. A mosquito buzzed and landed on my arm. I slapped and missed. I continued working on my tea, in no hurry to finish. When I finally did, Amber took my cup to the sink. I went back to fiddling with my beard. I could hear her own nervousness as she clanked about in the kitchen. I wasn't about to do a repeat of Colorado. This time I wanted her so bad I could hardly stand it. But first I had a decision to make. Sunglasses on? Sunglasses off? Sunglasses on? Sunglasses . . . *Oh, the hell with it.*

"Hey, Amber, why don't you come over here a minute?" I said, patting the spot beside me on the bed. She abandoned the dishes with a clatter, came over, and sat down next to me to the creak of bedsprings. She was dressed in jeans and a tank top, and I could feel the warmth of her skin against mine. I leaned over and kissed her softly on the shoulder. She leaned her head my way. I turned sideways, put my right hand on the small of her back to orient myself, and kissed her temple, tasting the sweetness of her hair. She leaned back, exposing her neck.

My glasses went flying and landed on the floor with a thud.

—◦—

Making love for the first time left us both glowing, all the pent-up awkwardness melted off our bones. Had I been able, I would have sprinted to the nearest mountaintop and shouted, "I love this woman!" Instead, I held onto her as if I'd never let go. We fell asleep that night crammed in her tiny bed in her tiny cabin, tangled in each other's arms. And then, just as I had the previous summer, I woke up late the next morning and hugged and kissed her goodbye. I was going fishing with John and Jaha on the Kasilof River, and my ride had arrived.

"I'll give you a call when I get back from fishing," I told her.

She'd heard those words before, and they gave her a chill. But unlike the summer before, I not only called after fishing, I came home to her with a forty-pound king in my cooler and a humongous grin on my face.

CHAPTER 17

Life Plan, Take II

Back at Arboleda, I rose as usual with the roosters, poured myself a cup of coffee, made my way to the front porch mine-sweeping with my feet, settled into my favorite morning chair, and began formulating a new life plan for myself. I'd made a major decision on my trip to Alaska. I was going to move back up and reclaim my life. I was going to give my relationship with Amber everything I had to give, which at the time wasn't much. That part had to change.

I'd said I intended to make something good out of the grenade life had tossed me. Now that I had someone besides myself to consider, I was highly motivated to make that "good" part happen. I had no idea how—I couldn't even match my socks—but I was determined to figure it out.

Enrolling in a school for the blind was on the horizon, but I wasn't quite ready. First, I had a lot more letting go to do. It wasn't always up to me to decide what to let go of or when to let it go. I was taken off guard on a regular basis, like getting a call out of the blue from the Alaska State Troopers regarding a certain box with my name on it.

"I have some things here that belong to you, some clothing you had with you the night of your accident," the trooper told me. "What would you like me to do? I could put them in the mail or I could dispose of them for you."

"Well, what have you got?"

"There's a green pile jacket, North Face, but it's in pretty bad shape."

"Like, does it just need to be washed or . . . ?"

"No, not really. Sorry, but it's, ah, it's a mess."

"No, I don't want that."

"There's a gray sweater here, but I don't think you're going to want that back, either."

"That's fine. Get rid of it."

"There's also a green ball cap."

I perked right up. "Definitely send me *that*."

"Hey, guys!" I shouted to Brian and Jeremy. "My Bonfire hat still lives! Wahoo!"

When the box arrived and Brian opened it and looked inside, there was nothing to celebrate.

"Geez, Dan, I really don't think you want this. I don't even want to touch it."

It had clearly been through the mauling with me. My chest sank. It was just a hat, but that hat had been such a big part of me.

"Just toss it," I told him. "Get it out of here."

I had to let go of certain friends, too. Some of my hardcore ski buddies were just that; all we ever did together was ski. They'd come around for a while but eventually they'd fade out of my life. I knew that. I understood. People move on.

Already I sensed a distance between me and John, but for a much different reason. It couldn't be easy for him to look at me. He'd stared that same bear in the eyes. He'd heard me being torn apart and had been powerless to stop it. I don't know how anyone could ever be the same after that. On my comeback fishing trip, I swear John, Jaha, and the two other fishing buddies with us that day, Nick Ohlrich and Nigel Fox, pooled their fishing karma and willed me to catch not just a fish, but that fish, my forty-pound king. John whooped and hollered along with the rest. But the night before when we'd all stayed together in Cooper Landing, John seemed unusually quiet and kept disappearing out the door. He had a hard time watching me bump into things, I think. He had a hard time seeing me need an escort to get to the outhouse and a cane to tap my way around a room.

After the bear, he left his ski-resort job, and several months later, his anthropology program at the University of Alaska. I worried that the bear had altered the course of his life. I'm pretty sure he'd disagree. I'm guessing, because we've never talked about it. As close as we had been in our philosophies, in our reverence for the land, in our understanding of the ways of the fishing junkie, we were opposites in that regard. I needed to explore every square inch of the emotional terrain surrounding my bear attack, to turn over every stone. John was more of the mindset that you leave that stuff alone. I needed to talk about it. He needed not to.

I missed him; we'd had so many laughs together. But if I thought too much about all that I missed, I wouldn't be able to get out of bed.

Amber was the exception to that rule. Missing her was like motivational rocket fuel. I was goofy in love with her, from her tenderness to her obsession with shoes. After craving her every day through four more months of long-distance phone bills, I planned my second trip up to see her over Thanksgiving. By then I had prosthetic eyes. My droopy right eye was still mostly swollen shut, and neither set of eyelids worked, so I couldn't blink, nor could I close my eyes when I slept, which I worried would be disturbing. Still, I kept hearing that my new eyes were a big improvement over my freaky green ones. That, I assumed, would be easier on Amber, although she never said a word about the way I looked. Not once. It would only be down the road that I'd find out how squeamish she had been about my wounds, especially early on when my newly rebuilt eyelids and sockets were oozy. I've never known anyone so willing to overlook that which is impossible to overlook.

Amber had done some upgrading of her own since my first visit. She'd moved out of her tiny cabin in Bear Valley and into a real house just across the way, a two-story with big windows and a deck overlooking Cook Inlet. She'd moved in as the housemate of a seldom-seen, North Slope oil-field worker with kids in Oregon, so he was rarely around. Besides having a place with lots of room and dependable heat and doors that didn't blow open and pipes that didn't freeze, her creaky twin bed was history. She now had a double futon, and I was eager to get to know it.

My spirits were flying as she drove us from the airport into the Chugach Mountain foothills toward Bear Valley, my left hand on her knee, her right hand on mine. Then the season's first snow began to fall.

"Oh, man, it just started snowing," she said, leaning toward the dashboard, gripping the top of the steering wheel with both hands.

"Really? Is it dumping or just flurries?"

"It's snowing pretty good. Big, fluffy flakes. I've got my studded tires on so no worries."

My body reacted on a cellular level, the way it would have before. *Ooooh, yes! Let the ski season begin!* Fresh snow, like a fresh run of sockeyes plowing upriver, was a call to action, and I'd never failed to respond to that call. The initial excitement quickly faded as it occurred to me that had I not crossed paths with that bear, I would have been grabbing my skis, my pack, my avalanche beacon, and my dog, and we would have been heading off to the snowfields and glaciers in the backcountry. Me and Maya, we would have been out there. I turned my head away as if to look out the window. Amber pulled up to her place, shut off her engine, and turned in her seat to look at me.

"Are you okay?"

I nodded. I opened the truck door and got out. As I did, I felt crystals the size of Corn Flakes land on my face. I took a step, then stopped and listened. Snowflakes piling on top of each other was my favorite form of silence. I stood there in the newly fallen snow, arms stiff at my side, the corners of my mouth battened down tight.

Amber offered her arm, I took hold, and she guided me inside. She opened a bottle of red wine and poured us each a glass, then went into the master bathroom, a place of earth-tone tiles, mismatched towels, and a roomy Jacuzzi. She opened up the hot-water faucet, poured in a shot of bubble bath, and started filling the tub. When it was ready, she led me to it. Our clothes hit the floor, I climbed in, and she climbed in behind me. She massaged my neck, arms, and shoulders. She wrapped her arms around me and held me tight against her chest. With my ducts obliterated no tears could fall, but I cried. I cried with my entire body. And I cried a long time.

Of all the letting go I had to do, the most pressing was having my tragedy be my identity. "Life is 10 percent what happens to you and 90 percent how you deal with it," as the saying goes. Despite all I'd lost, I was grateful I was still able to be grateful.

I was grateful to have experienced sight for the first twenty-five years of my life. I was grateful for the vivid memories that were mine to keep. Like diving into the Sea of Cortez in the middle of the night amid bioluminescence, and for a mind-blowing hour cavorting about in firefly soup. Like floating through a cave in New Zealand with thousands of glowworms dripping from the ceiling like beads of luminous dew. Like watching Alaska's summer sun slip below the horizon, electrify the clouds in pinks and blues, then rise again on nights I was so energized by the light that I'd forget to go to sleep.

I thought of a coworker from long ago who had seen so little with his own eyes. After returning from Malaysia to Cincinnati and graduating from high school there, I had taken a job as a street sweeper, picking up trash and cleaning up after problem drinkers' overindulgence. My workmate was supporting his family that way. Kenny had been born and raised in the city, had never ventured beyond it, and was the type of man who'd be scared of a deer. I would show up for work on Monday mornings and regale him with tales of climbing and caving at the Red River Gorge. He couldn't imagine it.

"You be hanging out there in the woods and stuff? Oh lordy, that's some crazy shit. I'd be pissin' my pants."

By twenty-five, I had seen more extraordinary things than most people have the opportunity to see in a lifetime, from the Great Wall of China to manta rays while swimming off a boat in Baja, nothing but manta rays above, below, and on both sides of me as far as I could see.

So now what? There were the Erik Weihenmayers of the world, blind people who do the seemingly undoable, in his case acrobatic skydiving, long-distance biking, and climbing Mt. Everest. Post blindness, I did a little telemark skiing and sea kayaking. I went rock climbing at Pinnacles National Monument and backpacking in the Sierras and around Big Sur. But I was no Weihenmayer. Those weren't the kinds of goals I had in mind for myself. After so many years on the go, I figured it was time for me to learn the art of being still.

For years I had been questioning what I had to offer the world besides boosting the economy by frequenting outdoor gear-head shops. The question burned deeper by my final year at Prescott, with a cathartic moment in the Tetons during a backcountry ski course with Scott McGee of the Professional Ski Instructors of America National Nordic team. One night at the lodge where our group was staying, my classmates and I assembled after dinner for an evening program. We sat on sofas and stretched out on the floor in long-john tops, polar-fleece pants, and down booties, and sipped tea and hot cocoa as our guest speaker, Scott Wood of Brigham Young University-Idaho, spoke to us about the value of adventure. Woven into his talk was the story of one of his former students, Suzie Francis, from a school trip into Arches National Park years before.

He told us how Suzie had made it her goal to treat the other students on that trip the way Christ would treat them, and how she'd endeared herself to everyone through her efforts. The second day in, one of the students found a small, secret cave, its entry obscured by brush, and they all went to investigate. Inside, Suzie buried herself in the sand like a kid at the beach. When it was time to go, she got up, shook herself off, and headed out.

Suzie died in a car accident that fall. Speaking at her funeral, Wood told us, was one of the hardest things he'd ever done. He returned to that area the next year with a new group of students, remembered the secret cave, and almost dropped to his knees when he saw Suzie's imprint still there, as if she'd just risen from the sand. Several of her friends were on that trip. They had a group cry and shared thoughts on how the way she'd lived her life had left a lasting imprint on theirs.

I was so moved by the story that after the session I skied off into the night, found a spot off the trail where I was sure I was alone, stabbed my poles into the snow, leaned into them, stared up at the moonlight filtered through treetops and sobbed. The story drove home how unpredictable life is, its potential to end without notice, and how there's only so much time to put it to good use. I pulled out my bandana, dried my eyes, stuffed it into my back pocket, and skied a couple of miles before heading back to the lodge. I crawled into my sleeping bag that night knowing I wanted to use my time on this planet to do something meaningful and lasting, to leave my own imprint in the sand.

Then along came the bear. Surviving the unsurvivable brought clarity. The old Dan was gone. The new one was a work in progress. I'd fought for this second chance and wasn't about to squander it.

One good thing to come of my tragedy was the bear bringing my biological father back into my life. Steve and his family lived in Salinas, a forty-minute drive from Arboleda, and we had been getting to know each other since my return to California. He had a doctorate in psychology, and had devoted much of his career to working with severely damaged kids. Maybe it was in my genes, but I was drawn to that kind of work. After a lot of soul-searching and talks with Lee Hagmeier, I decided to go back to school, to get a master's degree in social work at the University of Alaska. I wanted to learn how to help others navigate through tragedies of their own.

At the same time I was making the decision to go back to school, I was also facing a much riskier one, a decision with the potential to alter my future in either constructive or destructive ways. At the urging of many, my family and I had looked into filing a lawsuit for negligence against the state and federal agencies responsible for managing the area where I was mauled. The way we saw it, the policies and procedures, or lack of them, had created a dangerous situation at the Russian River for people as well as bears. Although there had been efforts to deal with the bear-magnet buildup of salmon carcasses along the Russian and Kenai rivers, they failed to go far enough. An increasing number of bears were using the area as a buffet line and teaching their young to do the same. You don't need a degree in wildlife biology to know that nothing good could come of that.

Conflicts between people and bears had escalated in the month leading up to my attack, including that fisherman who shot and killed a sow that charged him, in essence killing all three of her young cubs, too, since they ended up having to be euthanized. According to Craig Medred, who covered my mauling and its aftermath for the *Anchorage Daily News*, at one point thirteen bears were counted within sight of the Russian River ferry crossing, not far from where John and I had been fishing. "According to wildlife officials who have worked on the ground here for decades," Medred wrote, "no one in the past 25 years has seen this many bears at one time near the confluence of the Kenai and Russian rivers."

It was only after I was mauled that officials took aggressive action by closing the trails and riverbanks to nighttime fishing for more than a month, cracking down on anglers leaving food, coolers, and fish stringers unattended, and bouncing rubber bullets off brazen bears' butts.

Having the resources to make my life work would have taken a load off since at the time I didn't know if I'd be able to make a decent living. But money was not the sole motivation. A lawsuit had the potential to change management practices and perhaps prevent someone else from being mauled and bears from being shot. We found an attorney willing to take the case, but he warned me that it was going to be a rough ride, especially in Alaska where juries are disinclined to side against nature. Did I really want to spend a year or two or possibly more bogged down in a lawsuit? It was going to be an arduous process, and the public and the media would surely have a field day with me. I could just hear it: "What's he trying to do, sue the bear?"

The last thing I wanted was to be the laughingstock of Alaska. And I sure didn't want to drag Amber through it. Although we felt we had a strong case, I decided it wasn't worth it. I wanted to leave it all behind. I wanted to move my life forward, to move beyond the bear.

But first, I needed to feel better. Time would do its part, although the numbness in my face and the phantom pains in my eyes would probably be with me the rest of my life. I was still taking bomber antibiotics as a precaution against the MRSA that had taken up residence in me. I was sick of the constant itching. I was sick of feeling nauseous, sick of the spontaneous puking, once in the middle of a parking lot that came on so suddenly, I was mid-stride when I hurled. If I took the drugs indefinitely, they would hold the MRSA at bay. If I quit, I'd run the risk of a flare-up, of it spreading into my bloodstream, and possibly even killing me. I weighed my options. I had a life to get on with. I would take my chances. I was done with antibiotics.

Next, if anything was to come of this imprint-in-the-sand business, I needed to learn how to be a blind man. I needed to adapt the skills I had to life in the dark. I needed to learn how to make my way around a city, how to pay my own bills, and how to make my own peanut butter sandwich without mutilating the bread. I needed to learn ways of telling the difference between Blistex and Super Glue, Listerine and Mr. Clean, a piece of chocolate and a piece of Ex-Lax. The time had come for me to make my way to a school for the blind.

Jeremy Grinkey, my friend and caretaker at Arboleda, 2006.

I got a new set of prosthetic eyes, my second pair, in 2012.

In 2010, I returned to the Living Skills Center, now the
Hatlen Center for the Blind, to visit my friends, staff
members Arif Syed, Ron Hideshima, and Samir Shaibi.

CHAPTER 18

Blackbeard and the Blindies

Lee Hagmeier liked to say that he was the first blind person he'd ever met. The same was true for me, but that was about to change. After shopping around for a school for the blind, I decided on the Living Skills Center for the Visually Impaired in San Pablo, California, now called the Hatlen Center for the Blind.

I liked the school's size, only sixteen students at a time. I like that it had virtually no classrooms, no sign out front announcing its presence, and no indulging of those used to having others do for them what they were capable of doing for themselves. Committed to teaching students to live in the world rather than being sheltered from it, the center offered full immersion, with eight double-occupancy apartments for students, one for the night manager, two for offices, and another for a state-of-the-art, adaptive technology lab. These twelve apartments were part of a three-story, seventy-five-unit complex of sighted, working-class people and families. Rather than students going to the instructors, the instructors came to the students, working with them in their own apartments, teaching everything from how to cook, to how to clean a bathroom, to how to manage finances. Normally, it takes about a year to achieve a high level of independence. I was way too anxious to get back to Amber to stay that long. The center was willing to work with me at my own pace on an accelerated plan.

That fall, I packed up what I'd need for an undetermined length of stay. The apartment was furnished so I brought only the essentials—clothes, bedding, a French-press coffee maker, my laptop, my stereo, my guitar, a sixteen-track mixing board for recording music, and a couple of microphones in case there were any other musicians around. Brian and I loaded my things into boxes and carried them out to the back of my truck. Once everything was shoved in, I slammed closed the topper and felt my way to the passenger door, trailing my fingers alongside the truck. I swung the door open, Maya hopped in, and I climbed in after her, giving her a little hip check since she still wasn't used to me sitting in her seat. She crawled back into the extended cab with a snort. Brian slid behind the wheel, started the engine, and headed down the canyon to deliver me to the next chapter of my life.

We arrived in San Pablo in late afternoon on the Sunday before my first day of class. We had toured the place the week before, so we knew where we were going and had already picked up the keys. Arms loaded, we began the first of three trips up two flights of stairs to my third-floor apartment, with Brian shuffling his feet so I could follow with my ears. Before heading up with our last load, I let Maya out of the truck to do a couple of laps around the parking lot, which I later heard about from the building's management due to a strict no-pets policy. She'd be staying with Jeremy at Arboleda, along with her buddy Cloey, but I'd be seeing her on weekend visits. I crouched down to have a word with her.

"Don't you be giving Jeremy any trouble, you hear me, girl? No flying jump kisses unless by request. And no messing with the chickens. Got it?"

She licked my face and wagged her entire back end. I hugged her neck, then opened the passenger door. She hopped inside. I cupped her head in my hands, planted a kiss on her snout, and made sure her tail was out of the way before shutting the door.

I'd already met my roommate, an eighteen-year-old who'd been blind since birth, but he wasn't around that afternoon so we had the place to ourselves. We put away the groceries we'd bought along the way, and set up my stereo in my room, where it was back to sleeping in a twin bed for me. My apartment and its furnishings looked a bit tired, Brian told me, the walls as though they hadn't seen a fresh coat of paint since before I was born. Not that any of that mattered to me. We headed out to the back balcony to check out the scene from there. I heard sirens in the distance. I heard car brakes squealing, a woman screeching at her kids, an animated conversation in Spanish, a dog going ballistic. Leaning over the balcony railing, sunglasses flipped over the top of his head, Brian described my view.

"Not much privacy," he said. "Your neighbors can see everything that goes on out here. You're overlooking the parking lot and the Dumpsters, and I can see a liquor store and pawnshop down the street. Looks a little rough out there, Dan."

"Niiice," I said with a nod. So much for my sheltered existence. I'd wanted real world and I was going to get it.

We settled into plastic lawn chairs, popped open a couple of beers, and sat out there on the balcony taking in the sounds of the fidgety neighborhood. When Brian finished his beer, he sat a moment, a restless foot tapping against the leg of his chair. He sighed and stood up.

"I should probably head out," he said, both eager to get out of there and reluctant to go. We hugged goodbye. "Take it easy, man. If you need anything just give a call. Good luck with everything."

I didn't walk him out since I didn't know if I could find my way back. I stood on the balcony, gripping the railing, savoring the cool East Bay breeze. I heard the clank of the metal security gate, the opening and closing of the door of my truck, the start of its engine, the emptiness as it pulled away. Once the rumble of my truck merged into traffic, I turned, went inside, and with a hand out in front of me at my waist, slowly shuffled my way to my bedroom. I put on some Grateful Dead, made up my bed, and began pulling clothes out of my duffel bag and putting them into drawers and on shelves in the closet. After that, I put my things away in the bathroom, then the kitchen. When my boxes were empty, I sat on an unfamiliar couch in an unfamiliar living room in an unfamiliar city, picked up my guitar, and went to a familiar place in my mind.

My foray into the world of the blind, its language, culture, and politics would begin the next morning with a nine o'clock knock on my apartment door.

"You must be Dan Bigley." Her voice sounded warm and enthusiastic, which instantly put me at ease. I reached out to shake her hand. "Welcome, Dan. We're happy to have you here. Are you ready to get started?"

I was more than ready. This first day of my first class meant I was one step closer to getting back to Alaska, back to Amber.

I wasn't a stranger in a strange land for long. At twenty-seven, I was quite a bit older than the other students, who were closer to my roommate's age and had never lived on their own. Before the end of my first week, I'd become fast friends with two of the center's staff members, Arif Syed, who was sighted, and Samir Shaibi, who was not, both of whom were wicked musicians. At the time, Arif was the office manager, a laid-back jack-of-all-trades with a tidy black beard and bachelor's degree in environmental science from UC Berkeley. Samir was the after-hours supervisor, a fearless and charismatic former student with retinitis pigmentosa, a genetic condition that had slowly cinched down his field of vision until all he had left was about what one would see looking through a straw in a room full of smoke. I had invited Arif up first, to help me eat my homework, a chicken-and-rice casserole I'd made for my cooking class. He talked up Samir, so I invited them both next time. Out came the guitars, and we were a trio from then on. We were Blackbeard and the Blindies.

We shared meals, nipped a little Johnny Walker, and jammed together night after night, sometimes so late it was rough getting going the next morning. On weekends, I would escape to Arboleda, and now and then they'd come along for more of the same. We recorded a homemade CD of our Arboleda sessions with a Prescott friend, Evan Raymond, on bass, percussion, and harmonies. Blackbeard and the Blindies played for staff and students, and for whoever could hear us through the walls. We even got a little gig at an outdoor cafe in Sacramento that drew a contingent from the center, as well as my parents.

When I wasn't hanging out after hours or jamming with my two newest best friends, I was working my tail off. I was upgrading my cane skills by several notches. I was learning talking software like Window-Eyes and Kurzweil that would allow me to do Internet searches, balance my checkbook, use email and read the newspaper. I was learning how to deal with conveyor belts at grocery-store checkout lines, how to avoid product-placement booby traps, how to sign my name at the bottom of a check. I was learning how attaching Braille labels at home could help me tell ground pork from ground turkey, one medicine bottle from another, liquid laundry detergent from Liquid-Plumr.

Ron Hideshima, an accessible-technology instructor who'd lost his sight at the same age as me—in a car accident in Japan during a trip home from the states to be with his dying father—worked extra hours to get me up to speed on blind technologies and other wizardry I'd need for graduate school. I learned just enough Braille to realize the time and commitment it would take to become proficient, which made me appreciate even more the challenges Lee Hagmeier was up against in his day. I also picked up simple, no-tech tricks for managing mundane, day-to-day tasks like how to match my socks—buy all the same type and color, or connect them with a safety pin before tossing them into the wash. To tell shampoo from conditioner, I'd put a rubber band around one and not the other. To keep track of money, I'd fold my fives in half widthwise, tens in half lengthwise, and twenties and larger into thirds, and keep each in a separate compartment of a tri-fold wallet.

I'd been so intimidated at first, so afraid I'd be way behind all the others, most of whom had spent their whole lives blind or able to see only in dabs, blobs, or shards of shape, color, and light. Over time, I found the opposite to be true. Having had sight, I had a lot more awareness, a lot more understanding of the way the world looks, and therefore how to move and act within it. It soon became clear to me that too many parents underestimate, and even undermine, the capabilities of their blind children. When the time comes to make their own way in the world, they arrive at adulthood with a debilitating lack of confidence, independence, and will. One of the stories floating around the center was that of a man in his fifties who'd lived his whole life with his mother, and when she died, he didn't even know how to dial a phone. To us, that amounted to child abuse.

As I worked with my mobility instructor and a cane, my world gradually grew bigger and wider. My first challenge was to find my way around the apartment complex, then out to the street. With jackhammers, car horns, and faulty mufflers cluttering the airwaves, crossing my first busy intersection was heart-thumping, and every screech, squeal, and whoosh of traffic had me bracing for impact. I practiced over and over, each day going farther and farther, with my ears and cane as proxies for my eyes. Initially my instructor was at my side, then three feet behind me, then, as I gained confidence and skill, a half-block away until finally I was on my own.

My first solo trip to a place I'd never been before was to a fish market near Berkeley that I found based on directions I took over the phone. After a series of street crossings and a couple of bus transfers, I walked inside, did a mental fist pump, and walked out. I hadn't felt that much freedom since the bear. My instructor, who got there on her own, was waiting for me out on the sidewalk.

"You've got it!" she said. "Great job."

Over time I got good enough to make it all the way to Gilroy on Friday nights, a three-hour journey that involved a ten-minute walk from my apartment to a bus stop, a bus ride to a Bay Area Rapid Transit (BART) station, a squeeze through a ticket-accessible turnstile, a trip up an escalator to a platform, a BART ride into one side of San Francisco and out the other, a walk from that station to a Caltrain station, and then another train ride through San Jose to Gilroy, where Jeremy would be waiting to drive me back to Arboleda.

Heading out for the weekend, I'd sometimes have Jeremy pick me up in Fremont instead, which involved a transfer on BART but not a Caltrain ride. Getting from the Fremont station out to the street was the trickiest part. I had it wired, though my technique wasn't exactly graceful since it including bumping my cane, or even my shoulder, into this and that, here and there, as a way of orienting myself. I'd step off the train and wait at the platform until the rush of people had passed. Once the place had quieted down, I'd work my way forward until I tapped into a long row of seats, then I'd veer left until I found a wall that I'd walk along, at the end of which I'd hear the escalators, pull a U-turn around the wall, and step onto an escalator heading down to the station's lower level. At the bottom, I'd step off, work my way across a large open area until I'd tap into a glass display case in the center. Then I'd work my way to the left, pass a customer service desk, then veer right until I found the exit turnstiles. I'd go through, walk up a set of stairs to the street, and make my way along the curb to a bench where I'd sit and wait for my ride to Arboleda.

Learning to get around independently includes learning how to deal with those who are certain you're incapable of doing so. To find the door of the bus, sometimes you first have to find the side of the bus, and people have a hard time watching that. On one of my trips to meet Jeremy, I got off BART as usual, bumped into my row of chairs, as usual, and veered left. Everything was going fine. Just as I was about to tap into my wall, I felt a hand grip my shoulder from behind and yank me back.

"Whoa! Hey, I'm okay. Thanks, I'm fine. I know where I'm going."

The man did not speak English.

I collected myself and continued on, with footsteps trailing me not more than a couple of steps behind. Working my way along the wall, I got off course, distracted by my stalker, and bumped into an unfamiliar row of chairs. The man again grabbed my shoulder and aimed me in the direction he assumed I wanted to go.

I turned to face him. "It's cool, man. It's good. I don't need help. No help. Thank you." I pointed to myself, gave a thumbs-up, turned, and continued on my way. As I caned toward the escalators, the man was right there steering me by my shirt. By then I was fuming. I whipped around to face him. "Hey, leave me alone! No. More. Help."

I whipped back around and rode down the escalator. I could feel him right behind me. I got off, walked faster than usual toward the display case I needed to bump into to orient myself in the large, open space, and sure enough, just before I reached it, he grabbed my shoulder.

I yanked out of his grip and whipped around to face him with my cane raised above my head. "Dude! Leave me the fuck alone!" I hollered. I turned to face the customer service desk. "Please," I pleaded, "could somebody tell this guy to get away from me? That I don't need his help?" Hearing his footsteps scurry away was a tremendous relief.

Over time I would get better at dealing with situations like that, of well-meaning people, clueless about the ways of the blind, trampling my dignity. People were constantly pushing me this way and pulling me that, as if I were some kind of wind-up toy about to march off a cliff. It happened so often, that if I didn't learn to shrug it off, I would have become the very thing I never wanted to be—an angry man.

After spending Christmas with her family in Minnesota, Amber came to see me in time for us to celebrate another New Year's Eve together, a second chance at getting it right. The plan was for her to fly into San Francisco, rent a car, and drive to the Living Skills Center to see the place that was giving me back my independence. From there, we'd spend time at Arboleda, play in the city, and visit my folks in Carmel. Everyone at the center knew all about Amber. I spoke of her constantly. "Amber's going to love this," I'd tell my cooking instructor while making eggs Benedict or caramelizing onions for a New York Strip with Burgundy Sauce. "Can't wait to take Amber here," I'd tell my mobility instructor after a successful navigation to my favorite Mexican restaurant. Everyone knew about our late-night calls and my plans to move back to Alaska to be with her. So when she came to visit, I wanted to show her off, I admit it, and they wanted to scope her out, they joked, to see if she was good enough for "our Dan." But by the time she arrived, it was after hours. Disappointed, I figured everyone had gone home for the night.

"We should pop into the office a moment, see if anyone's still here," I said as we passed by on our way to my apartment.

We popped in. Amber, dressed in blue jeans and a snug button-up sweater, stopped in her tracks. I could practically hear her face flush and her shoulders stiffen. Just about the entire staff was lined up waiting to meet her, every one of them grinning.

"Hello, Amber. Welcome. Dan has told us so much about you. It's *so* nice to finally meet you."

CHAPTER 19

Back to the Future

I wrapped things up at the Living Skills Center in early February with a round of hugs for the house and the promise to keep in touch. It had taken a little over six months to get where I wanted to be in my quest for independence. From then on, life would be my teacher.

Soon after I'd moved from the center back to Arboleda, Amber flew down for another visit around Valentine's Day. I'd considered making her a romantic dinner, eager to show her how far my cooking skills had progressed from my pre-blind-school repertoire of microwaved frozen burritos and pizza delivery. Anything I could do for her versus the opposite, I figured, was a point in my favor. Candlelight was out since the risk-reward ratio of open flames doesn't pan out for a blind guy. Same for wine glasses. It's like you're just asking for it, and fine wine served in mason jars just doesn't cut it. The clincher was when my first solo practice run of the dish I wanted to make her, the New York Strip with Burgundy Sauce, came out more like Boot Leather Strip with Disaster Sauce.

I took her to Carmel instead, to one of my favorite sushi places, Robata's Grill and Sake Bar, a traditional Japanese inn-style restaurant with paper lanterns, a low ceiling, and a rustic wood interior. Due to poor planning, I called too late to get a reservation, so we were ushered into the overflow section, which couldn't have been better planning since we ended up with the whole room to ourselves. Amber was stunning that night in a silky, black dress with spaghetti straps and a diagonal hemline that started its plunge just below her left knee. She outclassed the hell out of me in the browns, beiges, ivories, and other dull-but-safe colors I'd taken to wearing to minimize fashion accidents. My black flip-flops didn't help my cause, either. As I often did in those days, I also wore my amulet, the prayer beads blessed by the Dalai Lama that my massage therapist, Ilene Connelly, had given me.

We ordered vegetable tempura and maguro, hamachi, unagi, and rainbow rolls with yellowtail by the pairs, and just enough hot sake to make everything we said seem funny. "Sake me, baby!" we'd say after draining our tiny cups, with each request for a refill more hilarious than the last.

I'd mastered chopsticks during my middle school years in Malaysia, and was still good enough to wield them in the dark. So I picked up a piece of sushi, and dipped it in soy sauce fortified with enough wasabi to deliver the desirable nasal burn. The moment it hit my mouth, I grasped the edge of the table with both hands, and turned my head to the side. "OH yeah . . . Oh-o-o-O. Whaaoh!" I gasped as I whipped my head back to center. I thumped the table twice with a fist. "Damn! Whoo, boy. That was a good one."

Amber laughed, then dipped her own piece, popped it into her mouth, gasped, and squished her nose against the palm of her hand until she was able to breathe.

As contemporary Japanese flute played softly in the background, it hit me all we'd been through to get to this point of spending our first Valentine's Day together. There were still many unknowns in our relationship, but I was living in the moment that night, and my heart felt like it might split at the seams. I leaned across the table, reached for her hands, brought them to my lips, and kissed them. Still holding on, I lowered them, rested my forearms on the table, and leaned in close. And then I just said it:

"I'm so in love with you."

"Mm, well, I . . ."

"It's okay, you really don't have to say anything. I don't mean to put you on the spot. It's just that I really want you to know how I feel. So there."

"Well, thank you. I'm just kind of funny about . . ."

"No, really. It's okay . . . I mean it. Hey, you're slacking. My sake cup is hurtin' over here. Sake me, baby."

"No, you sake me."

"That could land you in the burn unit."

We laughed as Amber refilled us both.

"Cheers," I said raising my cup.

"Cheers," she said clinking hers against mine.

I drained my cup, set it back down on the table with a clunk, and visualized her silky dress in a heap on my bedroom floor.

—◦—

As eager as I was to get back up north to be with her, I gave myself one more month at Arboleda to say goodbye in a way I'd been unable to say goodbye to Alaska after the bear forced me to go. I savored every day, beginning with my early morning songbird recitals over coffee, all the way through the great-horned-owl hooting matches back and forth across the canyon before I'd turn in at night. I thanked and said goodbye to everyone who'd helped me along my healing journey. I thanked and said goodbye to all my favorite trees and trails and benches tucked away in the thickets. I relished the time I had left with Jeremy; his being there for me had been a godsend.

Besides all the medical duties, appointments, and errands, he helped me dodge countless head bonks, swept up my trail of broken glass, and took me to shows, from Los Lobos to The Dead. Even before I was blind, I appreciated how the two of us could sit reading books together for hours without the need to talk.

During my final days at Arboleda, my old roommate from Girdwood came for a visit, to play music and help me pack for my move back up. Jamie pulled boxes from the backs of closets, unfolded their tops, and pulled stuff out for me to sort through, much of it untouched since the move down. We pawed through my outdoor gear, tools, books, CDs, and household this and that. What I wanted to send north, we set aside to be packed into my truck, which my stepdad would drive up the Alaska Highway. The rest went into a Salvation Army pile.

"You got a ton of photos here," Jamie said in that deep, subwoofer voice of his while mindlessly scratching the back of his unruly head of hair. He'd pulled a large Ziplock bagful from a box and sat there waving it back and forth awaiting my response.

"Just toss them," I said.

"Huh? Are you sure? I don't know, Dan, you might want to hold onto these."

"It's not like I'm ever going to look at them again. That's all they're good for, to look at. I don't need them. I don't want them. Really, they're pretty much worthless to me."

"Ahh, well, okay. But mind if I take a few?"

"Take all you want. Have them."

Jamie sat at the dining room table sorting through my life one shot at a time. He weeded out the ones with lousy lighting and those that seemed to have been snapped during some kind of seismic event. He kept the good ones from our Prescott and Girdwood days, including one of my favorites—me on telemark skis with a goofy grin on my face sailing over a ski jump I'd built in the front yard after a big snowfall in Prescott. The rest he set aside for my brother, for which I'd be grateful down the road.

As my departure day drew near, I was both ready and not. After a year and a half in California, moving on would be like shoving off from the safety of my own little island into a sea of unknowns. To get my life back I had to leave this refuge, where stress was banned, music was imperative, and nothing was expected of me other than to heal. I had to leave what had become comfortable and familiar, as well as those who'd been there for me day and night to talk me down from my anxiety attacks, to take me where I needed to go, to let me know my T-shirt was on inside out or that the potato salad I'd pulled from the back of the fridge was green and fuzzy.

What worried me most was my relationship with Amber. She was the major motivation for moving back up. We had hardly dated before the bear, and after, the little time we'd spent together had been on vacation. What if things didn't work out between us? I had no Plan B.

While I was fretting down in California, she was wrestling with fears of her own up north. "It's getting closer; Dan will be moving here soon," she wrote in the journal I'd given her at Christmas. "I am excited and nervous. Things are going pretty well and I'm falling deeper and deeper in love with him. Who'd a thunk it? It is challenging, though. I think I like the phone relationship so much because I totally forget that he can't see."

She did not elaborate on that, nor did she commit to writing the depth of her doubts. I know now a lot of questions were gnawing at her, like, what if having a disabled boyfriend got old? What if she grew to resent doing all the driving, explaining all the nonverbal jokes, dealing with all it would take for me to get through graduate school? What if my emotional trauma and anxiety attacks wore her down? What if she fell out of love with me? She'd fallen out of love before. But in my case, how do you live with yourself knowing you've hurt someone who's already been hurt beyond comprehension? Loving someone is a huge responsibility, and she wasn't sure she was up for the additional weight. She already had a full life—a challenging job as a counselor for Alaska Native high-school students, some straight from tiny, remote villages, a job that had her dealing with everything from college goals to pregnancy, domestic violence, and suicide. She had a lot of friends to keep up with and a high-maintenance dog with selective hearing and an unsavory attraction to the neighborhood chickens. She was afraid she'd have so much on her plate she couldn't handle a blind boyfriend. On top of all this, she had a case of garden-variety commitment phobia, which, given my track record with her before the bear, I had coming to me.

"It's just that I've been single for so long," she told me during one of our calls. "I'm not used to having anyone else to answer to."

As much as I wanted her to feel she could tell me anything, that was not fun to hear. What she was saying without saying it was that she was afraid I was going to slow her down or limit her freedom or take up too much of her time and space. I understood all that, but I can't say I liked it. I needed to prove to her that I could make it on my own. More importantly, I needed to prove it to myself. I wanted her to be my lover not my caretaker. So the plan was for me to rent my own place, for her to keep hers up in Bear Valley, for us to continue to date, and to see where things went from there.

Living at my cabin in Bear Valley was out. I'd be relying on public transportation, and it was way beyond range. I needed a place within walking distance of a bus stop, a place that would let me have Maya. A month before my move up, Amber found me one—the top floor of a two-story house on five wooded acres, a property shared with three rental trailers off Huffman Road in South Anchorage.

One thing I didn't have to worry about, at least for the time being, was how to make things work financially. I'd become eligible for insurance benefits at work only days before the bear, and I would eventually push the edge of a one-million-dollar policy. Life insurance, also through work, provided a couple hundred dollars a month in disability pay. Since I was unemployed, I also received a monthly check from Social Security Disability Insurance. Plus I had tenants in my cabin, so I had rent coming in. The Division of Vocational Rehabilitation would pay my school expenses as long as I was going for the express purpose of pursuing gainful employment. Other services would also help me along my way.

The official restart of my life began at the beginning of spring in a place that felt nothing like it. I landed in Anchorage with two bags and my dog, half stoked, half apprehensive about starting over in a slippery, sprawling city with many weeks to go before shedding its winter coat of snow and ice, a city I'd once known well but now couldn't tell one end from the other. The morning after a steamy reunion with Amber at her house, she delivered me and Maya to my new place, a twenty-minute drive downhill from her own.

"You might want to brace yourself," she said as we drew near. "Your driveway is kind of insane." I held onto the oh-shit handle above the door as we jostled and slammed through a minefield of potholes, ice crunching beneath the wheels of her truck. "Your house is definitely an upgrade from your Girdwood place," she told me, "but the property wouldn't win any landscaping awards."

"Do you mind describing it?"

"Okay, so your address is at the top of the driveway spray-painted onto a half-sheet of plywood. There are a couple of driveways off the main one that shoot off to two of the trailer houses. The third one is right across from your house, and it's classic. Lawn ornaments everywhere—dead vehicles, appliances, and who knows what beneath the snow. It basically looks like your neighbors have one of those perpetual garage sales going."

"Lovely," I laughed.

"Oh, and there's an industrial-size Dumpster at the end of the main driveway."

To me Dumpster translated to bear magnet. "Guess I'll need to carry a shotgun when I empty the trash," I joked.

Amber parked in front of the house, and I let Maya out to explore. The distant drone of the Seward Highway, I noted, would take some getting used to. Amber then guided me up the steps, across the porch, and into the top floor of a house so full of emptiness it made my ears ring. The only things in the place were my mattress and box spring, which Amber had reclaimed from a friend who'd held onto them for me.

After Amber showed me around, we started hitting the thrift stores, where over time we picked up a kitchen table and chairs, a couch, a dresser, and other odds and ends that would turn my bare space into a home. Using some of my Living Skills Center tricks, she helped me mark the settings on my appliances with those raised plastic dots meant for keeping cupboard doors from banging, and with adhesive Velcro cut into different shapes. We added a dot to the start button on the microwave, thin strips of Velcro to mark the various temperature settings on my stove, and another dot so I could tell how far to twist the dial on the washing machine. She helped me organize my clothes to minimize wardrobe disasters. Braille labels told me what was what in the cupboards. Obsessive-compulsive arrangement helped me find things in the fridge—condiments on this shelf, dairy on that, rubber band around the salad dressing, no rubber band around the barbecue sauce.

At Office Max, I bought an office chair and one of those build-it-yourself computer desks. We spent hours wrestling that thing, with me holding the parts in place while Amber screwed them together, alternating between laughing and swearing and laughing and teetering on the verge of winging the pile of "easy to assemble" body parts out the window. Only after it was fully assembled did we realize we'd built a ship in a bottle, that there was no way we'd ever get that beast out of the room without undoing all we'd just done. After that, there was nothing to do but pay my mattress a visit.

My game plan for the coming months was to take some time to adapt to this new life of mine and to work on my grad school application. I needed to get dialed into services offered by the Alaska Center for the Blind and Visually Impaired and the Division of Vocational Rehabilitation. I needed to get used to coming home to nobody but Maya. There was no end to all I needed to do. With Amber working all day, I had a lot of time to devote to such things. I didn't even have my guitar for the first couple of weeks, until my stepdad showed up with my truck.

After learning my way around my new place, I started learning my way around Anchorage using public transportation. Regular bus service would cover the basics, but there would be times I'd need to use AnchorRIDES, a shared, door-to-door van service for seniors and people with disabilities. First, I needed to be assessed to see if I qualified. AnchorRIDES picked me up and took me to headquarters, where I provided the required doctor's note verifying that I was blind, demonstrated I was capable of walking up all of three steps, and that

I could handle going up and down a ramp. I had arranged to use the service as my ride home, as well. After passing my assessment, I caned my way to a bench at the Anchorage Transit Center to wait for my departure. I waited and waited and waited. After about an hour, I caned my way back to the office to ask, "Did you guys forget about me?" Assured they hadn't, I caned my way back to my bench and waited some more. All told, I waited an hour and a half for my ride to show. It took another half hour after that to get home. How was this going to work for graduate school, I wondered. In California, public transportation was so well wired, I rarely waited more than ten minutes. Getting myself around Anchorage was going to be even harder than I'd thought.

Once I was more or less settled into my new place, I had some rounds to make. By then, Dr. Kallman had become a partner in Dr. Ellerbe's practice, and they invited me in for lunch with some of the staff I'd gotten to know during my outpatient days living in the hotel. Kallman greeted me with the kind of hug you'd expect of an old friend.

"You're the kind of guy who makes being a doctor worth it," he told me. "I feel blessed that I was the one on call that night."

I got a lump in my throat thinking of all the two of us had been through together and the impact we'd had on each other's lives. Ours, I knew, would be a lifelong bond and friendship.

I also returned to the intensive and progressive care units at Providence hospital. Everyone had been so good to me, from those who held my hand during painful procedures to the nurse who played guitar and sang at my bedside when I was still barely able to move. Amber and I were in the building for an appointment to address some stomach issues I'd developed, and decided on a whim to drop by to see if anyone was around who'd taken care of me.

At the security doors at the ICU, I explained who I was and why I was there, as my brother had on the worst day of his life nearly two years before. The doors clicked and swung open. We walked in.

"Why don't you wait here a moment and let me go see if I can find anyone who was around back then," the nurse said.

As word got around the unit, a few who remembered me gathered around near the nurses' station. I held tight to Amber's hand and tried not to choke up. I rocked back on my heels and started in.

"It's hard to know exactly what to say when thanking someone for helping save your life. 'Thank you' doesn't seem powerful enough." I paused a moment and lifted my chin, distracted by sounds that were way too familiar. I refocused and continued. "It's all because of your efforts that I'm even standing here. I just want you to know how much I appreciate everything you did for me, and for my family."

No one said a word for a moment. Then one of them spoke up.

"Thank you, Dan. So often we never hear from people once they leave here."

"We never know what happened to them," another said. "It's rare for a patient to come back to thank us. It really means a lot to us. So thank you for taking the time."

I wasn't done. I had to return to the Russian River to try to make peace with the place where I came so close to dying. Amber had three girlfriends visiting from Minnesota that summer who wanted to go fishing, so that's where we decided to take them. I wasn't looking forward to it, but if I wanted to move on it had to be done. I steeled myself, and made sure I brought my prayer beads along.

I'd spent so much time coming and going from Cooper Landing, I knew the way by heart. I knew exactly where we were at every major curve along the Sterling Highway. I knew we were approaching the turnoff to the Russian River Campground before the car started to slow. After winding through the campground, we pulled into the Grayling parking lot and I dug my fingernails into my knees. I sat quietly a moment before climbing out of the car. It was the same kind of bluebird day that one had been—T-shirt warm with just enough breeze to keep mosquitoes grounded. A riptide of memories started dragging me under. I shook them from my head. Amber's friends were there to have a good time, not to get caught up in my post-traumatic drama. As everyone geared up, I stood leaning against the car, facing the treetops, soaking up the sounds of fishing preparations—the swish of neoprene waders, the rattle of fishing poles, the pop of the cooler lid.

For once I wasn't interested in fishing. It was more important for me to speak with the land since obviously we hadn't parted on good terms. I loved the Russian too much to spend the rest of my life avoiding it. This would be a solo mission, not something I needed to share with any of the others. Not even Amber.

"You sure you're okay going down there?"

"I'm as sure as I'm ever going to be. I have to do this, you know."

"Okay, but if it gets to be too much, just say the word and we're out of here."

"I appreciate that, but I am ready for this."

"Well, if you change your mind . . ."

"I won't."

I suggested a hole upriver from the parking lot where she and her friends could avoid the hordes at The Sanctuary. As we clomped down the same set of stairs I'd been hauled up on a backboard two summers before, I struggled to find the balance between thinking too much and thinking too little. Walking toward the junction with Angler Trail, I could feel the thick brush closing in on me. A bear could pop out at any moment, but fear wasn't going to help me if that happened, and fear wasn't going to help me move forward in life. Besides, the statistical chances of being mauled twice in the same place had to be overwhelmingly in my favor. That's what I told myself, anyway.

We turned left at the junction, then headed upriver, as John and I had when we first backed away from the bear. My hands clenched into fists as we approached the spot where the bear came at me like a rocket. *Keep going, keep going, keep going.* A little farther, in the vicinity of where the bear had dragged me, my shoulders stiffened, my fingernails dug into my palms, and my heart took off in a sprint. *Don't think, just keep walking. Just walk on by.* I redirected my attention toward the chatter of the river. Just a few more steps, and ground zero was behind me.

When we reached the hole I had in mind, I found a spot to sit along the riverbank while Amber and her friends got after the reds. I rolled up my pant legs, unlatched my sandals, kicked them off, and baptized my feet in the current. I sat down, leaned against my pack, and kneaded the riverbank gravel with both hands, letting the sand and pebbles flow between my fingers. I felt around for some stones and plunked them one by one into the water.

Ker-plunk.

Ker-plunk.

Ker-plunk.

I pushed aside my pack and lay down flat on my back. With the sun warming my face and the Russian washing my feet, I listened to the river rush by and the rustle of leaves in the breeze. I lay there the rest of the afternoon feeling the earth alive and ancient beneath me, fingering my prayer beads.

I doubted I could ever make peace with that haunted patch of ground down the trail; what happened there was too horrific. What was important was to try. The more I walked by it, the less power it would have over me. I hoped someday to return to the exact spot with John and Jaha, to say a prayer and place flowers on my grave. That, I hoped, would be the moment all three of us could cast the bear out of our lives once and for all.

Lee Hagmeier had done a similar closing ceremony, only not until some forty years after his bear. He and Doug Dobyns, the childhood friend who was with him that day, had been bonded for life by what they'd been through together, one at the threshold of death, the other shouldering the burden of trying to keep his friend from passing through it. They were in Juneau at the same time for the first time since their "bear misadventure," as Lee calls it, and decided to return to the site together to confront what had happened and to carve their initials in a tree. *I'm still moving forward, thank you very much,* Lee thought as they approached the area. Ten years later, he would hold a reception in Juneau commemorating the fiftieth anniversary of his attack, to thank the people of his hometown for all their support through the years.

After my own bear misadventure, forty-four years after his, Lee started a ritual of calling me every year on the anniversary of my mauling to check in with me, to wish me well, and to remind me how lucky we both are to be alive.

While on this roll of tending to unfinished business, another issue I faced that summer was the need to deal with my cabin in Bear Valley. Since I'd never be able to live there it was time to let it go. With a heavy heart, I put a two-line, for-sale-by-owner ad in the classifieds. It wasn't going to be easy parting with the place, so it was important that it go to the kind of people who'd love it as much as I did. TJ and Audrey (Cotter) Miller were the ones. TJ was working on his master's degree in adult education at UAA and would later teach outdoor leadership there, and Audrey was in nursing school. They had exactly the same vision for the place that I'd had, to turn it into a real house and raise a family up there someday. They wouldn't just admire the view, they'd play in the mountains out the front door. Even though some guy offered to pay cash on the spot, I wanted those two to have it enough to do owner financing.

Heading home from the title company after closing, feeling a little low, Amber and I were wishing we'd suggested having a beer together when we pulled up behind them at a stop light. TJ got out of his truck and jogged back to our car. Amber rolled down her window.

"You guys want to go have a beer or something?" he asked.

We laughed. "We were just thinking the same thing."

They followed us back to my place, we cracked some beers, and that was the beginning of what would become a deep friendship. As it's turned out, I've never had to say goodbye to my cabin. Amber and I have been up there countless times for dinners and jam sessions and walks with the dogs. And New Year's Eve at the Millers' has become a tradition. Once again, I felt the universe was looking after me.

I felt it even more strongly as Amber started spending more and more time at my place. It surprised us both how quickly we grew closer in ways that transcended my blindness and the disarray beneath my glasses. She'd show up with her pajamas, toothbrush, and a change of clothes. Then she'd show up with all that plus Hobbit. It got to where she wouldn't go back to her own house for several days at a time. When she did go home, it was just to do laundry or grab some more clothes. Then she started doing laundry at my house. Then she started stockpiling her clothes.

"Would you mind if I brought some things over to keep here in your closet?" she asked.

I just grinned at her. "We could probably save a bunch of money if you'd just move in down here."

Practically speaking, she already had. But she was ready to make it official, and gave notice up the hill. The more mornings we woke up together, the more love had trumped her doubts, until it drowned out the noise in her head.

"There's no way of knowing what's going to happen down the road," she said of her decision, as if I, of all people, didn't profoundly know that. "So why not go with what feels right?"

"I hear ya."

"Whatever happens between us, at least we can say we gave it our best shot, don't you think?"

"No question. That's all anyone can do. Even after what happened, I can't see going through life never taking risks. There's more than one way not to be alive."

Having Amber off during summer break, from early June until school started in September, was exactly what we needed to cinch it. We crammed as much fun as we could into that summer, hitting all the fairs, music festivals, and bonfires we could manage. We danced around our living room. We danced around the living rooms of others. We danced in the rain and danced under the midnight sun. And somehow, when Michael Franti & Spearhead came to town, I ended up dancing with Franti—if you could call it that.

Before Franti's Bear Tooth show, he'd performed for the kids and staff of my pre-bear employer, Alaska Children's Services. Jim Maley, head of the organization, a Deadhead from way back and a jam-band fan like me, must have told him my story because Franti recognized me up front by the stage. During his encore song, "Sometimes," he started tweaking the lyrics while bopping my way.

Sometimes, I feel like I could do anything,
Sometimes, I'm so alive, so alive.
Sometimes . . .

Amber nudged me. "Dan, he's right here in front of us."

Sometimes, sometimes, I sit in the dark alone,
Sometimes . . .

"Oh my god, he's singing to you, Dan. He's reaching out for you. Reach your hands up. Reach up. A little more to the left . . ."

I reached up, and Franti pulled me up on stage and wrapped me up in a huge hug. He spoke into my ear. "I know who you are, and I know what you've been through. Let's dance." So we started dancing, well, jumping up and down while hugging each together, anyway, looking like two guys who'd just won the lottery. The next thing I know we're at the mike and he's singing so I started singing, too—if you could call it singing. (Had I known, I would have skipped the tequila.) I probably sounded like Peter Boyle in *Young Frankenstein* attempting "Puttin' On the Ritz," but he didn't seem to care. A memorable scene was made more so when, singing and hopping about with my arms around Franti, my white cane went flying as if I were announcing to the crowd, "It's a miracle; I can see!"

Among other revelry that summer, Amber and I hiked in the Chugach Mountains, scrambling in steep sections on all fours while Maya and Hobbit jammed their noses down every pika hole within a quarter-mile radius. We strolled down the Homer Spit, shuffling our feet in the sand and listening to waves lap the shore. We stopped by the Salty Dawg Saloon, a classic Alaska watering hole carpeted in wood chips and wallpapered in dollar bills autographed with Sharpies. We camped along the pristine, cyan waters of Kenai Lake, where for the first time since the bear I threw my head back and howled at the moon.

It goes without saying Amber and I did a lot of fishing that summer. Halibut fishing in Resurrection Bay and salmon fishing along the Kenai Peninsula. By then Jaha was co-owner of a guiding business, Alaska Drift Away Fishing. He took Amber king fishing for the first time on his favorite river, the Kasilof, where she hooked into a magnum and was so excited she didn't mind that it got away. But it wasn't until my brother came for a visit and he and I took her fishing for reds that she began to understand my fishing obsession. We took her to that favorite spot on the Kenai River, the one John and I had fished earlier the day of the bear. At the time the daily limit was six per angler, and she and I were nailing them right and left, with Brian running back and forth between us, bonking them in the head and getting them onto stringers. We were hauling them in so fast, he couldn't keep up.

It was right about then that Amber and I started finishing each other's sentences. It was obvious to us and everyone around us that we made a great team. When Jeremy and Paige came to visit, they started calling us Danber. And when it was the two of us and our two dogs, we were Danber Mayobbit Biglevitz.

As the summer started winding down, Amber began thinking about going back to work and I got serious about my graduate-school application, but not before celebrating my birthday in late August. Birthdays take on a whole new significance when you've come so close to never having another one. As my twenty-eighth approached, I put some serious thought into how I wanted to honor it. I decided returning to the Brown Bear Saloon would be most fitting. Although the name is unfortunate, it was the perfect place to celebrate, not only that I was able to have another birthday, but also coming full circle with Amber. So we made plans to return to the Turnagain Arm bar where we'd stopped the night of the beluga convergence and sparks between us first flew.

The place hadn't changed a bit. We walked in and there was the same bartender and the same duo of decrepit dogs sacked out on the floor. We sat at the same table, and ordered the same beer.

A couple of days earlier, Amber had come up to me in the kitchen and said, "Close your eyes and open your mouth."

"Very funny."

"No, seriously, just open your mouth."

"Ahh, I don't know if I should trust you."

"What? You don't trust me? Why wouldn't you trust me? Come on. Be a man. Trust me."

"Okay, but this better not hurt."

I opened up and she popped a bacon-wrapped scallop into my mouth.

So when Amber went up to the bar to get us another round, I dug a little something out of my pants pocket. She set the beers on the table and sat back down.

"Amber, close your eyes and open your mouth."

"Huh?"

"Close your eyes and open your mouth."

"Forget it."

"What? You don't trust me?"

"It's not that I don't trust you, but I don't trust you." We laughed. "Besides, how are you going to find my mouth?"

"Yeah, good point. Okay, then how about you close your eyes and hold out your hand instead."

She held out her hand. I slipped a ring on her finger.

"Amber, will you marry me?"

"Wait a minute, are you serious?"

"I'm dead serious."

"You're not just messing with me?"

"Would I do such a thing?"

"Yes. I mean, yes, I will. I would love to marry you."

My whole body began to tremble. I lunged across the table just as I had a different life ago and held both of her hands in mine. This time I didn't let go. Then I rose to my feet, found my way up to the bar, and rang the bell; the next round was on me. "Hey, everyone, my girlfriend and I just got engaged! Wa-hoo!"

The room erupted in cheers. The dogs raised their heads off the floor, looked around, dropped their heads back to the floor, snorted, and went back to sleep.

After what happened, I tried to set Amber free. I failed.

CHAPTER 20

Ungulate Landmines and Statistics Sinkholes

No one has ever accused me of being old school, but on a meet-the-parents trip to Minnesota, I got her father's permission before asking Amber to marry me. I'm sure Frank and Diane Takavitz had all the same questions Amber and I had: How was this going to work when I couldn't even mow the lawn, let alone, at the time, make a living? And what if we had children? How does a blind dad watch the kids while mom makes a dash to the grocery store? How does a blind dad change diapers? Eesh. The thought was too gross to consider. Amber and I had a simple answer to such questions: No idea. Despite all the unknowns, Frank didn't hesitate: "We'd love to have you in our family." As proof, he bestowed upon me one of his treasures, a home-run baseball from a Minnesota Twins game that was smacked right to him in the bleachers above left field. I kept it on my dresser next to my prayer beads.

Amber's belief in me, and the vote of confidence from her family, added more fuel to the fire of my ambitions. Amber trusted me to find my way, for us to find ours, and I wasn't about to let her or her family down.

Lee Hagmeier found his way, and he faced much more daunting obstacles in his day. If I got into graduate school at the University of Alaska, I had all this talking, high-tech gadgetry to help me along. The university's Disability Support Services, the Alaska Center for the Blind and Visually Impaired, and other services on and off campus would have my back. When Lee started college in 1962, other than financial aid, he had no such services. The technology he relied upon amounted to a Braille writer and reel-to-reel tape recorders. On top of being blind, he was also deaf in his right ear, a result of the spinal meningitis I had dodged but he hadn't. Losing hearing on one side lopsided his audio orientation, particularly in places as busy and noisy as a college campus.

At Chico State, nearly thirty years before the Americans with Disabilities Act, he'd had to white-knuckle his way through a world disinclined to accommodate him. Between the Division of Vocational Rehabilitation and a trust fund established by the Territorial Sportsmen of Juneau, his tuition, books, supplies, and the cost of hiring readers was covered. But Lee had to figure out his own system for making things work.

He recruited readers from his dorm and through campus bulletin boards. He used a state prison's volunteer program to create his own books on tape. He'd get lists of textbooks from his professors well in advance, buy the books, and mail them to the prison, where inmates would read them aloud and send back reel-to-reel tapes.

His typewriter-like Braille machine was much too noisy to use in class, so he'd record lectures, then back in his dorm room he'd listen again, constantly turning the recorder on and off to take notes on his Braille writer. To do a term paper, he and a reader would hit the library together to gather research materials. He'd have these read to him while he took notes. He'd write his paper in Braille, hire a Braille translator to put it into writing, have a reader read it back to him so he could make corrections, pay someone to type it up, then have it read to him one final time before turning it in. As cumbersome and time consuming as this process was, he graduated summa cum laude with a degree in psychology in 1967. He then moved on to the University of Washington in Seattle, where he got his master's degree in vocational rehabilitation in 1969 and his PhD in educational psychology in 1973.

I would have things so much easier than Lee did. Even so, graduate school would make blind school seem like summer camp.

In the middle of fine-tuning my application essays, I went through yet another surgery, my last, although I'd made that claim before. The tendons that attach the eyes to the nasal bridge had been torn off by the bear, which left me with an anchor problem. Although initially the reconstructed area around my eyes had been reasonably symmetrical, as I healed contractile forces pulled my right eyelids down, leaving my prosthetic eye on that side drooping lower than the one on my left and looking like it was melting off my face. Also, I was all sunken-in at the temples. Due to lack of blood flow, atrophy of the fat pads covering the muscle there left me looking like a walking cadaver.

If this bothered Amber she never mentioned it, but it did bother me. Most people told me I looked fine, given the circumstances. I didn't see how. My face felt bizarre to me, swollen in some places, hollow in others, my eyes all out of whack. It wasn't like I expected to come out of it looking like *GQ* cover material; I just hoped to look less alien. Although a surgeon as talented as Dr. Kallman can only do so much with a face as exploded as mine, I wanted to look as good as possible for Amber. And I didn't want people I'd be dealing with at school or in my future profession to be distracted by my looks. So I had surgery number six to even up my eyes and plump up my temples with implants. Afterward, Amber got stuck gooping my sutures with antibiotic ointment, a chore that made her a little queasy but one she did without complaint.

While recovering, I made plans to tackle two prerequisites I'd need before starting my graduate program should I be accepted: a human development course and statistics. I would be accepted only if I managed a B or better in both of these classes, so no pressure or anything. The first one I wasn't so concerned about, but statistics? I couldn't imagine anything more visual with all its equations, symbols, charts, graphs, and tables. The vocabulary alone gave me a headache: central limit theorem, sample mean (X bar), p-value, quantile, correlation coefficient.

As school loomed, I spent my first Christmas with Amber suffering from a bad case of discrete-variable angst. With a fire in the woodstove, a round of hot buttered rums in hand, and the Grateful Dead on the stereo, we put up our first tree together, a Fraser fir from "Minnesota Bob," one of the few independent roadside tree vendors left in the city and a little taste of home for Amber. I held the tree upright in the stand, trying to get it straight while she stood back and directed.

"A little to the left, a little more, now back the other way a touch. There. Now don't move."

She anchored the tree in place, gave it a drink of water, and wrapped a gold-colored tree skirt around its base. I then fed her tinselly garlands and twinkly lights as she strung them around and around the tree. She'd bought maroon and gold balls and beaded ornaments with dangles at Fred Meyer, which we divvied up and hung on the tree. If she redistributed any of mine, she did it on the sly.

"It's crazy that I'm starting school in a couple of weeks," I said as I passed her the onion-dome topper.

"How are you feeling about it; do you feel ready?" she asked from atop the stepladder. She took the topper from me and impaled it on the tree.

"I have no idea what 'ready' should feel like. I feel ready to give it my all. My all may not be good enough, that's what I'm worried about." I tried to laugh but it came out like a nervous wheeze.

"Then we'll figure out what's next. I'm not worried about it, though. I know you can do this."

"I hope you're right." I backed away from the tree, sank into the couch, and began fiddling with my beard as anxiety swelled in my chest. Amber climbed down off the stepladder, sat next to me, and put her hand on my knee.

"You can't think that way, Dan. It will just get you off to a bad start. No matter how hard it gets, you will find a way to make it work. I've learned that much about you."

I had good reason to worry. I was still relatively new at blindness, and I hadn't taken a math class since high school. Our future was riding on how well I did the coming semester. It would be my litmus test. Blowing it was not an option.

Nervous about getting lost, afraid of feeling like a bumbling fool, I spent several days and many long hours memorizing and practicing my routes from one class to the next, to the library, to Disability Support Services, to the bookstore, to the coffee kiosks, back and forth, over and over, only to show up the first day of school to discover the room had been switched and I was standing in some engineering class.

Things spiraled downward from there. By the end of my first day of statistics I was already overwhelmed. By the end of my second, I'd come to the realization that sitting in class was going to be of no help to me whatsoever. Virtually the entire class took place via overhead projector or on the board. I got nothing out of it. Nothing. While the professor and all my classmates worked out problems on the board, I sat there with my laptop taking notes that would later make no sense. The squeaking of felt-tip marker on the projector glass and the tapping of chalk on the board were like exclamation points after every detail I missed.

My first in-class panic attack slammed me halfway through class number two. It started with my professor's voice morphing into something distant, as if she were lecturing from a culvert. My palms turned sweaty, and my heart began beating like hooves on pavement.

Oh no. Not here. Not now. Just breathe your way through it. Breathe, breathe, breathe. Damn, I've got to get out of here . . .

My arms and legs were noodles. I'd crawl if I had to, to get out the door, to take refuge in the men's room. Then I thought better of it. The last thing I wanted was to draw attention to myself. If I managed to make it as far as the men's room, I might pass out, hit my head, and be dead before anyone found me. If I was going to lose it, I'd be safer staying put. So I just sat there poker-faced and lock-jawed, my stomach a pit of fire, fingers frozen on my laptop keyboard, hoping nobody would notice.

The worst of the attack passed in twenty minutes. But my nerves were sizzled by then. When the professor wrapped up class, I'd recovered enough to rise up on wobbly legs, gather up my things, and cane my way out the door.

At the start of the second week, I asked my professor if I could learn the material on my own, show up for tests, and skip taking up space in her class. The time it took getting to and from school, I reasoned, I could apply to studying. As much as she wanted to accommodate me, that was a no-go since attendance was part of my grade. Unless I came up with some kind of alternate plan, I was going down.

At home at night, I tried bulldozing my way through my homework with three pieces of technology in front of me—a talking computer, a talking calculator, and a voice recorder for recording the order of operations, to keep track of where I was in the equation.

The variance is the sum of the squared deviation of the scores from the mean divided by the number of scores minus one.

Even state-of-the-art technologies have their limits. I started relying on Amber way too much. She would read a problem to me, and I would record it. I'd then tackle it one step at a time, keeping track of where I was on my computer while doing the math on my talking calculator, and Amber reminding me of what, say, the value of N had been. I also had to learn complicated computer software programs for creating charts, graphs, tables, and histograms. Since Amber was way more computer savvy than I was, I drafted her help with that, too. Reading aloud my statistics textbook and walking me through light-year-long equations was the last way she wanted to spend her evenings and weekends. She did it, but not always graciously. She was giving of her time, but she was no martyr. The long, tedious sessions made us both grumpy.

"You know, you're not that much fun to be around," she'd tell me when I was short with her. "Maybe you should go for a nice, long walk. If you don't, I will."

Then the semester got harder and the workload increased. I started falling behind. As bone-deep frustration set in, I became a regular at UAA's Disability Support Services, where Director Kaela Parks became a tireless advocate for me. We tried different strategies, including a sighted assistant accompanying me to class. That was no help. I started working with a tutor. That helped but not enough. I often stayed up half the night trying to stay on top of my workload. When I did sleep, I thrashed about and hollered. I don't know how many times Amber shook me awake: "Honey, wake up. It's okay. You're having a nightmare." I'd come to and find my bedding twisted around me, sheets and pillow soaked with sweat. Not damp, soaked, and soaked so thoroughly I'd have to flip my pillow over and lay towels beneath me to get through the rest of the night.

As if that wasn't hellish enough, caning to and from class in perpetual pitch darkness kept me on edge. Hearing footsteps crunching in the snow would trigger my post-traumatic stress response and nearly rocket me out of my skin. In California I'd worried about being bitten by a black widow spider. In Alaska, I worried about being stomped by a moose. Somewhere around a thousand of them spend their winters in the Anchorage bowl. They could show up anytime, anywhere. I nearly caned right into one on my way home from the bus stop one day after school. Shoveling the walkway up to our porch one time, I had no idea a moose was standing right behind me until Amber banged on the window and hollered for me to get inside. For all I knew, I'd been shoveling snow right in its face. Now and then someone ends up in the hospital after being kicked or trampled, including a six-year-old boy who was kicked in the head moments after getting off his school bus. In the 1990s, two people were stomped to death in Anchorage, one in a backyard, the other in the heart of the UAA campus, and these were people who could see.

Between the crushing pressure of school and walking around without eyes in a city inhabited by thousand-pound land mines, for the first time since the hospital I ended up on antidepressants, plus homeopathic remedies for stress. They took the edge off my nerves and gave me enough space from my fears to allow me to think.

I vowed to keep changing strategies until I found one that worked, one that relied a whole lot less on Amber. In addition to my one tutor, I got another. And then another. Working at one point with three different tutors, three nights a week, plus a little Amber on the side, I figure I poured three times the number of hours into that class as most of my peers.

The one who made the most difference was my tutor Andy Page, an assistant professor at UAA's College of Education, who volunteered his time and used a hands-on, kinesthetic approach to help me "see" the histograms, bell curves, and other graphics I needed to grasp. He would explain things, then have me put a finger on my computer screen, and with his hand guiding mine, trace the lines and curves. I had to convince him I had 100 percent comprehension of each concept before we'd move on to the next, and he wouldn't be convinced until I knew it well enough to explain it back to him. He held me to a high standard, but he was also tuned into signs of cognitive overload—my restlessness, lockjaw, and deep sighs—and would end our sessions before reaching the point of diminishing returns. Day after day, night after night I kept at it. Finally, things started to click.

My statistics instructor, Linda L.D. Smith, proctored my quizzes and exams so she could see how I did my work. She would read me the questions, and I would work through them with my recorder, talking calculator, and talking software on my laptop. I did lousy on my first weekly quiz, a little better on my second, pretty good on my third, great on my fourth. By the time midterms came along, I walked out of my testing session knowing I'd nailed it. My grades climbed out of the gutter and kept going up.

At the end of the semester, Amber and I kept checking Blackboard, UAA's password-accessible website, in an obsessive-compulsive way waiting for final grades to post. Amber found it first.

"Damn, Dan, you did it. You passed, all right. You got an A."

"Wahoo!" I hollered with a fist pump. "That's one big, fat boo-yah!" (an endearing term I'd picked up from Jaha).

I immediately called my parents in Carmel. Next, I called Andy to thank him profusely for his commitment to helping me. He got all choked up.

"You sure do deserve it for all the hard work you did," he told me. "Your perseverance and discipline blew me away. I don't think I've ever had a more determined student."

When I received the letter from UAA informing me that I'd been accepted into graduate school, I felt battle-ready. Finding my way well enough to ace statistics gave me the confidence I needed to get through ·my master's program, plus a two-year internship as a clinical social worker. Three years after I walked into the wrong classroom my first day of school, I came out the other side with not only a master's degree, but a 4.0 grade point average.

During the graduation ceremony at UAA's Wendy Williamson Auditorium, a burst of applause came as each name was called. When my turn came, I took hold of a classmate's elbow and we walked across the stage to pick up my diploma. I'm not sure if people knew me as that-guy-who-got-blinded-by-a-bear, or whether just seeing someone who was blind getting his master's degree was what sparked the enthusiasm, but the applause was exceptionally vigorous and kept going and going. I nearly lost it. I later heard from Amber that many audience members stood and that some were in tears. Andy Page was among them.

Hearing that bedrock of support from the community, I knew my days of fearing failure were over. I would never again visit the graveyard of who I'd been before.

CHAPTER 21

Blind Date with a Dog

THE WHITE CANE HAS ITS ADVANTAGES, NONE I APPRECIATE MORE THAN its lack of a bladder. Finding my way by cane can be inelegant and slow, sometimes maddeningly so. But a cane doesn't have to be taken outside to relieve itself multiple times a day in a city where temperatures and wind chill factors make a mockery of winter coats and barge right through to your bones. A white cane would never succumb to a spontaneous bout of diarrhea in a hotel elevator. Nor would it zero in on the Minnesota Twins home-run baseball my future father-in-law had given me and mistake it for a chew toy.

Nevertheless, after white-caning it for more than two years, I got a call from Guide Dogs for the Blind notifying me that I had a dog waiting down in Oregon. Off I went to doggie boot camp, fifteen hours a day, six days a week, four weeks straight, to learn how to drive one of these prodigious animals. Leaving Amber for a month would be tough. With our wedding fast approaching, we'd just bought a house and had our celebratory, new-homeowner pizza on the floor the night before I left.

My family had first looked into guide dogs while I was still in the hospital, but I wouldn't begin to qualify until I had a handle on travel by cane. The privately funded, nonprofit Guide Dogs for the Blind, one of several such organizations, provides dogs for free to people who are blind or legally blind as long as they meet certain criteria, among the most important being a fondness for dogs. Each dog represents hundreds of hours of work and commitment, from the volunteer breeders and puppy raisers to the professional, licensed trainers. These Rhodes Scholars of the canine world are eager to do their jobs. The organization doesn't want them going to people more inclined to bond with a couch than a dog.

After moving back to Alaska, I filled out an application that included the question, "What is the cause of your blindness?" The online version of that inquiry was followed by an auto-list of more than ninety possible responses, and "mishap with bear" wasn't one of them. Next came an hour-long telephone interview, followed by a home visit to evaluate my competence for taking on such a dog—my personality, home life, activity level, and mobility independence since one thing guide dogs can't do is consult Google Maps to chart out routes. As a team, the dog is the pilot and you're the navigator. The woman doing the evaluating watched me cane about my neighborhood and around campus while assessing my skills and the safety of my routes.

I got a second home visit a few months later to see how I'd do with an imaginary dog called Juneau. The trainer played the dog by pulling on the dog end of the harness while I held onto the handle. Booking along at more than twice the speed I was used to walking with a cane didn't come as a complete surprise. Test-driving someone else's dog is kind of a no-no, but I was curious, so back in California I had tried out a friend's guide dog on a short, straight stretch of sidewalk. When I told that dog "forward," he forwarded so fast, he just about forwarded me right out of my flip-flops.

During this visit, the trainer also checked out the consummate Maya, who got along with every dog she'd ever met, and the insubordinate Hobbit, who could be a real ass. I was too forthcoming about his personality defects. Hobbit was territorial around food and would clobber Maya upon occasion if she got between him and even a chili pepper dropped on the floor. I got a follow-up phone call over that. Hobbit had been flagged as a potential problem.

"If bullying becomes an issue between Hobbit and your guide dog, would you be willing to re-home Hobbit?"

I about dropped the phone. My answer to that wasn't no, it was hell no, although I'm sure I said it nicer. Hobbit was Amber's dog, and they came as a package. She'd picked him up her first summer in Alaska on a hitchhiking trip down the Kenai Peninsula. He was a cute puppy then. And he was free. By the time his delinquent side emerged, it was too late; she was committed. Apparently being unwilling to part with the dope wasn't a deal breaker because the next call I got informed me that I was in.

Although Guide Dogs for the Blind is headquartered in San Rafael, California, I did my handler training at the organization's Oregon campus southeast of Portland in a town called Boring, named after an early settler who I assume did not live up to his name. I had some idea what to expect, but there's so much more to bringing a guide dog into your life than knowing which end goes into the harness. A guide dog alters the way you interact with the world, since the type of information you get through a harness is much different than through a cane. A cane gives you sounds and textures and shapes. Something that goes *ping* at the tip of the cane creates a mental picture, as does something that goes *thud* like a sack of rocks. When all obstacles in a room are accounted for, you can create a map inside your head. Copy machine here, unidentified sack-of-rocks thing there. Canes provide a tactile connection between you and your environment, which you don't get with a dog since a dog will guide you around obstacles. You don't know if you just avoided a fallen tree branch or a drunk passed out on the sidewalk. Not that lack of such detail is problematic; it's just different. Most of the time you just want to get where you're going. With a dog, instead of moving through the world like a pinball, you move through the world like someone who knows exactly where he's headed.

At the training center, my cohorts ranged from an auto mechanic to a mother of two, all blinded by something from that list of ninety-plus ways. What we had in common was we'd all fallen down stairs, had talked to trees after people wandered away without notice, and had felt up strangers by accident. Once, reaching for a car-door handle, I'd goosed Amber's sister, Lynsey, so badly she shrieked and went airborne. Some of us liked to laugh; others had forgotten how. My roommate told creepy infidelity stories and refused to shut the bathroom door when he peed, which, at six in the morning, sounded like he was relieving himself beside my head. That alone made it a long month.

We spent our first week dogless while we learned the basics—how to care for a dog, how to talk to a dog, and how to read a dog's mind. We worked with dogs, not our own, so we could get the hang of it and feel the communication that takes place through the harness. From day one we worked on trust. If you don't trust your dog the marriage is doomed.

Guide dogs are almost scary smart, some smart enough to tell whether the person holding the harness is blind or just pretending to be. If it's the latter, they can get lazy. "Oh, come on, you're not blind. Gimme a break." Guide dogs are smart enough that trainers sometimes have to do their work blindfolded.

They're also smart enough to exercise "intelligent disobedience." They're programmed to listen and obey, but if I'm standing on a sidewalk and tell my dog "forward," but going forward would put me in the path of a runaway hotdog cart, that dog is not going to budge. "Nope, I'm not doing that," he'd inform me. If he sees me about to be creamed by a car or some kid on a skateboard, he'll pull me backward or yank me off to the side. My job is to take his word for it, because guide dogs are first and foremost dogs, and a dog is just as interested in saving its own skin as mine.

At the end of the first week, Dog Day finally arrived, the day we'd receive the dogs that would be going home with us. All I knew was that mine was a black Labrador retriever named Chandler. The trainers asked us to leave our doors propped open that afternoon, and one by one they brought us our dogs, our free, eighty-thousand-dollar dogs. I sat in my room anxiously waiting my turn, listening to the sounds of toenails clacking against linoleum and students going giddy down the hallway as they met their matches. The toenails worked their way closer. I sat on the edge of my bed, tapping my feet. More toenails. More shrieks of joy. A playful woof. Then I heard panting and a commotion at my door. My dog had arrived, the dog that would be my conjoined twin. In he trotted, his unruly tail thumping each side of the doorjamb as he entered my room all bonkers to meet somebody new.

"Dan, this is Chandler," the trainer said. "He's a good lookin' boy, and quite the talker. Aren't you, Chandler?" She handed me his leash. "He's all yours, and vice versa. Spend some time getting to know each other. We'll meet up in about an hour to take the dogs out, and then we'll get back to work."

Once she left, I got down on the floor. Chandler put his front paws on my shoulders and proceeded to give my face a bath. He felt lean and long-legged, with a streamlined snout. I held his head in my hands, scratched his velvety ears, kissed his forehead, and got a bonk on the nose. *Woooo-woo*, is what he had to say about it. It took me all of thirty seconds to fall in love with that dog.

"Chandler, you and I are going places," I told him. "Sure hope you like to go fishing."

He whapped his tail hard against the floor, which I took to mean, "How soon can we go?"

We spent the rest of our free time together on the floor playing fetch and tug-of-war and knock-the-blind-guy-over-and-pounce-on-his-head. And then with me lying on my belly, turning my head from one side to the other, back and forth, back and forth, we played a game I called escape-from-the-killer-face-licker.

Chandler was the perfect dog for me, enthusiastic, but chill and mellow when he needed to be, a real Joe Cool. A black dog with a white patch on his chest, he looked like he was dressed in a tuxedo, I was told. Amber and I would be getting married a month after he and I got home, and I imagined him wearing a bow tie at the wedding.

I'll never forget the first time we crossed a street together. With a trainer standing by, I listened for the sound of traffic braking as the light went from green to yellow to red, then vehicles slowing to a stop. When all was still I gave the command: "Okay, Chandler, forward."

We stepped off the curb in unison, and off we went without hesitation in a perfectly straight line, past the lineup of idling vehicles, across the sun-baked asphalt, until Chandler stopped to show me we were at the opposite curb, and then we stepped up together. Right there on the sidewalk, I got down on my knees, wrapped my arms around his neck, buried my face in his fur, and cried. That was the moment it really sank in, the profound difference this dog was going to make in my life.

My elation was short lived. I loved Chandler, and as far as I could tell the feeling was mutual. Off duty, he'd get so excited he'd make that *woooo-woo* sound of his, a sound I'd never heard any dog make. At night he'd try to crawl into bed with me, and when I'd sit on the floor he'd climb into my lap. But on duty, he wasn't feeling it; he seemed mopey and distracted. For whatever reason, he wasn't motivated to work for me. He let me know this right off the bat during an early training session inside a mall. We were headed down one side, passing by storefronts and kiosks, navigating around baby strollers, huddles of teenagers, and retail buffs bulging with purchases. We were trucking along just fine, not bumping into anything or anybody, when all of a sudden Chandler detoured, and I felt a strong pull on the harness that had me practically jogging to keep up. As I was taking this in, wondering what it was about, I heard the mall's central fountain getting louder and louder until it became evident that we were headed straight for it. Maybe Chandler was thirsty. Maybe he was going for a swim and taking me with him. Either one was no good. Soon after, I was called into the office.

"Dan, we know this isn't what you want to hear, but we don't think Chandler is the right match for you."

"Oh?"

"He's a great dog. He's a sweetheart. He's proven himself over and over in training, and we know he's going to make an excellent guide for someone someday. But it's not like him to stop short of a curb or in the middle of the block the way he has been lately."

My heart plunged to the bottom of my stomach. "Is it me? Am I doing something wrong?"

"Not at all. It's nothing like that. We do our best as matchmakers but we don't always get it right. Although it's obvious you love Chandler and he loves you, the work chemistry isn't there. We know this isn't going to be easy for you, but we can't have your safety depending on a dog whose heart isn't into his work. We have another dog, one of the top dogs in his group, that we think will be a much better match in the long run. What do you think? Are you willing to give him a chance?"

I felt flattened, like all the air had been squeezed out of my lungs.

"I'll have to trust your judgment," I finally said. "I want what's best for me and for Chandler."

"That's great. Thanks for understanding. I know this is going to be hard, but why don't you go get him, bring him back here, and we'll swap him out."

I returned to the office with my dog and went back to my room with an empty leash. Losing Chandler was a punch in the gut. I tried not to take it too personally, but I really felt like I'd failed him. The reason it didn't work out between us, I now think, was because of Chandler's pride. The longer you work with a guide dog the better you get, and I was a neophyte. Chandler was used to traveling with professional trainers. As soon as I got behind the wheel he could tell I barely knew what I was doing. Maybe he felt he deserved better. Or maybe I'd stepped on his paws too many times. Of course I'll never know, but six months later I would read in the organization's newsletter of his graduation with somebody else.

A half hour after saying goodbye to Chandler, I was called back to the office to meet his replacement—a stocky, sixty-five-pound yellow lab named Anderson. He was just as excited to meet me as Chandler had been, and an even bigger lickaholic, one who'd lick your face raw if you let him. He'd come straight from the kennels, so the first thing I did was take him to the bathing area to clean him up. It should have been a bonding time, but I have to be honest, I didn't feel that instant connection I'd felt with Chandler. It was hard to fall in love with a new dog when I'd barely begun grieving the loss of my previous one. Rather than spontaneous love, I grew to love Anderson over time.

They were different in many ways, each with their own strengths and weaknesses. Chandler was amazing with "find" commands. As long as he'd been there a time or two, I could say, "Chandler, find a bathroom," and he'd take me down a corridor, into the men's room, and straight to an empty urinal. Anderson was more likely to take me down a corridor, into the men's room, and up to a urinal that somebody was in the process of using. On the other hand, Chandler was like a four-wheel-drive pickup truck. Anderson was a Ferrari. The first ride I took with him was like *Vrrrrooom.* I practically had to hold onto my hat. He loved his job and was eager to work with me.

He aced his distraction tests, too. He walked right by the loose cat and other anarchists of the animal world brought in for training purposes. He kept his cool amid the chaos of ducks, and ignored the annoying chattering squirrel. He even held his head high as he passed by the trail of sliced deli ham that trainers had laid in his path.

Trainers have all kinds of tricks for teaching students to trust their dogs. Like getting behind the wheel of a car and coming at us as if they're going to run us down. In one session, they came at us five times in five different ways—running a red light, backing out of a driveway, and other fun-filled scenarios. Dogs don't naturally go in reverse, but guide dogs do. Either that or they hit the gas and pull us full-speed out of harm's way. Anderson nailed them all.

At the end of my four weeks, the volunteer who'd raised him from a puppy, Angela Schwab, came from Colorado with her fiancé and brother to watch us graduate together. It's a proud moment for puppy raisers to watch their dogs make guide-dog rank since many don't make the cut, ending up instead as "career change" dogs, doing search and rescue or pet therapy or going back to live with those who raised them. She told me stories of Anderson's hellion puppy days, gave me a photo album of his puppyhood pictures, and brought him his favorite puppy toy—a chew ring that he loved tossing into the air that would occasionally land around his neck. After caring for him for a year, putting him in a crate and sending him off to guide-dog school had been bittersweet. She'd worried about who would get him, and was relieved to hear that he'd be going to school and eventually to work with me, that he'd be going hiking and camping and fishing.

After graduation, she took us to the Olive Garden for dinner, where Anderson was the perfect gentleman beneath our table. At the end of the night, we said our goodbyes back at the school. We hugged, and then she bent down and hugged Anderson one last time. After we turned and headed down the long corridor to my room, I could sense her standing there watching us go.

Bringing Anderson home changed the family dynamics. Amber is one of those women who feels compelled to do it all herself, and on a certain level, she got displaced. When I wasn't using my cane, "hopping on" to her elbow, as I call it, had been my primary mode of transportation. Now it was me and Anderson. When she was along, unless we were in wide-open spaces, she'd have to walk behind us; otherwise he'd be looking for enough room to accommodate all three of us. Since Amber is easily distracted, she's walked me into things, like display pyramids at grocery stores. Anderson, I'd tell her, wouldn't do that.

"Fine," she'd say. "Sleep with Anderson then."

So having a guide dog as a roommate took some getting used to. So did a lot of things. If there was no sidewalk, as is the case in many parts of Anchorage, I'd have to walk on the left side of the road, even if I was just strolling through our neighborhood, because in that situation Anderson was trained to face traffic. I couldn't just make a beeline across the cul-de-sac to my neighbor's house. I'd have to be robotic about it. I'd have to make a ninety-degree turn, then walk straight across the street.

The adjustment was just as hard for Anderson. At guide school, it had been just the two of us. Once I got him home, he seemed taken aback to discover I came with a pack. Amber and I introduced him to the others slowly and cautiously. They bonked noses and inspected posteriors. After they'd exchanged information and everything seemed cool, Amber took off for the store.

Anderson's attention to me must have gotten Hobbit's goat because as soon as I was alone, I heard this terrible screech at my feet. Hobbit had jumped Anderson on the deck and was giving him a brutal hazing—just in case he had any doubts about who was in charge around there. Dogfights sound much worse than they are, but you would have thought Anderson was being skinned alive. I'm absolutely certain he had never been in, or even around, a dogfight in his life. I have no doubt he was dumbfounded that another dog would behave in such a manner. I reached down, grabbed Hobbit by the scruff of his ornery neck, pulled him off, and herded him inside. Anderson bolted.

I knew he was somewhere in the backyard, which was fenced, but I had no idea where, and he wouldn't come when I called. I had to wait until Amber got home to find out he was hunkered down in the farthest part of the yard, in a corner backed up against the fence, just sitting there, head slumped, staring at the house. I felt sick about it.

I'd like to say they've since worked it out, but it's more like Anderson has learned to dodge hot-headed Hobbit like he would an oncoming car or any other hazard. I wouldn't call them friends but they've learned to tolerate each other.

Anderson may tread lightly around Hobbit, but he's fearless around traffic and golden at crossing roads. He's pretty good at figuring things out, too, although he gets frustrated and a little panicky when he can't. In an unfamiliar area, when he can't figure out what I want and I'm not entirely sure myself, he'll just start showing me things. He'll take me to the bottom of an escalator: "Is this what you're looking for? No?" He'll take me to an open doorway: "How about this?" If I can't help him out, he'll tell me through unmistakable body language: "Okay, this is getting annoying. Where the hell is it you want to go? No, I'm not going to let you walk into a wall to get your bearings. No, I do not see your point."

Crowded cafeterias and restaurants, with their mazes of tables and chairs, are a problem. Anderson is trained to tune into spaces big enough for us to walk through side by side, so he's not going to let me turn sideways and squeeze between two tables. If he doesn't see an opening, he'll park it. I'll say, "Forward." He'll say, "Nope." But I'll still need to get through. Just about the time he'd be dialing 9-1-1 if he could, I'll drop his harness, he'll instantly heel, and I'll start feeling my way out of the jam, hoping not to touch anyone's head or privates, and then I'm the one in the lead, the blind guy leading his guide dog.

A refresher in the power of positive reinforcement came the day we were on campus working our way from one building to another when we came to an intersection of sidewalks that's challenging under the best of circumstances, and we'd just had our first big snow dump of the year. It was still snowing and nothing had been shoveled, so the campus was one big blanket of confusion. I got disoriented and started looking for a way to get my bearings. "Anderson, find it," I said; find anything I'm familiar with, was what I was thinking. He took me to some door, but I didn't know it. He took me to another. I didn't know that one, either. He took me out to some post-holed path others had blazed, but that didn't feel right. Then he threw in the towel. We were lost. We were just standing there stuck. In a snowstorm. In the cold. The way snow muffles sound, I couldn't hear anything or anybody. I got frustrated and lost my cool.

"Damn it, Anderson! We need to go somewhere, I don't care where. Let's just *go*."

I felt his head sink. This is a dog that thrives on doing a good job, and I'd shamed the spirit right out of him. I was instantly remorseful. I reached down and patted his side, but it was a bit late for that. Five minutes passed, then ten. At last I heard footsteps in the snow.

"Hey there, sorry to bother you, but we're a little disoriented. Do you mind telling me where the BMH building is from here?"

A couple of minutes later we walked into class twenty minutes late.

I felt terrible about losing it with Anderson, and was determined to make it up to him. I took him back to campus the next day with a pocket full of treats to practice that route, to make it successful and fun for him, to rebuild his confidence. Every time he got something right, I praised the hell out of him. "Anderson, halt," I'd say. "Anderson, okay." That's his cue that he can take a break from guiding, that it's okay to celebrate. I scratched his ears and patted his rump and praised him so much he was dancing around and I was dancing with him. Anderson, it seemed to me, knew this was my way of apologizing. He was pumped and proud and forgiving.

I will always have issues with Anderson that I don't have with a cane. He's a dog, he's got quirks. Like refusing to do his business on any kind of artificial surface, which is a problem when we travel. One time in Los

Angeles, I walked several blocks from my hotel trying to find him a spot. Then I heard some guys standing at a street corner talking. I walked up.

"Hey, do you guys know where I can find some grass?"

"Ah, yeah, man, no problem. We can set you up."

Pause.

"Oh. I mean, for my dog here. He's really got to go."

Silence.

"Naaah, man. Around here? Nah. We don't know nothin' about no grass."

With a guide dog, it's important to have a sense of humor. I mean, what else can you do but laugh when you find out, as an acquaintance of mine did, that you've been walking about in public with your girlfriend's bra wrapped around your dog's neck?

This is an old joke amongst we guide-dog people, but it really does happen all the time: People ask, "Is that a blind dog?"

"Actually," we say, "he sees just fine. It's me who's blind."

Anderson is my eyes, my companion, my protector, and my security blanket. As a blind person out in the community, I feel a fair amount of awkwardness and anxiety in social situations. Unless someone is talking to me, it's lonely out there, especially in a room full of people. It's hard to start conversations without a meeting of eyes or a nod of recognition. With Anderson beside me, I always have a friend. When I'm alone, surrounded by people, I can always bend down and give him a pat. And having Anderson makes it easier for people to strike up a conversation with me.

"Nice dog. I have a Lab at home, too. What's his name?"

There's a huge distinction between a blind man with a cane and a blind man with a dog. When people see a blind man with a cane tapping along the side of a building, they assume he needs help. When I use a cane, strangers are constantly grabbing my arm and trying to take me somewhere, like they're the bellboy and I am a luggage cart. With Anderson, that never happens. He takes me straight to the door. Or straight down a sidewalk without bashing into sandwich boards or parking meters or hanging flower baskets. People no longer see me as a blind man with a cane who needs help, but as a blind man with a dog who's doing just fine.

My guide dog, Anderson, and me, 2012.

CARL BATTREALL

FAMILY PHOTO

A great day of king fishing with Jeremy "Jaha" Anderson, and my brother Brian Bigley, 2011.

With Alden at Lake Tahoe, 2008.

FAMILY PHOTO

DEBRA MCKINNEY

On the beach with Acacia near my parents' home in Carmel, California, 2010.

CHAPTER 22

Family Man in the Dark

THEY SAY THAT SEEING YOUR BRIDE THE DAY OF THE WEDDING BEFORE she starts her walk up the aisle is bad luck. If that's true, it seemed logical to me that never seeing your bride would tip the odds in favor of the more desirable kind. Besides, relying on your hands to "see" the woman you love wrapped in skin-tight satin isn't so bad.

Amber and I chose July 7 as our wedding day. The location was obvious; it had to be Arboleda, not only the center of my healing journey but the place from which we'd fallen in love all over again by phone. The week leading up to our ceremony, family and friends trickled in, coming from Alaska to Florida and many points between, to help us celebrate what three years before none of us could have imagined possible, least of all me. Cloey the Arboleda dog announced each new arrival the moment he heard the crunch of gravel at the top of the driveway. He'd run to investigate while the neighbor dogs provided backup. Within my circle of friends, it was the first time many of us had seen each other since our Prescott days, back when I was "Cedar," the chronically smiling nature boy without a single worry cell in his body, back when I was more interested in watching a sunset than a movie, and was prone to sleeping in my truck in ski-area parking lots to get first crack at fresh powder. As we greeted each other, the ones who hadn't seen me since the bear held onto me longer than others.

With a growing number of revelers, we began training for the big day in earnest, starting the day with Bloody Marys and ending it with late-night feasts and jam sessions around the stone barbecue pit. I still grin when I think of my bachelor party, which began inside a behemoth Hummer limousine en route from Arboleda to San Francisco—with stops at Pier 23 for happy hour and Blowfish for sushi dinner—and ended eight hours later with me in my rumpled, white-linen suit conked out on Chris Van Ness's shoulder, one of my buddies spilling out of the limo dressed in someone else's jacket, and another missing his boots.

The day before the wedding, a rental crew dropped off tables, chairs, and other supplies, as well as parts for a large dance floor and stage for the seven-piece ensemble, Vinyl, that we'd hired for the reception. Lee and Christy Hagmeier, who had driven down from their new home in Lacy, Washington, arrived that afternoon. Although we'd e-mailed and talked on the phone a fair amount, it was the first time Lee and I had been together since I was clearing the cobwebs of a coma out of my head.

"Hello, Dan. It's Christy," his wife said, walking up to give me a hug. "It's so nice to finally meet you."

Then, with her hand against the back of Lee's arm, she gently guided him forward and helped him and me find each other. I reached out for Lee's hand, clasped it, drew him in, wrapped my other arm around his back, and gave him a one-armed, back-slapper hug, a slightly awkward one since we'd misjudged each other's heights, he being five-foot-eight and me, six-foot-four. In addition to being shorter than I'd imagined, he was quite a bit thinner, although that should have been no surprise since, at sixty-four, he was still a devout hiker and runner. Standing there face to face with the only person who knew exactly what I'd been through, it hit me like a flash flood how far I'd come since the day we'd met and I was so weak all I could muster was a thumbs-up.

"There's still a lot of life worth living," he'd told me that day. "It may not seem like it now, but you have a great deal to look forward to." Now here I was not quite three years later proving him right, on the eve of my wedding day.

The next morning, the place was abuzz with preparations. The caterers arrived and took over the kitchen. The bar got set up and the wine delivered. Kegs of beer got wrestled into tubs of ice. Friends and family helped set up the area for the reception, to be held beneath a canopy of live oaks and old-growth sycamore trees. They arranged tables and chairs, draped white linens over the tabletops, and plunked centerpieces down in the middle. Climbing up and down a ladder, a lighting man strung lights all through the trees and down the driveway, and my friend, Kevin Gregory, who does stage sound for Yonder Mountain String Band, got the sound system up and ready. My soon-to-be father-in-law got set up to invoke his Slovenian late-night wedding tradition of passing out cigars and blasting polka tunes after the band called it a night.

Amber and I had made camp in the master bedroom upstairs, but were getting ready in separate rooms with our respective entourages, which included our best friends, Jay McCollum as best man and Bekkie Volino Robinson, who'd married one of the Photonz, as matron of honor. I'd agreed to the dark suit, no problem, but lost the footwear battle of wills to Amber, Queen of Shoes. So no flip-flops for me.

Midafternoon, Amber and I met up in the Secret Garden, a jade-colored lawn with a backdrop of grapevines, fruit trees, and lavender bushes that trimmed the place in purple. My Prescott friend and spiritual mentor, Blair Carter, presided over our ceremony, as he had over my vision at the Russian River, of my loved ones circled around once I'd made the decision to live. It was there, in the blue place, I came to realize we are never alone, that those who love us are omnipresent in some alternate dimension, or whatever you want to call it. They were with me at the doorstep of death. They helped guide me back. Blair and his girlfriend in college, Martha McCord, also showed up like guardian spirits in the psychedelic circus of my drug-induced coma. Standing with Amber in front of those two and a lawn-full of family and friends, I was overcome by that same vortex of love that kept my heart beating the night of the bear.

As Blair and Martha filled the air with the harmonic tones of Tibetan singing bowls and my former roommate, Jamie Berggren, played didgeridoo, Amber and I exchanged secret vows. We shared the moment between just us, expressing our love for each other, holding hands, leaning in close, whispering words meant only for each other to hear.

There's always been something familiar about you, Amber, as if we've always known each other, as if we loved each other in another lifetime and were meant to find each other again in this one. I adore and cherish you, and will do everything in my power to create the best possible life for you, for us, and for the family we hope to create. I will forever be faithful to your best interests, and support you on your life's journey. Nobody knows better than we do how uncertain life can be. But there's one thing I am certain of: I will love you more tomorrow than I do today. I love you Amber Takavitz. I love you with every cell of my body.

Two months after the wedding, I was propped up in bed with my morning cup of coffee when I heard Amber calling out from the bathroom:

"Ahh, honey?"

We weren't going out of our way to get pregnant. We just weren't going out of our way not to. We'd had many discussions about our hopes of having kids someday, "someday" being the key word. Just because we wanted it to happen didn't mean it would. We had several friends who'd been trying and trying without luck, so we didn't expect it to be any different for us. We were so convinced that "someday" was down the road that we'd just stocked up on pregnancy test kits from Costco.

Amber was getting ready for work that morning when, feeling a bit off, she took a moment to try out one of those strips. Afterward, she set it on the bathroom counter, turned on the faucet, washed her hands, grabbed a hand towel, glanced down at the test, and stared in disbelief as a plus sign emerged. She blinked hard, picked it up for closer inspection, and instantly felt feather-headed.

"You're not going to believe this," she called to me, her head poking out of the bathroom doorway. "This thing says I'm pregnant."

I sat straight up in bed, nearly sloshing my coffee in my lap. "What!? Are you serious? Are you sure?"

"I'm pretty damn sure. It's a plus sign, not a minus. That means we're pregnant."

"We're having a baby? Us? You and me? A baby? Holy cow."

We were simultaneously stoked and terrified, the way a first-time skydiver must feel stepping into thin air. I lifted up the covers; Amber crawled back into bed beside me. We held onto each other as we tried to imagine our lives furnished with car seats and strollers. About an hour after Amber left for work, the phone rang.

"Can you believe I'm pregnant? Me. Pregnant."

"I can't, but it's awesome. I couldn't be happier."

Amber's pregnancy came so soon after the wedding, it had our families stopping to do the math. Both her parents and mine had concerns about me as a father. Like, how does a dad with no eyes keep an eye on his kids? And how does a blind dad keep from knocking his toddlers down the stairs? (That one, as it's turned out, was good reason for worry. Unfortunately I've heard that *thump-thump* sound a time or two.) Both of our families knew we had big challenges ahead, particularly for Amber who'd be carrying more than her share of the load. Still, they were thrilled for us.

Amber and I took prenatal and birthing classes together. We read a pile of books on childbirth and parenting. Amber did expectant mom exercises, prenatal yoga, massage, and chiropractic. She drank enough raspberry leaf tea to float a boat. When we found out our baby was a boy, we named him Alden, meaning "old friend." Every night before drifting off to sleep, I'd scrunch down under the covers, lean over, and whisper into Amber's bellybutton.

"I hope you let your mama sleep tonight, Alden. No kicking a soccer ball around in there until tomorrow morning, okay, buddy? Can't wait to meet you. Goodnight, Alden. I love you."

Amber, one of those pregnant women who glowed and relished every aspect of the experience, had her heart set on a home birth with a midwife, and self-hypnosis and guided imagery as pain control. About a week before Alden was due, we were just sitting down to dinner at Bekkie and Ben Robinson's place when Amber disappeared into their bathroom. We waited and waited. I took a bite of my salad. I fidgeted with my fork. I took another bite.

"Hey, Amber, you okay in there?"

"Ahh, Bekkie, could you come in here a minute?"

She scooted back her chair, got up, and strode to the bathroom.

"I'm really sorry, but I've made a big mess."

"Oh my god, Amber, your water broke."

"But I've made a mess. Do you have something I can use to clean this up?"

"What are you talking about? Don't you worry about that. You're going to have a baby."

As I heard this back and forth from the dinner table, I set down my fork and laughed out loud, not only because it was so Amber not to want to inconvenience anyone, but because it meant we were only hours away from holding our son. Amber wasn't feeling any contractions yet, so she cleaned up and joined us, and our dinner became a celebratory one. We stuffed ourselves, not knowing when we'd get the chance to eat again. Afterward, we gave our midwife, Laura Gore, a call.

"Why don't you head home and try to get some rest," she advised us. "You'll need it when the time comes."

Back home we were too excited to sleep. Instead, we tried various techniques to induce labor, including Amber walking up and down the stairs and around and around the block, then up and down and around some more. For hours we tried everything in and out of the books to coax Alden to get a move on so he could be born at home. It wasn't to be. Twenty-four hours after her water broke, we had no choice but to go to the hospital due to the risk of infection. Amber was in tears; after her unflinching commitment to natural childbirth, she was going to have the birthing experience opposite of what she'd wanted.

"I feel like a failure," she sobbed.

"Oh Amber, no. Please don't think that way," I told her, rubbing her back. "That's the last thing you are. It wasn't in the cards is all."

At the hospital, after eight hours on a Pitocin drip, Alden was still holed up tight and Amber was writhing in vise-grip contractions. Suddenly, the number of those tending to her went from one, to three, to what sounded to me like a crowd, with everyone speaking in medical lingo and terse tones.

"Dan, we're going to have to ask you to move aside."

Amber and I had been holding hands, and she'd squeezed mine so hard during contractions that it ached. I let go and took a couple of steps backward.

"Everything's going to be okay, honey," I assured her. "You're in great hands."

"Here's what's happening," the doctor explained. "Amber's contractions have been getting stronger but the baby's not budging. The contractions are squeezing him and squeezing him, and his heart rate has dropped to a level where we feel it's best to go in and get him."

I'd had a lot of practice so was able to keep my panic under wraps. I stood stiffly off to the side as everyone else in the room hustled. I heard the rustling of bed sheets and the snapping of Latex. I heard Amber sobbing. Someone rattled papers for her to sign authorizing a Cesarean. I tugged hard on my beard and chewed my lower lip.

In the operating room, scrubbed and dressed in a paper gown, cap, and booties, I stood beside Amber with her hand in mine. Sitting up on the operating table, she groaned as the epidural needle slid into her spine. A nurse helped her lie down on her back. With an oxygen mask over her face, she was unable to speak. She pulled it off, turned her head to the side, and threw up.

"Hang in there, Amber. We've just about got him."

The next thing I heard was a robust wail. *Our son!* The instant I heard Alden's cry, my throat swelled and I was unable to speak.

"He's gorgeous, a real keeper, Dad," I heard someone say. "Ten fingers and ten toes, and just as pink as he can be. He's perfect."

A nurse took Alden from the doctor, carried him to the side, cleaned him up, and bundled him in a blanket. Then I heard her soft-soled shoes coming my way. I held my arms out but was thinking: *You're going to hand that thing to me? But . . . that's a baby! I don't know what to do with a baby.* As I felt the weight of his warm little body in my arms I started to cry.

"Hey there, little guy," I said in just above a whisper as I gently rocked him in my arms. "Hello, Alden. We've been so excited to meet you. It's so great to finally have you here. Mama and Daddy love you so much."

With Amber wheeled off to the recovery room, I held Alden until I had to hand him over for his trip to the nursery to get his vitamin K shot and the rest of the standard newborn routine. Our midwife, who'd stuck with us through the delivery, offered an elbow. I took hold and she guided me back to him. As we walked through the nursery doors, I heard someone singing, and my throat seized up again.

"Happy birthday to you. Happy birthday to you. Happy birthday, dear Alden. Happy birthday to you."

Our midwife showed me to a rocker. Once I was settled in, she gently lifted Alden out from under the warming lights, wrapped him in a blanket, and brought him to me. I pulled off my shirt, unwrapped Alden's blanket, and held my son's perfect little body against my own battle-scarred one.

———

By the time I finished my master's program, Amber was seven months pregnant with our second child, our daughter Acacia, named for the trees Amber had lived among in Africa. I had two clinical internships behind me, one with Anchorage Community Mental Health, the other with my pre-bear employer, Alaska Children's Services. I entered the job hunt with straight-A transcripts and a glowing letter of recommendation from Dr. Elizabeth Sirles, director of the UAA School of Social Work:

"It is not an exaggeration for me to say that Dan is the best student I've worked with in my fourteen years at UAA. He has excellent communication and interpersonal skills, a professional demeanor, an inquisitive mind, and a solid grasp of the theories and knowledge base for clinical social work practice. He has emerged as a leader with his peers and is respected by students and faculty alike."

So I looked pretty good on paper. But potential employers wanted to know how I'd actually do the job, even with Anderson as my eyes. None had the resources or desire to look after me. I assured them that accommodating me would not be their problem, that I'd bring to the job all the mobility and technical support I needed through the state Division of Vocational Rehabilitation and the Alaska Center for the Blind and Visually Impaired. Their people would make everything accessible to me, and help me learn my way around the office, from my mailbox to the copy machine to the microwave in the break room. My computer tech would set me up with what I needed to handle paperwork and other office tasks. Those considering me must have liked the sounds of that because before I'd even picked up my diploma I had two job offers. A week after my walk across the stage at graduation, I began my new career as a clinician with Denali Family Services working with some of the most severely emotionally disturbed kids in the state.

On the home front, Alden had been doing such a stellar job of teaching me the ways of the blind dad that I had some tricks by the time Acacia joined us in July. Mastering the art of the diaper change was not one of them. At times, it was like trying to gift-wrap a flopping salmon in the dark. If we're talking diaper blowout, my changing sessions typically culminated with a bath or shower for one or both of us.

By then, I had acquired a tolerance for cacophony and survived enough near heart failures to know that just because a child may sound like he's auditioning for a Stephen King movie doesn't mean he's seriously hurt. Among the worst was the day Amber was away and I was giving Alden a bath when he suddenly leapt up, slipped out of my hands, pitched forward, and did a face-plant on the faucet. First came that dreaded silence as he stockpiled enough energy to launch a scream missile. Then he unleashed his fury with enough power to propel his lungs right out of his chest.

"Oh, Alden, I'm so, so sorry. Oh my god, you okay, little buddy? Oh man."

I prodded his face with the tips of my fingers in search of blood. But he was dripping wet, so I couldn't tell if he was coated in blood or bathwater. I dried him off, patting his face as gently as I could. No blood. No concave anatomy. The face-bonk had smarted but was not life-threatening. It didn't even require a Band-Aid. Something about being torn up within an inch of your life brings perspective to these things.

By the time he was two, Alden had already picked up that there was something different about me. At the National Federation of the Blind convention in Dallas, sharing a hotel with two thousand blind and visually impaired people, he cracked us up by walking into walls, then laughing hysterically, over and over. Before he was three, he knew, as did all three dogs, to get out of the way when he saw me coming. Or to at least speak up.

"I'm here, Dad."

"Nice job, Alden. Thanks for letting me know."

He knew the way I saw things was through my hands.

"Dad, I got this really cool car."

"No kidding? How cool is it? Can I see it?"

He'd bring it over and put it in my hands.

"Wow. This is one cool car. Check out those tires. Awesome. No wonder you like it. What color is it?"

Alden knew I needed help finding things.

"Hey, Alden, time to go. Where are your shoes?"

"Here they are, Dad," he'd say as he'd bring them to me.

This didn't become painful until he started asking why I couldn't see.

"How come your eyes don't work? Are they broken?"

"Yeah, Daddy's eyes are broken. Daddy doesn't see the way you and other people do."

"If you wear your sunglasses can you see?"

"No, my sunglasses don't help at all."

"Maybe tomorrow you can see?"

"No, I won't be able to see tomorrow, either."

"If you go to the doctor, then you can see?"

"No, Daddy's probably not going to be able to see ever again. It's called being blind. Close your eyes. Close them tight. Are they closed?"

"Yep."

"You're not peeking are you? You have them covered with your hands?"

"Yep, Dad. I promise."

"That's what it's like for me. I can't see anything. Nothing at all. It's like walking around with your eyes closed all the time. What do you think of that?"

I could almost hear the concerned look on his face. I could tell he didn't think highly of it at all. I was putting him to bed one night, lying next to him atop his dinosaur quilt, when he told me what he wanted to be when he grew up.

"I'm going to be a big fireman so I can help you because you're blind," he said, his hand upon my cheek. "If there's a fire, I can save you. Or I can save you if you climb up in a tree and get stuck because I'm going to be a big fireman."

I had to laugh. But he kept asking why I was blind, and it got to the point where my answers weren't cutting it. He wanted to know what had happened to me. Here I was schooled in how to have difficult talks with kids, and I didn't know what to say to my own son. I didn't want to make up some story, like that the Eyeball Fairy forgot to bring me some, or that I'd lost them in a poker game. I decided to be as honest as I could short of giving him nightmares.

"Why are you blind, Dad?"

"Well, here's what happened. I was out fishing one day, and I saw a mama grizzly bear. She thought I was dangerous, so she was scared of me. She thought I was going to try to hurt her babies, which I wasn't, but because she thought I was, she bit me. She was just doing what mamas do. She was protecting her babies. Just like Momma keeps you safe, that bear was trying to keep her babies safe, too."

Alden was silent a while.

"You mean the bear poked you because she was very mad, and that's how you got blinded?"

Close enough. I didn't want to give him more details than he needed.

"Hmm, yeah. A bear got scared of me and she poked me. That's how I got blinded."

Since I'm a big believer in honesty, in this case dished out in small doses, I wouldn't do it any differently. But the result is that Alden isn't just afraid of monsters in the closet, he's also afraid of bears in the woods. Sometimes he's afraid to go to bed at night because he's worried about what's lurking outside his window.

"There's a bear out there, Dad, and it's going to poke me in the eye."

The summer he was three, we were at soccer practice when he wandered away from his team. Amber watched him walk over to the fence, grab hold with both hands, rest his forehead against the chain links, and peer out into the woods.

"Alden, what are you doing, buddy?" she asked when she reached him. "Don't you want to get out there and play?"

"No, I don't want to play. I'm watching out for bears."

The world is not a safe place. No matter how kind you are to others, no matter how much good you try to do in life, sometimes bad things happen. Sometimes horrific things. I'd learned that at twenty-five. I just wish Alden hadn't had to learn it at three.

My family: Amber, Acacia, and Alden, 2011.

CHAPTER 23

Whale Watching Blind

*Be careful what you water your dreams with. Water them with worry
and fear and you will produce weeds that choke the life from your dream.
Water them with optimism and solutions and you will cultivate success.
Always be on the lookout for ways to turn a problem into an opportunity
for success. Always be on the lookout for ways to nurture your dream.*
—LAO TZU

I HAVE MOMENTS I FORGET I'M BLIND. I'LL BE OUT SLEDDING WITH THE
kids and take off post-holing through the snow, with the ever-vigilant
Anderson loping after me like a border collie trying to herd in a renegade
sheep. I'll run and run, just like I did with Jay in the Red River Gorge
back when I was blinded by the lunacy of youth rather than for real, when
we almost ran off a cliff. Or I'll take Alden's hand and the two of us will
dash through a field together whooping like a couple of four-year-olds.
At times like these, I feel like I've sprouted wings. Then reality will rear its
ugly foot and stick it out in front of me. Playing squirt guns with Alden
one time, all it took was three running steps to find a lawn chair the hard
way and end up all bloody and bruised.

Blindness is a callous teacher, with pain and embarrassment as
powerful motivators. I'm not a model student in that regard. I'm still
pulling head-bonkers and face-smashers on par with being punched in
the face by a three-hundred-pound man. Sometimes I clock myself hard
enough to send me crawling into bed for the remainder of the day. After
toweling off from a shower one morning, I was going for my clothes on
the floor when I bashed my forehead so hard on the edge of the sink I
gave myself whiplash.

On the other hand, I've earned a black belt in patience. And, because I do so much of it, in waiting. Waiting for rides. Waiting for Amber to find something I need. Waiting at parties for someone to talk to me. I'm always waiting.

Strange things happen to those who do an inordinate amount of waiting. People assume you have nothing better to do than sit still when nothing could be further from the truth. One winter day when I was still in school, I was waiting after a counseling appointment for a lift back to campus. There was no place to sit while waiting, so I made myself at home near the building's foyer, cross-legged on the floor with Anderson and my laptop. I could hear the front doors opening and closing, accompanied by a rush of cold air. Listening to people coming and going, I heard a man stepping off the elevator yammering away on his cell phone. His monologue grew louder and more annoying as he came my way, then stopped in front of me. I lifted my head. "Hold on a sec," he told the person on the other end. He bent down and thrust a five-dollar bill into the palm of my hand. "Here. Why don't you go get yourself a burger." He resumed his phone conversation and pushed his way out the door. I sat paralyzed a moment, the bill burning the palm of my hand.

Did that guy just give me money? I'm blind so he thinks I need a hamburger?

"That was nuts," I said to Anderson. "How about you go take that guy's leg off." Anderson's tail began to thump against the floor. I stuffed the bill into my pocket, and later passed it on to a neighbor kid raising money for a school sports trip.

Blindness has not only restructured my relationship with time, it's restructured my perception of space and all that resides within it. I live in a world of disembodied voices and faceless people. Even the Amber I interact with on a daily basis is a presence, a personality, a voice and energy that I love rather than a two-legged, curvy woman with blue eyes and a shoe fetish. I am aware of where she is in a room but I don't need to visualize her to feel a connection. I save that for special times, like when she slips into a pair of heels and that little black dress of hers, and clasps a string of pearls around her neck. Times like that, with my hands upon her hips, I see her perfectly.

I see her face when she busts up laughing. I see her face when she's reading bedtime stories to the kids. Dip-netting for red salmon at the mouth of the Kenai River, I see her face every time she gets a hit in her net and goes, "WoOOoo!" Faces fade over time, but I've made a practice of remembering hers. To me, Amber will always be twenty-three.

My relationship with my own face is a troubled one. We are estranged. All these years later, I still have dead-nerve zones and phantom pains in my nonexistent eyes. I sometimes get the sensation of blood running down my right cheek, but when I go to wipe it away, nothing's there. Our bodies are resilient but they can also hold a grudge. I miss my old self like a lost twin, but I don't see the point of trying to remember a face that no longer exists. When I inspect the damage with my fingertips, from the titanium bridge of my nose, to the metal-hard edges of my eye sockets, to the patchwork on my forehead, what I feel is detached.

Marlene Buccione, one of my nurses during my last surgery, is one of the few who knows what my face looks like on the inside. She recognized me and my scars at the pool one evening during a family outing at Alyeska ski resort, introduced herself, and told me that in thirty-six years of working as a surgical nurse, I was the only patient who made her cry. She'd never seen so much hardware inside one head. My CT scan looked like RoboCop, and there I was in the recovery room afterward giving her a smile and a thumbs-up.

In facial trauma as severe as mine, healing is a lifelong process, with scars that are constantly remodeling. The area around my prosthetic eyes is still on the move, sunken in places, bulging in others. Fortunately, I can hide the chaos behind dark glasses, which I do whenever I'm in public or around people I don't know well. Dr. Kallman—Dr. K, as I call him now that we're as much friends as we are doctor and patient—would jump at the chance to make me look better.

"When I see you my usual reaction is, I wish I could do more; I really wish I could," he told me one Saturday afternoon over lunch at Café Amsterdam, not far from where we first met in the emergency room. "Sometimes I feel disappointed. The healing process has left you with some distortion of your features that wasn't there initially. The piece of bone missing in your forehead—that the guys in San Francisco took out because it became nonviable—I'd like to put some kind of implant there, not only to re-establish the contour, but to protect the brain. And I'd like to make your eyelids tighter. Tissue has died, and as time goes on, things have started to sag a little bit. We could conceivably tinker with you indefinitely, trying to make this or that a little bit better. With facial trauma, there's almost an infinite number of tweaks we could do."

I have no doubt he could make me more presentable to the general public. But I've had my fill of anesthesia, scalpels, stitches, staples, bandages, and drugs that make me loony tunes. My family loves me the way I am. My friends and coworkers see past my skin. Unless a medical issue arises, I'm not interested in having my head opened up anymore.

Strangely enough, I have regained a little of my lost sense of smell. Dr. Kallman, who is intimately familiar with my obliterated nasal anatomy, can't explain it. Even so, I swear I can smell coffee brewing and burgers on the grill. Yet, wave a jar of kimchee under my nose and I wouldn't know it. Gasoline, ammonia, dead skunk in the middle of the road—nothing. I don't care if it makes no sense; if all I get is a thimbleful in a full world of smells, I'll take it.

Besides never having seen my own children, what sucks most about the blindness piece of my injuries is when people who don't know me assume I'm incapable. Like buckling my seat belt for me. Like asking if I need help putting on Anderson's harness. One evening I came down the porch stairs with a bag of trash, walked across the driveway to the garbage can, lifted the lid, dropped the bag inside, put the lid back down, then heard a neighbor stroll up.

"Man, how'd you do that? We've been watching you, and I had five bucks you were going to fall on your face."

"Um . . . I was just . . . taking out . . . the trash." What I wanted to say but never would was, "You should see me chew gum and play the stock market at the same time." Or better yet, "You should see me preparing a multimillion-dollar foster-care budget.

Budget analysis is just one piece of my current job description. After a little more than a year as a clinician, I was promoted to director of therapeutic foster care, and am now overseeing sixty homes for Denali Family Services, the largest provider of therapeutic foster care in the state. These are kids who drew the short straw in life. Some were born miswired, or with fetal alcohol syndrome, or addicted to crack in the womb. Too many have had adults in their lives cook meth, commit suicide, get murdered, or be sentenced to prison. The traumas some of these kids have been through at the hands of those they should have been able to trust the most puts a random assault by an overly protective mother bear in its place.

I get a lot of recognition for being a fighter, not just for my life, but for my quality of life. Five years after my attack, the Governor's Committee on Employment and Rehabilitation for People with Disabilities presented me with an Alaskan of the Year award. Prescott College and the University of Alaska have given me Distinguished Alumni honors. Because I have made a full, rich life for myself, people respond to me like I'm something special. I just do what I have to do. The alternative would be to live in a straitjacket of misery. Life isn't too short to live that way, life is too long. The same spirit and will that kept me going at the Russian River keeps me going today. The bear took my face and eyes, not my dignity, and not my ability to dream, and dream large.

"Most patients with severe facial injuries, their lives implode and they withdraw from the world," Dr. Kallman once told me. "What sets you apart from the average patient in my mind is we did our best to give you another chance and you have run with it."

The first time someone called me an "inspiration," I was still in bandages, unable to speak, and moving like an old man with two-by-fours for legs who'd taken an auger in the middle of his forehead. I was living in the hotel, with my parents in the adjoining room, and home-healthcare nurses coming and going. I was still trying to comprehend what had happened to me. But mostly I was still in survival mode, and just trying to make it through what each day required of me, which amounted to a lot of lying around in bed. So when one of my nurses told me I was an inspiration, I didn't take it well.

I'm so glad my misfortune is an inspiration for you. I'm so happy my pain and suffering and the loss of my eyes makes you feel all warm and fuzzy inside.

Although I never crossed paths with the woman again, she became a teacher of mine, and an integral part of my healing journey. The bitterness I felt that day illuminated exactly the kind of man I did not want to be. Being angry at the world, or wallowing about in the quicksand of "why me," had the potential to ruin my life far more than being blinded by a bear.

Wrapping up a stellar day of fishing one moment, waking up blind the next forced me in the most fundamental way to examine where my life was headed and consider what kind of man I did want to be. It forced me to reevaluate and reorder my priorities. As Alaskan author Kim Heacox puts it in his moving memoir, *The Only Kayak*, "Living a life unexamined is far riskier than sleeping on a beach with bears."

Since my eyes are gone and never coming back, I have chosen to embrace acceptance. Since I no longer take each breath for granted, I have focused on being grateful for what I have: My wife, my children, my friends, my work, my community, my potential to help others find strength and hope. If not for the bear, I would, no doubt, still be an adventure-hopping vagabond and commitment escape-artist. Amber would have considered me a lost cause and moved on a long time ago. Alden and Acacia would never have been born.

As the man I've become since the bear, I can say with certainty that being a husband and father has brought me greater joy and fulfillment than any peak I've bagged or turns I've carved in backcountry powder. The career path I've chosen challenges and rewards me in ways I may otherwise never have known. I have learned to accept what life offers, and have discovered that misfortune can lead to fortunate things.

My daughter, Acacia, is now the age Alden was when he first started asking about my eyes. She recently started calling me her Big Blind Daddy, although she still doesn't quite know what that means.

"Daddy, are you blind?" she asked me the other day.

"Yep, I am blind."

"Are you happy?

"Yep, I am happy.

She paused a moment, then asked: "So, you're blind *and* you're happy?"

Staying upbeat takes vigilance. It takes hard work. It takes humor. I'd be sunk without my ability to laugh at myself. When pushing a cart through a home-improvement box store and I hear on the PA system, *Customer service needed in the blind-cutting area*, I can turn to Amber and say, "Quick, to the blind cutting area! That's the perfect job for me!"

I can laugh about the time we were camping, and I was just about to drift off to sleep, when Acacia started exploring my face, one of my prosthetic eyes dropped out, and she snatched it up in her tiny hand and squealed, "I got Dada's eyeball!"

I can laugh about the time I was getting dressed after a workout at the Alaska Club and couldn't figure out why my boxer shorts were so tight until I realized I had opened the wrong locker and was standing there in someone else's underwear.

It's harder to laugh about accidently touching a coworker's breast. Twice. Or the day I showed up to lead a group therapy session with troubled teens, clueless that I had dog crap all over my shoes and pants because I couldn't see nor smell it.

I miss the way I used to play in the backcountry. I miss it so much it aches. But I've come to appreciate it in different ways. No more psychedelic sunrises or clouds of shorebirds playing crack the whip. But I can still soak up the sensations and soundscapes of the natural world. When I'm in a drift boat now I love hearing bald eagles crying overhead, Arctic terns squabbling over fish, and the river passing beneath the boat. When vacationing in Mexico with my family, I love going whale watching, and get as excited as everyone else on the boat, as if I'm actually seeing whales. Because I am seeing whales. I hear their exhale geysers and the whaps of their tails. I see every one of those whales. The way I choose to think of it, the bear that blinded me gave me a new way to see.

Lee Hagmeier continues to inspire me. At seventy, he still travels the world, unfortunately mostly without Christy, whose health limits what she can do. Just in the past few years, he's rafted and hiked the Grand Canyon, and has visited Guatemala, Ecuador, the Amazon, the Galapagos, and a few places between. He's poked around Mayan ruins, visited ornate cathedrals, and hiked thirteen miles along a volcano. He's enjoyed the company of condors as they surfed the thermals along a ridge, and met a gargantuan tortoise named Lonesome George, whose shell came to the middle of his thigh. "Holding a tarantula was novel," he recently wrote me. "She was very polite." To get in shape for these trips, besides running and hiking, he tromps up and down ten flights of stairs, twenty times a shot, with a twenty-five-pound sack of flour in his backpack, his "flour child," as he calls it.

Like Lee, I refuse to let blindness keep me from seeing the world.

❦

I often get asked to tell my story. So I do, at assemblies, meetings, and conferences, to a variety of groups and organizations in and out of Alaska. I've told it to kids at McLaughlin, Anchorage's youth detention center. I've told it to delegates at the USA/Canada Lions Leadership Forum. I've told it to peers at the Minnesota State Services for the Blind. Despite what life throws at us, I tell them, we have the power to rise above it. I heard a line one day during a training session at work, and try to pass it on as much as I can: "The bigger my life, the smaller my disability."

Because I've put my story out there, and served two years as president of the Southcentral Alaska chapter of the National Federation of the Blind, I hear from people. I hear from those who are going or have gone blind. I hear from survivors of devastating illnesses and accidents. Now and then, I hear from other bear-attack survivors. One of them is Allena Hansen, a California woman who was severely mauled by a predatory black bear in July 2008 while she was working on her ranch in the Southern Sierras. In addition to other devestating injuries, the attack damaged her vision.

"We're curiosities, you and I, having survived the unsurvivable—chosen to survive the unsurvivable—when most other unfortunates throughout history who, finding themselves in similar circumstances perhaps wisely did the rational thing and just let go," she wrote me. "It certainly would have been a lot easier to die when we had the chance and not have to endure the torment of questioning our decision—let alone the physical aftermath every day.

"The actual attack, in retrospect, appears to have been the easy part. It's the reconstruction and psychic aftermath that seemingly presents the bigger challenge."

It's true that we are and always will be curiosities. But I have never questioned my decision to live. I've stayed true to the promise I made to myself at the Russian River that night, to never to look back with regret.

In my Prescott days, I spent a lot of time meandering through the redwood forests of Big Sur, hiking along trails and rock-hopping up and down riverbeds. One time I came upon a six-foot remnant of a redwood tree that had clearly been burned up in a fire, broken apart, then flooded out and washed down the canyon, where it became wedged mid-river between two boulders. The floodwaters had long since receded, and so the burned up, broken apart, flooded out, trapped-between-two-boulders remnant of a redwood tree now hovered four feet above the current. From that remnant of a redwood stood a new, fifty-foot tree hovering four feet above the river. I like to think of it as a branch of that old, battered tree that refused to die, now rising toward the sky like a clenched fist.

When I think of where the bear has taken me, I think of that redwood tree hovering above the river. From the remains of my former self, I am growing. I am reaching for the sky.

Acknowledgments

DAN BIGLEY

There are far too many people I'd like to acknowledge and thank for their roles and contributions in my life's story to list them all here. I would not be here, alive and well, if not for the many people who were involved in my heroic rescue, my surgeries, my care in recovery, my rehabilitation, my training as a blind man, and the care of my psyche, those who helped to heal my soul and kept me from sliding into bitterness. My life itself would not be possible if it were not for your acts of courage, your commitment of service to humanity, and your compassionate giving and kindness toward others. Your roles in my life's story have galvanized my faith in the human spirit, and there are no words sufficient for me to express my gratitude and appreciation.

I'd like to thank the wonderful people of Alaska and beyond for your prayers, your thoughts, the letters of support, and more. I'd like to thank the man who offered one of his own eyes in hopes that I may see again. Then, to my family and friends who left their own lives behind to be at my side when it wasn't clear if I would live, and to those who stayed at my side until I had grown wings and had a whole heart once again.

Thanks to my friend and coauthor Deb McKinney for her dedication to this project and for helping me tell my life story. To my parents and brother, thank you for your twenty-four-hour vigilance at my side. The love you brought and surrounded me with was perhaps the greatest variable in the outcome of my healing journey. To my beautiful wife, Amber, and my children, Alden and Acacia, you are the life in my heart and the joy in my soul, and together the life we share as family is my greatest dream come true.

DEBRA MCKINNEY

I am deeply grateful to Jim Welch, who unknowingly set this book project in motion. Without him, I would not have met Dan Bigley. I owe a world of gratitude to Dan for the trust he placed in me to help him tell his story. I am grateful to the entire Bigley family, and to Dan and Amber's couch, where I woke up many mornings after work sessions that went late into the night.

It would be a daunting task to try to list all the teachers, coaches, writers, editors, whip-crackers, and verbosity death squads who've inspired and mentored me, but I take a deep bow to the late John Forssen, my journalism teacher at Hellgate High in Missoula, Montana, who began the process of making a writer out of me. Another shout-out to the heavens goes to Foster Davis, my writing coach at Poynter Institute who became a dear friend. Endless thanks to Kathleen McCoy and others at the *Anchorage Daily News* for helping me grow.

Thanks to my Fairbanks family, Kathy Lenniger, Pam Weaver, Mike Bowman, Barb Sivin, and Ron Harper, for their wisdom, feedback, and endless enthusiasm for this project. Same to my daughter, Genia Cliffton, to Richard Murphy, Dori McDannold, Jill Crosby, Gina Hollomon, Fran Durner, Douglass Bourne, Geoff Penrose, Lara Stone Penrose, and so many others. Even more of the same to my judicious advisors and readers: Tom Kizzia, Craig Medred, Peter Hoople, Barbara Hunt, Linda Billington, Jamie Berggren, Lynn Hallquist, Chris Volk, and Shelia Toomey, despite her proclivity for slashing out entire pages. And to Jeff Fair, not only for his critiques, but for supplying "Mother Yukon's Glossary of Editing Terms" and other laughs when I needed them most.

I am grateful to many for sharing their areas of expertise, including Dr. James Kallman, Dr. Carl Rosen, Stephen Herrero, Joel Reynolds, Carol Ann Woody, and Evelyn Hemmingsen. A toast to Kirsten Schultz Brogan and Crystal Bailey at Providence for their help chasing down details. And another to Martha McCord and Carl Battreall.

I am grateful to Lee Hagmeier for sharing his own remarkable story. And to my father and stepmother, Walter and Carol McKinney, for their tireless encouragement, and for providing me a writer's retreat on their lanai overlooking the Pacific Ocean. Same goes for Michael Miller, my friend and Mac guru, who'd take my panicked calls day and night, and to Web-master extraordinaire, Alan ElSheshai.

Our literary agent, Elizabeth Evans, awed us with her sage advice, generous investment of time, and unfaltering belief in us. And big thanks to all those behind the scenes at the Jean V. Naggar Literary Agency. Warm thanks, too, to Holly Rubino for finding us a home at Globe Pequot/Lyons Press, and to Janice Goldklang, David Legere, Sheryl Kober, Justin Marciano, and the rest of the *Beyond the Bear* team.

I'm only mentioning him last because it makes me all weepy. My husband, Paul Morley, deserves an armload of merit badges for his unwavering support throughout this project, from serving me dinner at my computer to dragging me outside to watch the sun set. His love, patience, and belief in me are a gift I will never take for granted.

About the Authors

Dan Bigley was awarded an 2008 Alaskan of the Year Award by the Governor's Committee on Employment and Rehabilitation for People with Disabilities. He, his wife, and two young children live in Anchorage, Alaska.

Debra McKinney, now a freelance writer, was part of a team that won journalism's highest honor, the Pulitzer Prize for Public Service, for the *Anchorage Daily News.* She and her husband live in Palmer, Alaska.